Coaching Students with Executive Skills Challenges

The Guilford Practical Intervention in the Schools Series

Kenneth W. Merrell, Founding Editor
Sandra M. Chafouleas, Series Editor

www.guilford.com/practical

This series presents the most reader-friendly resources available in key areas of evidence-based practice in school settings. Practitioners will find trustworthy guides on effective behavioral, mental health, and academic interventions, and assessment and measurement approaches. Covering all aspects of planning, implementing, and evaluating high-quality services for students, books in the series are carefully crafted for everyday utility. Features include ready-to-use reproducibles, appealing visual elements, and an oversized format. Recent titles have Web pages where purchasers can download and print the reproducible materials.

Recent Volumes

Social and Emotional Learning in the Classroom, Second Edition:
Promoting Mental Health and Academic Success
Barbara A. Gueldner, Laura L. Feuerborn, and Kenneth W. Merrell

Responding to Problem Behavior in Schools, Third Edition:
The Check-In, Check-Out Intervention
Leanne S. Hawken, Deanne A. Crone, Kaitlin Bundock, and Robert H. Horner

School-Based Behavioral Assessment, Second Edition:
Informing Prevention and Intervention
*Sandra M. Chafouleas, Austin H. Johnson, T. Chris Riley-Tillman,
and Emily A. Iovino*

Child and Adolescent Suicidal Behavior, Second Edition:
School-Based Prevention, Assessment, and Intervention
David N. Miller

School Supports for Students in Military Families
Pamela Fenning

Safe and Healthy Schools, Second Edition: Practical Prevention Strategies
Jeffrey R. Sprague and Hill M. Walker

Clinical Interviews for Children and Adolescents, Third Edition:
Assessment to Intervention
Stephanie H. McConaughy and Sara A. Whitcomb

Executive Function Skills in the Classroom:
Overcoming Barriers, Building Strategies
Laurie Faith, Carol-Anne Bush, and Peg Dawson

The RTI Approach to Evaluating Learning Disabilities, Second Edition
*Joseph F. Kovaleski, Amanda M. VanDerHeyden, Timothy J. Runge,
Perry A. Zirkel, and Edward S. Shapiro*

Effective Bullying Prevention: A Comprehensive Schoolwide Approach
Adam Collins and Jason Harlacher

Social Justice in Schools: A Framework for Equity in Education
Charles A. Barrett

Coaching Students with Executive Skills Challenges, Second Edition
Peg Dawson and Richard Guare

Coaching Students with Executive Skills Challenges

SECOND EDITION

PEG DAWSON
RICHARD GUARE

THE GUILFORD PRESS
New York   London

Copyright © 2023 The Guilford Press
A Division of Guilford Publications, Inc.
370 Seventh Avenue, Suite 1200, New York, NY 10001
www.guilford.com

Printed in the United States of America

Last digit is print number: 9   8   7   6   5   4   3   2   1

The authors have checked with sources believed to be reliable in their efforts to provide information that is complete and generally in accord with the standards of practice that are accepted at the time of publication. However, in view of the possibility of human error or changes in behavioral, mental health, or medical sciences, neither the authors, nor the editors and publisher, nor any other party who has been involved in the preparation or publication of this work warrants that the information contained herein is in every respect accurate or complete, and they are not responsible for any errors or omissions or the results obtained from the use of such information. Readers are encouraged to confirm the information contained in this book with other sources.

Library of Congress Cataloging-in-Publication Data

Names: Dawson, Peg, author. | Guare, Richard, author.
Title: Coaching students with executive skills challenges / Peg Dawson,
   Richard Guare.
Description: Second edition. | New York, NY : The Guilford Press, [2023] |
   Series: Practical intervention in the schools | Includes bibliographical
   references and index.
Identifiers: LCCN 2022048275 | ISBN 9781462552191 (paperback) |
   ISBN 9781462552207 (cloth)
Subjects: LCSH: Executive ability in children. | Executive ability in
   adolescence. | Children—Life skills guides. | Child development.

About the Authors

Peg Dawson, EdD, is a psychologist on the staff of the Center for Learning and Attention Disorders at Seacoast Mental Health Center in Portsmouth, New Hampshire. She also does professional development training on executive skills for schools and organizations nationally and internationally. Dr. Dawson is a past president of the New Hampshire Association of School Psychologists, the National Association of School Psychologists (NASP), and the International School Psychology Association, and a recipient of the Lifetime Achievement Award from NASP. She is coauthor of bestselling books for general readers, including *Smart but Scattered, Smart but Scattered Teens, Smart but Scattered—and Stalled* (with a focus on emerging adults), and *The Smart but Scattered Guide to Success* (with a focus on adults). Dr. Dawson is also coauthor of *The Work-Smart Academic Planner, Revised Edition*, and books for professionals including *Executive Skills in Children and Adolescents, Third Edition*.

Richard Guare, PhD, is Director of the Center for Learning and Attention Disorders at Seacoast Mental Health Center in Portsmouth, New Hampshire. Dr. Guare's research and publications focus on the understanding and treatment of learning and attention difficulties. He is a neuropsychologist and board-certified behavior analyst who frequently consults to schools and agencies. He is coauthor of bestselling books for general readers, including *Smart but Scattered, Smart but Scattered Teens, Smart but Scattered—and Stalled* (with a focus on emerging adults), and *The Smart but Scattered Guide to Success* (with a focus on adults). Dr. Guare is also coauthor of *The Work-Smart Academic Planner, Revised Edition*, and books for professionals including *Executive Skills in Children and Adolescents, Third Edition*.

Preface

We published our first coaching manual, a slender 29-page volume, in 1998. It was our first attempt to operationalize a proposal made by Hallowell and Ratey (1994) in their now classic book, *Driven to Distraction*. This was the first book we know of that was written for a lay audience about adults with attention-deficit/hyperactivity disorder (ADHD). They suggested that these adults might benefit from working with a coach to address some of the challenges imposed by their attention disorder. We found the idea intriguing and wondered if kids with ADHD would similarly benefit from coaching. This led to *Coaching the ADHD Student*.

Our interest in ADHD led us to executive skills, and this domain has occupied our attention for almost 25 years now. We have written books for professionals, for parents of children with executive skills challenges, and for adults who may be struggling with these same challenges. The first edition of this book, *Coaching Students with Executive Skills Deficits*, enabled us to marry our interest in coaching with our interest in executive skills, as we realized that the coaching model we had developed to treat students with ADHD would lend itself to students struggling with executive skills challenges more broadly.

In the more than 10 years since we published the first edition, we've continued to coach and to train coaches, and our understanding of the process has deepened as a result. This deeper understanding has led us, among other things, to change the title. We have moved away from a deficit model in our approach to executive skills. From our clinical work, we now understand that it is normative for people of all ages to have stronger and weaker executive skills. We think it is more accurate to describe people as having executive skills *challenges* rather than executive skills *deficits*, and for this reason, we have changed the name of the second edition of this book to *Coaching Students with Executive Skills Challenges*.

This volume builds on the first edition, but we have made some rather substantial changes based on the coaching work we have done and feedback from the coaches we have trained.

Whereas we focused on coaching teenagers originally, we now recognize that coaching can be adapted for use with younger children—even children as young as preschool age. We also now give greater prominence to strategies such as motivational interviewing and other therapeutic techniques such as cognitive rehearsal strategies. All of these approaches, when incorporated in our coaching model, provide coaches with more tools to enhance the likelihood that coaching will be a successful experience.

We have always felt that coaching works best—in fact may *only* work—when the student is a voluntary participant. If anything, we now have an even greater appreciation for the *collaborative* nature of coaching. Coaching involves two experts (the coach and the student), each with their own domains of expertise, working together to map out a course of action that will help the student achieve goals that are important to them. This, we believe, is the true power of coaching.

OVERVIEW OF THE BOOK'S CONTENTS

This manual is divided in four units. Unit I provides the theoretical and research background that supports our coaching model. Chapter 1 is a brief overview of executive skills, placing them within a developmental context, with a particular emphasis on how they emerge throughout childhood and adolescence. Since coaching as we envision it is an intervention strategy for students with executive skills challenges, any discussion of coaching must be preceded by a solid understanding of executive skills development.

In Chapter 2, we turn to the theoretical and research base upon which our coaching model was developed and that demonstrates its efficacy. Coaching involves multiple components, each of which has a strong research base to support it, and we summarize that research here, covering topics such as motivational interviewing, goal setting and future orientation, cognitive rehearsal strategies, and evidence from the literature on self-determination, self-regulation, self-management, and self-monitoring. We also summarize studies that provide support for the efficacy of coaching as a behavioral intervention.

In Unit II, we present our coaching model, starting with a general introduction (Chapter 3), followed by chapters outlining the steps for coaching middle/high school students (Chapter 4) and elementary students (Chapter 5). Chapter 6 presents authentic case examples that show coaching in action with younger and older students.

In Unit III, we dive into specific coaching techniques. Chapter 7 explains motivational interviewing, and how the techniques associated with this therapeutic approach can be applied to coaching. The research on motivational interviewing has been done primarily with teens and adults. For those who coach younger students, Chapter 8 discusses the communication tools that are helpful for those working with this age group.

For many coaches, the techniques that are central to coaching efficacy may be new and require practice to learn. Chapter 9 presents tools and techniques that coaches can use to analyze their coaching sessions to better understand their skill acquisition and to help them identify places for improvement.

Chapters 10 and 11 cover in more detail two of the coaching steps outlined in Chapters 4 and 5. Chapter 10 is a more granular discussion of how to engage in goal setting and action planning with students. Chapter 11 presents a variety of progress monitoring techniques with examples and explicit instructions for how to measure progress and outcomes of coaching.

Unit IV focuses on coaching strategies and adaptations of these strategies for specific groups of students. Chapter 12 presents strategies that coaches can use to support executive skills development. They fall broadly into three categories (the ABCs of coaching), and the chapter provides a wide array of strategies that coaches can put in their toolbox. Since many of the strategies we describe are ones that are often used by teachers and tutors in a more directive fashion, we spend some time discussing how coaches can employ these strategies in the more collaborative way that is a key feature of our coaching process.

The next two chapters focusing on "special coaching applications." Chapter 13 addresses how coaching can be used to supplement special education services for students with disabilities. We focus on ADHD, autism spectrum disorder, and intellectual disabilities, since these groups have some common features that benefit from specific adaptations. Our basic model of coaching involves one adult coaching one student, but there are other models that hold promise—and that may be more cost effective. Chapter 14 describes group coaching, a model in which one adult coaches small groups of students, and peer coaching, in which students are trained to coach each other. There is research to suggest that both of these models can be effective in addressing both academic and behavioral challenges.

In our last chapter, we return to self-determination and the way coaching can help students achieve a greater sense of self-efficacy. We also address the fact that coaching doesn't work for every student. We describe the obstacles that may interfere with coaching's effectiveness and offer suggestions for how coaches should address them.

We recognize that it may take more than just reading this book for people to acquire the skill sets they need to be effective coaches. Some may want to seek additional training, and we have included training resources for motivational interviewing (Appendix 20, p. 191). In addition, we encourage readers to further explore the techniques of implementation intentions, mental contrasting, and mental rehearsal in the works of Gollwitzer, Oettingen, and Brier (Brier, 2015; Gollwitzer & Oettingen, 2012). But we also believe that people who've had years of experience working with students in a therapeutic or teaching role may be able to use this book to move toward a model that enables students to participate fully in designing a future that works for them.

Note: Throughout this book we use *they/them* as a designation for both individuals and groups. We do this to avoid potential bias and the awkwardness associated with using terms such as *he/she* or *her/him*. This approach has come to be seen by grammarians as acceptable, and we hope the reader understands our rationale.

Contents

THEORETICAL AND RESEARCH BACKGROUND

CHAPTER 1

The Development of Executive Skills in the Brain

Biology and Experience

As is the case with many of the child's abilities, there are two main contributors to the development of executive skills—biology and experience. In terms of the biological or neurological contribution, the potential for executive skills is essentially innate, already a part of the brain's wiring at birth. This is similar to the manner in which we develop language. Of course at birth, executive skills, like language, exist only as potential. That means the child's brain has within it the basic neurological equipment for these skills to develop. But then a number of factors enter the picture, influencing how these skills actually develop.

For example, any type of major trauma or physical insult to the brain, particularly one involving the frontal lobes, would adversely affect executive skills development. Genes also play a major role, and therefore the genes that the child inherits from their parents likely impact these skills. If parents didn't have good organization, time management, attention, or other skills when growing up or now, there's a reasonable chance that the child will evidence these weaknesses.

As for the environment, anything that is biologically or physically toxic during infancy or childhood can affect the development of executive skills. Environmental toxins could include anything from lead exposure to child abuse. Low family income and disadvantaged economic circumstances have been shown in repeated studies to adversely impact brain development and executive skills in children (Blair & Raver, 2016; Troller-Renfree et al., 2022). For example, these economic circumstances can lead to less parental interaction with children, decreased responsiveness to children's distress, and harsher parenting. This results in increased stress for the child.

Chronic, significant stress is known to adversely impact the development of executive skills as well as the availability and use of executive skills that a child already possesses. Maternal depression further contributes to these interaction problems and is an additive stress factor for both mother and child. The third element in this triad of disadvantage is low educational attainment. While any one of these factors can adversely impact brain development in children, taken together they can result in a condition of sustained stress for child and mother, as well as, in extreme cases, a stimulation-deprived environment for the child. Collectively, these conditions are correlated with weaknesses in the development of executive skills.

On the other hand, with a reasonably typical neurological substrate and minimal adverse environmental factors, brain development should proceed as designed.

NEUROLOGY: GROWTH AND DEVELOPMENT + EXPERIENCE = EXECUTIVE SKILLS

Before we consider the developmental sequence, however, we need to look briefly at the way executive skills relate to the brain and brain development. At birth, the child's brain weighs about 370 grams or about 13 ounces. By late adolescence this has increased to about 1,300–1,400 grams or about 3 pounds. A number of changes in the brain account for this significant growth. Broadly speaking, growth of the brain over the course of development occurs through the generation of nerve cells (neurons) and their supporting cells (neuroglia). These cells are the building blocks of the nervous system. In order for nerve cells to "talk" with each other, they develop branches, called axons and dendrites, which allow them to send and receive information from other cells.

When we talk about the material that makes up the brain—neurons, dendrites, axons, and so forth—we can think about this in terms of shadings of the brain, that is, gray and white matter. The white matter of the brain acquires its shading through a process called myelination and represents bundles of axons that connect different regions of the brain and allows them to communicate. Myelin is a fatty sheath that forms around the axon and provides insulation that helps to increase speed of transmission of nerve signals. Thus, the "conversations" (as nerve signals) carried by axons between neurons are made more efficient by this process of insulation. Myelination begins in the earliest stages of development and, in the frontal lobes, continues well into young adulthood. The myelination process is one of the key features of frontal lobe development, and the time course of this process parallels the time course and development of executive skills, which extends to nearly the third decade of adulthood.

Gray matter, in contrast to the white matter of myelin, is made up of nerve cells or neurons, dendrites, and the connections between them called synapses. Unlike myelin, the development of gray matter is a bit more complex. For example, the adult brain has about 86 billion neurons. The majority of these neurons are present in the infant brain at birth. And in early childhood (2 years), the number of synapses exceeds by 50% the number in the adult brain. If the development of gray matter continued at this pace, the adult brain would be enormous. Instead, a different phenomenon occurs. There is an initial increase in gray matter (some neurons and particularly synapses) in infancy and early childhood. This increase peaks before age 5 and then there is a gradual reduction or "pruning" of these connections (Society for Neuroscience, 2018).

The initial increase occurs during a period of rapid learning and experience in early childhood. The pruning process allows the child to consolidate skills, and the gray matter connections that are not needed or used drop away. This period of consolidation continues until a second period of significant development that begins around age 11 or 12, the initiation of another period that we recognize for rapid learning and development. This increase is again followed by a period of reduction through pruning over the course of adolescence and into young adulthood.

Research indicates that this growth spurt in the brain prior to adolescence occurs primarily in the frontal lobes and particularly in the prefrontal cortex. Thus, it is as if the brain is preparing itself both for the development of executive skills and for the significant demands that will be made on executive skills during adolescence. Geidd (2004) has also suggested that a "use it or lose it" process may be occurring in the frontal lobes during this time. Neural connections that are used are retained, while those that are not exercised are lost. If this is the case, then the practice of these skills is important not only for learning self-management but also for the development of brain structures that will support these skills into later adolescence and adulthood. During this period of brain growth, teachers and parents can play a critical role in guiding the learning and development of executive skills.

Thus, there is a parallel between development of the brain and development of the child's ability to act, think, and feel. This parallel is especially important in understanding how executive skills develop and what areas of the brain are most critical for these skills. Researchers now generally agree that frontal brain systems (the frontal/prefrontal cortex along with connections to adjacent areas) make up the neurological base for executive skills.

SEQUENCE OF DEVELOPMENT

At birth we do not have executive skills that are developed or available for immediate use. Rather, in the postnatal period immediately following birth, while the basic elements of the neurological substrate that will support these skills is available, these skills begin to become behaviorally evident as the infant develops and interacts with their environment. In this way, the development of executive skills has similarities to the development of language; the neurological substrate for both language and executive skills exists at birth but they develop and take on their unique characteristics only as the infant develops and interacts with their particular environment.

Assuming that there is no insult to the brain and that experience is reasonably typical, these skills will unfold over time. As they unfold, they're influenced by the genes that we inherit from our parents as well as by the biological and social environments in which we live. If, for example, our parents did not have good organization or attention skills, chances are increased that we will have executive skill challenges in this area. If we are raised in biologically or socially toxic environments, for example where there's lead exposure or psychological trauma, there is an increased likelihood that our executive skills will be adversely impacted. However, assuming that there are no significant genetic anomalies and no significant exposure to physical or psychologically toxic environments, executive skills will begin to develop and present themselves in the infant's behaviors soon after birth in a slow development until adulthood.

Research in infant development indicates the emergence of executive skills, in rudimentary form, at about 6 months of age. For example, response inhibition is evident in an infant's attempt to reach for and grasp an object. In experiments involving eye tracking and eye gaze to stimuli of interest, infants are able to both direct their attention toward an object and inhibit the redirection of attention when a distraction is present (Reynolds & Romano, 2016). The same study also documented the emergence of visual working memory in infants of the same age. This working memory provides infants with the ability to hold in their minds objects, people, and locations that they cannot sense in their immediate surroundings.

These basic executive skills of response initiation/inhibition, sustained attention, and working memory provide the infant with the early capacity to self-direct their behavior. The emergence of a fourth executive skill, emotional control, adds another significant component to this capacity for self-direction. While smiles, which may represent an expression of happiness, emerge earlier, by 6–8 months of age the infant also begins to evidence negative emotions such as fear.

Taken together, these four executive skills enable the infant to direct their behavior either toward or away from objects, people, and locations in their environment. The development of emotional responsiveness underlies the development of emotional control. Combined with the skills of response initiation/inhibition, sustained attention, and working memory, as the child develops an increased capacity for locomotion, emotional responsiveness to different stimuli in the environment forms the basis of approach–avoidance behavior. The development of that behavior allows the infant to increasingly choose the situations in their environment that they would like to move toward or away from.

Considering how these skills begin to work together as they emerge in infancy gives us a window into how these skills will develop over time. In both early discussions and more recent ones on development of executive function skills, Barkley indicated that inhibition "sets the occasion for the occurrence" (2014, p. 412) of other executive function skills. He has described the components of inhibition as including the following:

1. The ability to delay or prevent a response leading to an immediate consequence so that some later-occurring consequence may impact behavior.
2. The ability to stop ongoing behaviors when they prove unsuccessful.
3. The ability to manage distractions or interruptions that could interfere with the work of other executive skills.

What Barkley discussed is a much more sophisticated development in inhibition than the 6-month-old is capable of. However, we do see response initiation and inhibition as fundamental to the development of executive skills over time because it is these behaviors that underlie interaction with the environment. But it is the other executive skills that provide the context for the infant's behavior. In order to explore their environment, the infant must be able to envision, in working memory, what is beyond what they can immediately see. If they initiate a response toward some recalled object or person, they must direct their attention to what they see in order to determine if it is what they expected to see. If it is not, then they must rely on a previous experience to determine whether what they are now attending to is something they want to approach or avoid. Thus, in the act of crawling in a particular direction, in a way that appears to a parent as purposeful, the infant exhibits the type of interaction with the environment that will determine their development of executive skills over time.

While an individual's genetic makeup has a strong influence on their acquisition of executive skills, the good news is that environmental factors play a significant role as well. As will become apparent in the next chapter, executive skills are closely associated with academic performance and overall adjustment. An executive skills coach with a firm understanding of how executive skills develop and how that development can be influenced through environmental modifications and through direct instruction and practice can help students with executive skills challenges build both academic success and the self-confidence that accompanies that success.

CHAPTER 2

Theoretical Underpinnings for Coaching

In their book *Driven to Distraction*, Hallowell and Ratey (1994) include a description of an intervention for adults with attention disorders that they refer to as "coaching." At the time we read that description, we were operating off a "case manager" model for helping students with attention-deficit/hyperactivity disorder (ADHD) navigate the complex channels of middle school and high school. We immediately recognized that the concept of a coach, using the same sports analogy that Hallowell and Ratey employ, fit better the needs of ADHD students. They didn't need someone to *manage* them as much as they needed someone to work with them as a *coach*, in a collaborative and supportive fashion.

Once we recognized this as the metaphor we wanted to work from, we surveyed the literature to find empirical evidence both to help us design our coaching model and to support its efficacy. In the years since we wrote our first coaching manual, we have recognized that the process is suited not only to students with ADHD but to any student who is struggling in school due to executive skills challenges. We have also looked to refine our model by incorporating evidence-based practices in both the behavioral and the cognitive-behavioral fields for strategies that will enhance the coaching process. What follows are descriptions of several strands of research that contribute to our understanding of coaching and to why we believe it is an effective intervention.

GOAL-DIRECTED PERSISTENCE VERSUS CONTEXT-DEPENDENT SUSTAINED ATTENTION

As noted previously, executive skills take two to three decades to fully mature, and one of the latest developing skills is *goal-directed persistence*. This executive skill actually incorporates

8

other executive skills: the ability to set a goal; developing a plan to achieve the goal; keeping the goal in mind over the length of time required to fully implement the plan; and sustaining attention long enough to navigate through distractions to achieve the goal.

In younger children, and those with developmental delays in the acquisition of executive skills (such as youngsters with ADHD), goal-directed persistence is a long time in coming. With diminished future orientation and goal-directed persistence, as Barkley (1997) articulated so well, individuals with ADHD are under the control of the immediate environment. This means that they have little difficulty sustaining attention to tasks that are novel and intrinsically interesting, and for which extrinsic consequences (rewards and penalties) are immediately imposed. These youngsters, for instance, attend well when playing video games, watching favorite television shows, or engaging in other preferred activities. They also tend to be successful in classrooms where the subject matter is of particular interest to them, or the teacher's instructional style is engaging or entertaining.

Unfortunately, it is very difficult for these individuals to sacrifice an immediate reward either to gain some longer-term reward or to avoid some later harm. They are under the control of what is happening *right here and right now*, which Barkley (2014) called context-dependent sustained attention. When there is a conflict between immediate activities (e.g., playing *Fortnite*) and long-term goals (getting a good grade in chemistry), youngsters who struggle with goal-directed persistence have little incentive to set aside the immediate fun activity in favor of the effortful work required to achieve a long-term goal.

Recent research studies suggest that favoring immediate rewards over long-term goals is not limited to children and adolescents with ADHD. For example, van den Bos, Rodriguez, Schweitzer, and McClure (2015) and Icenogle and colleagues (2019) suggested that a key characteristic differentiating adolescents from adults is the incomplete development of *future orientation and with it, goal-directed behavior*. Due to limited experience as well as ongoing brain development, teenagers tend to choose immediate versus delayed rewards, despite well-developed reasoning skills.

Research by van den Bos and colleagues (2015) and Luerssen, Gyurak, Ayduk, Wednelken, and Bunge (2015), among others, suggested the reason for this is the incomplete development of fiber tracts connecting the striatum with the dorsolateral prefrontal cortex (dlPFC), where development will continue into the third decade. These researchers also noted that improvements in future orientation and goal-directed behavior are the result of top-down processing that occurs as the dlPFC exercises increased control through the development of these fiber tracts. Palminteri, Kilford, Coricelli, and Blakemore (2016) offered additional evidence for this developmental difference between adolescents and adults using a behaviorally based reinforcement learning paradigm. They concluded that adolescents, in comparison to adults, tend to rely on immediate rewards and are less able to consider the alternative or aversive consequences that these actions may produce.

These researchers, among others, did not suggest that decision-making favoring immediate rewards is characteristic of all adolescents at all times. Rather, they noted that differences in brain development and experience can have a significant impact on adolescent decision making and the ability to delay gratification. Luerssen and colleagues (2015), for example, noted that weaker functional connectivity between the reward centers in the brain (nucleus accumbens) and the prefrontal cortex results in more immediate reward seeking. Abela, Duan, and Chudasama (2015) reported a similar finding for weak connections between the hippocampus, which is associated with memory and future planning, and the nucleus accumbens, which results in difficulty with delayed gratification.

Murty, Calabro, and Luna (2016) noted that stored experiences accessed from the hippocampus are gradually integrated through improved connections with the prefrontal cortex over the course of adolescent development, eventually resulting in adult levels of cognition, including future orientation and planning. Their research suggests that disruption or delayed development in tracts connecting the hippocampus, nucleus accumbens, and prefrontal cortex negatively impacts delayed gratification, future orientation, and attainment of future goals.

Why is this important? Klein, Robertson, and Delton (2010) suggested that past experience is a key component for future planning and there is research to support this (Underwood, Guynn, & Cohen, 2015). Research also suggests that accessing these past experiences through working memory benefits future planning and goal-directed behavior and that this takes place via developing hippocampal–prefrontal cortex connections. From our perspective, this means that developing experiences of successful goal planning can be stored as memories for future use and that these experiences may enhance the development of underlying neurologic pathways.

The time perspective of future orientation is an essential component of the ability to delay gratification and set future goals and plans. It is also key to positive adolescent development and can play a significant role in overcoming adverse early experiences and the development of self-efficacy and self-control (Zinn, Huntley, & Keating, 2020).

COACHING INTERVENTIONS

We believe that interventions need to be keyed to behaviors that will facilitate attainment of future orientation and goal-directed persistence. Our coaching model seeks to do just this, particularly in Phase 1 of our process, in which students are asked to identify long-term goals and begin to design action plans to achieve those goals.

Future Orientation and Goal Setting

Future orientation and goal setting are critical components of coaching and they go hand-in-hand. Extensive empirical research (see Locke & Latham, 2002, for an excellent overview) has documented the value of goal setting in promoting high levels of performance. While much of this research has been done with adults in a work environment (Locke & Latham, 2002), there is ample evidence that the same rules apply to children and youth in the school environment as well (see a review by Schunk, 2003). More specifically, Watkins (2019), in a study with first graders, found that goal setting combined with data tracking resulted in improved reading performance. Dotson (2016), in a study involving 328 fourth- and fifth-grade students, found that goal setting had a significant effect on reading performance.

According to Locke and Latham (2002), goals serve four primary functions. First, they *direct* behavior—toward goal-relevant activities and away from goal-irrelevant activities. Second, they *energize*—high goals lead to greater effort than low goals. Third, they encourage *persistence*. And finally, they motivate individuals to discover or use task-relevant knowledge or strategies.

Coaching, in all its forms, is built around goal setting. Whether we're working with a second grader on task completion, a fifth grader on social skills, or a high school student on passing classes, the process begins by having students set goals.

Table 2.1 summarizes key findings about the most effective ways to employ goal setting to improve performance.

Locke and Latham (2002) concluded by affirming that the efficacy of goal setting is well documented and that the process plays a significant role in producing high performance. They also succinctly summarized the conditions that impede the effectiveness of goal setting. These include "not matching the goal to the performance measure, not providing feedback, not getting goal commitment, not conveying task knowledge, setting a performance goal when a specific high-learning goal is required, not setting proximal goals when the environment is characterized by uncertainty, or not including a sufficient range of goal difficulty levels" (p. 714).

Motivational Interviewing

According to Ryan and Deci (2017), the drive for self-determination is a basic human need. They identified three essential elements for achieving this:

- *Autonomy:* People need to feel in control of their own behaviors and goals.
- *Competence:* People need to gain mastery of tasks and learn different skills.
- *Connection or relatedness:* People need to experience a sense of belonging and attachment to other people.

The goal of our coaching model is student self-determination. This requires a particular style on the part of the coach—one that promotes student self-control, a sense of competence, and a relationship of trust. Motivational interviewing (MI) embodies this style. As Naar-King and Suarez (2011) explained, the job of the coach "is not to take responsibility for change, but rather to support and guide while seeking to elicit the young person's own ideas for change" (p. 17). The coach is able to accomplish this by providing a menu of choices and information, by inquiring about the student's perspectives, and by encouraging personal choice and responsibility. The goal is to create an environment of "supportive autonomy" (Williams, 2002).

MI aligns well with our coaching process, and we have incorporated it as a foundational element. In Chapter 7, we expand on the components of MI and how they can be implemented throughout the coaching process, along with training information and resources.

Cognitive Rehearsal Strategies

In the development of our coaching model in the mid-1990s we incorporated correspondence training as an integral component. As defined by Paniagua (1992), *correspondence training* refers to a chain of behaviors that "include a verbalization or report about either past or future behavior and the corresponding nonverbal behavior" (p. 229). In other words, when individuals make a verbal commitment to engage in a behavior at some later point, this increases the likelihood that they will actually carry out the behavior. In our original model, for instance, we asked students to report what tasks they intended to accomplish before the next coaching session and to specify when they intended to accomplish them.

TABLE 2.1. Keys to Success with Goal Setting

What the research says	Guidelines for practice
Specific goals are more effective than urging people to "do their best."	Help students make goals that are measurable (e.g., spend 45 minutes studying for a chemistry test; complete math homework during sixth-period study hall).
There is an exception to the above: When a task is complex, urging people to do their best may produce better results than setting specific goals because it reduces evaluative pressure and performance anxiety.	Help students determine whether the goal they want to set is "simple" or "complex." Encourage them to make some of their goals complex but allow for a looser evaluation of results (let them use a "pass/fail" grading system for these goals).
Complex tasks are more likely to be achieved if accompanied by short-term interim goals (also called *proximal goals*) that specify steps to be followed to achieve the complex task.	For complex tasks, always build in a planning component that specifies steps to be followed and establishes interim goals for each step. Proximal goals act as an "early warning system" to let the student know whether the long-term goal is feasible.
When people are trained in proper strategies, they will use those strategies for high-performance goals. If they lack those strategies, however, they will perform better with easier goals.	Make sure that students have the strategies they need to carry out goals. If necessary, teach them the steps they will need to follow to achieve goals.
When individuals can control how much time they spend on a task, hard goals prolong effort, but there is often a trade-off between time and intensity of effort.	Give students a choice of working faster and more intensely for shorter periods of time or more slowly and less intensely for longer periods of time; help them identify which pace works best for them.
Goals can either be assigned or set participatively. Assigned goals may be as effective as those set by someone else, but only when the purpose or rationale for the goal is provided and understood. In general, when individuals are allowed to set their own goals, they tend to set higher goals and to have a higher level of performance in achieving those goals.	Since the goal of coaching is self-determination, it is better, whenever possible, to have students set their own goals. They may need help with this in the beginning, in which case suggesting a goal, along with a rationale for it, may be helpful.
People with high self-efficacy (confidence in their abilities) set higher goals than those with low self-efficacy; they are also more committed to achieving those goals and are more likely to identify effective goal-attainment strategies.	With students who have experienced a lot of failure and who lack confidence in their ability to achieve goals, encourage them to set easier goals in the beginning and to gradually increase their reach.
Self-efficacy can be increased (1) by ensuring adequate strategy training; (2) by role modeling; and (3) through persuasive communication that expresses confidence in the individual's ability to achieve a stated goal.	All of these are roles that coaches play in the course of the coaching process.

(continued)

TABLE 2.1. *(continued)*

What the research says	Guidelines for practice
Learning goals (goals regarding what skills or knowledge an individual hopes to acquire) produce different results than performance goals (what tasks individuals want to complete) do. When students set difficult learning goals, goal specificity is critical.	There is a place for both learning and performance goals, particularly with students who are failing in school because they fail to complete tasks that are assigned to them. Coaching often focuses on performance goals, but good coaches look for ways to incorporate learning goals as well, since these are often accompanied by a higher level of motivation and intrinsic interest.
Performance feedback informs individuals about progress toward goals. Goals plus feedback is more effective than goals alone.	This is another reason for helping students create measurable goals. Daily coaching sessions should incorporate performance feedback (e.g., How many of the goals you set yesterday were you able to achieve? You said you wanted to earn a grade of 85 or better on your math test. Were you able to?).
Performance feedback is enhanced when accompanied by attributional training—that is, training students to attribute their success to effort or strategy use and to attribute failure to lack of effort or strategy use rather than to lack of ability.	Coaches should ask students, "To what do you attribute your success (or failure)?" and should steer them toward explanations that involve behavior they have control over (e.g., "I tried hard" or "I studied for a long time") versus other explanations (e.g., "I got lucky" or "It was an easy test").

Bevill-Davis, Clees, and Gast (2004) concluded that correspondence training held some promise but that additional research was needed. In subsequent research, Gollwitzer and Oettingen (2012) noted that while strongly committing to a goal is a necessary step for goal-directed behavior, it is not a sufficient step to reach goal attainment. In their view, successful goal pursuit may be hindered by factors such as failing to initiate or sustain attention to a task or overcommitting oneself. In addition, they noted that people may continue to engage in unsuccessful strategies or pursue unattainable goals. To address such issues they developed a strategy called "implementation intentions with mental contrasting" or MCII (Oettingen & Gollwitzer, 2010).

According to Brier (2015), implementation intentions are basically a set of self-instructions that constitute a behavioral planning strategy. Brier noted that these instructions can help students "translate an intention first into an action-oriented commitment and, subsequently, into a set of clearly specified goal-directed behaviors" (p. 38). Mental contrasting is a technique designed to enhance the effectiveness of implementation intentions by having the student anticipate possible obstacles to the goal and planning strategies to overcome these.

These techniques work in the following way: The student is first asked to verbally spell out, in detail and as vividly as possible, the best outcome they can envision if they carry out their intention successfully. The student is then asked to think about, in detail, what specific obstacles could stand in the way of successfully achieving the positive result they desire. Student and coach then collaboratively plan how to address these obstacles if/when they arise.

More than 90 independent studies of more than 8,000 individuals have demonstrated medium to large effects on goal achievement (Brier, 2015). Of relevance for our coaching model, students from middle school, high school, and college populations have evidenced enhanced goal attainment using these techniques. Duckworth, Kirby, Gollwitzer, and Oettingen (2013), in a controlled study involving 77 disadvantaged fifth-grade students, reported significant improvements in attendance, conduct, and report card grades for students in the MCII group. Velasquez-Sheehey (2015), in a study with 118 urban high school students, noted significant improvements in academic performance (end-of-quarter grades) for students in the MCII condition. Oettingen, Kappes, Guttenberg, and Gollwitzer (2015), in a study involving university students, reported improvements in time management to address academic problems in the MCII group.

A third technique under the rubric of cognitive rehearsal is mental simulation. This technique involves students mentally imagining the behaviors they will engage in and the situation in which this will occur in order to reach their goals. More specifically, the individual is asked to mentally imagine the specific situation, objects, emotions, and actions, in as much sensory detail as possible, that will take place when they engage in the intended behavior.

According to a study by Knäuper, Roseman, Johnson, and Krantz (2009), the addition of mental simulation to verbally mediated implementation intentions further increases the likelihood of goal achievement. Creating an active, specific image of the behavior and the situation the individual plans to engage in increases the likelihood that when they enter the actual situation, it will trigger the plan they rehearsed. Interestingly, when individuals mentally rehearse an action plan, they activate the same areas of the brain they will use when they actually engage in the behavior. That's one of the reasons athletes, among others, rely on mental rehearsal to improve performance.

Self-Regulation/Self-Management

The ultimate goal of coaching is to enhance the self-regulatory capacities of youngsters, so that they are no longer reliant on others to cue them, coach them, or reinforce them for using their executive skills to achieve personal goals. *Self-regulation* has been defined as "the internally-directed capacity to regulate affect, attention, and behavior to respond effectively to both internal and external environmental demands" (Raffaelli, Crocket, & Shen, 2005, pp. 54–55).

Self-regulation applies to a broad array of behaviors designed to facilitate the acquisition of self-control and self-direction in a variety of contexts. A related concept, self-regulated learning, is also relevant to this discussion, since coaching is frequently designed to promote *self-regulated learning* more specifically. This has been defined as "the self-directive *processes* through which learners transform their mental abilities into task-related academic skills" (Zimmerman, 2001, p. 1). In other words, "students are self-regulated to the degree that they are metacognitively, motivationally, and behaviorally active participants in their own learning process" (Zimmerman, 1986, p. 5).

Self-regulated learners are able to use an array of cognitive strategies to accomplish academic tasks. They also have the metacognitive skills to understand what any given learning task requires, so that they can select the most appropriate strategies to accomplish the task. In addition, they are able to monitor their performance and make adjustments based on shifting situational demands.

An important component of self-regulation and self-regulated learning that is sometimes overlooked in the literature is the regulation of motivation. Wolters (2003) noted that students use metacognition to process, construct, or understand academic content; regulating motivation, however, involves a student's "willingness to process information, construct meaning, or to continue working" (p. 192). Metacognitive strategies involve *how* one performs a task, according to Wolters, while motivational strategies relate to *why* and *how long* one engages in a task. For many students with executive skills weaknesses, lack of motivation has as much or more to do with their inability to apply themselves to academic tasks than with their lack of cognitive or metacognitive skills. Thus, coaching is as much about helping students activate motivational strategies as it is about cognitive or metacognitive strategies. Table 2.2 summarizes research on strategies to enhance motivation regulation (see Wolters, 2003, for a more complete discussion of these strategies).

Self-management refers to a set of strategies students use to alter their behavior in order to achieve behavioral or academic goals. These strategies include self-monitoring, self-evaluation, self-instruction, and self-reinforcement. Table 2.3 provides descriptors and examples for each of these strategies.

Self-management of behavior in classroom settings has been the focus of research since the late 1960s (Fantuzzo & Polite, 1990; Fantuzzo, Rohrbeck, & Azar, 1987), with some impressive results supporting this approach to changing student behavior in the classroom. Fantuzzo and colleagues identified 11 different elements within self-management interventions where students can be responsible for the management of the intervention. These include (1) selection of target behavior; (2) creation of an operational definition of the target behavior; (3) selection of primary reinforcers; (4) setting the performance goal; (5) administering the prompt to engage in the target behavior; (6) observing the target behavior; (7) recording the occurrence of the target behavior; (8) evaluating whether the performance goal was met; (9) administering secondary reinforcers when the goal is met[1]; (10) administering primary reinforcers when the goal is met; and (11) monitoring occurrence of behavior over time using charts or graphs. Ways to incorporate elements of self-management into coaching are depicted in Table 2.4.

Studies Investigating the Efficacy of Coaching

When we first developed coaching as an intervention strategy, we were fairly confident that it would work because of the research supporting key components of coaching. We conducted a pilot study at a high school in Portsmouth, New Hampshire, in which we trained school personnel, including guidance counselors and special education aides, to act as coaches for five students (10th and 11th graders) with ADHD who volunteered to participate in the study. After completing a long-term goal planning session, they met with their coaches daily to make study plans consistent with their long-term goals. Although the study included no control group, we were able to compare the grades these students had earned the year before coaching began with the grades they earned during the two marking periods in which coaching took place. Table

---

[1]The authors' definitions of primary and secondary reinforcers appear to deviate from the more commonly accepted definitions of these terms. Technically, a *primary reinforcer* is biologically predetermined to act as a reinforcer, such as food or water. A *secondary reinforcer*, also called a conditioned reinforcer, is anything that acquires reinforcing properties by being paired with a primary reinforcer, such as token, points, or money.

TABLE 2.2. Keys to Success for Enhancing Motivation

What the research says	Guidelines for practice
Students who reward themselves for achieving goals or accomplishing tasks are more productive than those who punish themselves or do not self-consequate.	Encourage students to identify a way to reward themselves when they achieve a goal or accomplish individual steps toward achieving a goal. This might include something they can look forward to doing when the task or subtask is completed.
The use of self-talk has been associated with higher levels of task engagement and performance outcomes. Mastery self-talk is associated with greater use of planning and self-monitoring strategies and with self-reported effort. Performance self-talk is associated with rehearsal and regulation strategies and with classroom performance.	Teach students how to use both mastery self-talk (e.g., "I'm going to work at this algebra problem until I understand how it works!") and performance self-talk (e.g., "Great job. I stuck with my math homework and didn't quit until I finished it!").
Individuals can improve task performance through the use of interest-enhancement strategies to make tasks more enjoyable, interesting, or challenging.	Help students identify ways they may turn tasks into games, challenge themselves to complete tasks within self-selected time limits, or find a purpose for doing the task (e.g., by creating a question they want to answer in a reading assignment or forming an opinion regarding key points covered in a reading assignment and looking for evidence to support or refute their position). For some students, social engagement enhances interest in any learning task; encourage them to study with a friend or partner.
Some students engage in "self-handicapping" strategies (such as leaving assignments until the last minute or pulling "all-nighters"). Although these students report that this motivates them, research is equivocal, and the practice may be associated with creating a cycle of low effort and low task performance because students may use procrastination as an excuse for poor-quality work.	If students say they work best under the pressure of immediate deadlines, coaches may want to challenge this belief. Explain that a large body of research supports the superiority of distributed practice (spreading the work out over time) versus massed practice (doing all the work at one time, such as cramming for exams).
Proximal goals and self-set goals increase student motivation for task completion and performance.	See Table 2.1 for practice suggestions.
Motivation can be enhanced through emotion regulation techniques.	Teach students ways to decrease negative emotions (e.g., through relaxation techniques or thought stopping) and increase positive emotions to support the task at hand (e.g., by focusing on the pride they will feel in their efforts or their sense of accomplishment at completing a challenging task).

TABLE 2.3. Types of Self-Management Strategies

Type	Description	Example
Self-monitoring	Student recognizes occurrence of target behavior and records some aspect of the behavior.	Student checks off whether paying attention at the sound of electronic tone occurring at random intervals.
Self-evaluation	Student compares their behavior to previously established criterion set by self or adult (e.g., teacher or coach).	Student compares neatness of homework to example representing criterion performance.
Self-instruction	Student uses self-talk to direct behavior.	Student generates list of motivating or problem-solving statements to get through homework ("You can't walk away from this" or "If I can't figure it out, I'll ask my dad for help").
Goal setting	Student selects behavioral targets to work for.	1. Finish homework by 9:00 P.M. 2. Study 30 minutes per night for four nights for biology test. 3. Ask two teachers to write college recommendations by end of school day on Friday.

2.5 depicts the results. As can be seen in the table, whereas before coaching, the majority of grades students earned were C's, during coaching, the majority of grades they earned were B's or better.

A study that looked at the impact of our coaching model on math homework completion and accuracy on high school students with ADHD (Merriman & Codding, 2008) also produced promising results. Using a multiple-baseline approach with three 9th and 10th graders, students established both long- and short-term goals related to homework completion and accuracy rates and participated in daily coaching sessions in which each student met for 10–15 minutes with their coaches to perform the following tasks: (1) score and graph on an Excel spreadsheet percentage of math problems attempted and completed accurately for the prior day's homework assignment; (2) review and evaluate the student's success at following the previous day's plan and meeting the goal; (3) establish a new plan for the day; and (4) determine a new short-term goal if the previous goal had been met. Systematic fading was incorporated into the process by reducing the frequency of sessions to every other day once long-term goals were reached and to once a week when homework completion and accuracy rates stabilized across four coaching sessions. Coaching was discontinued when rates remained at high levels for four additional sessions.

Study findings showed that, prior to coaching, the students were submitting an average of 29% or fewer homework assignments with average accuracy ratings of 29% or lower. Compared to baseline performance, the percentage of problems completed and accuracy increased for all three students, and two of them met their long-term goals and were able to fade and then dis-

TABLE 2.4. Elements of Self-Management

Element	What does student participation look like?
Selection of target behavior	Student helps identify what behavioral problem needs to be addressed.
Definition	Student is involved in developing operational definition of the target behavior (e.g., "Keep hands to self during circle time").
Selection of primary reinforcers	Student is asked to identify possible reinforcers; helps create a reinforcement menu.
Performance goal	Student helps set a reasonable goal for the target behavior (e.g., "Remember to raise my hand x percent of the time").
Instructional prompt	Student helps decide the best way to remember to prompt for the behavior (e.g., use of kitchen timer or random self-cuing for on-task behavior).
Observation	Student is responsible for monitoring the target behavior.
Recording	Student is asked the best way to record the presence or absence of the target behavior.
Evaluation	Student is at least partially responsible for determining when the goal was met (may include a system for verifying accuracy).
Administration of secondary reinforcers	Student gives themself points or tokens for exhibiting target behavior.
Administration of primary reinforcers	Student chooses reward from reinforcement menu when they have accumulated enough points or tokens.
Monitoring	Student is responsible for charting or graphing performance over time.

Note. From Dawson and Guare (2009; based on Briesch & Chafouleas). Copyright © 2009 The Guilford Press. Reprinted by permission.

TABLE 2.5. Effect of Coaching on Report Card Grades

Percent grades earned	B or better	C	D
Before coaching	19	61	19
During coaching	63	32	5

continue coaching with continued success. The third student showed improvement over baseline but did not improve enough to meet their long-term goals.

A second study applied our coaching model to the development of social skills in children with ADHD (Plumer & Stoner, 2005). This study is described more extensively in Chapter 14, but it is noteworthy because it extended coaching to a younger population (late elementary school) and employed peers as coaches. As a result of coaching, not only did positive social behaviors increase significantly for the three students who participated in the study, but the gains appeared to generalize to other settings and involved children other than the peer coaches.

More recently, Vilardo and DuPaul (2010), in an unpublished study, used coaching with cross-age tutors to improve peer interactions in first-grade students exhibiting symptoms of ADHD. In this study, four children, two girls and two boys ages 6–7, were matched with four older children, ages 8–9, to work on prosocial skills. The children set long-term goals and then met with their coaches, who were trained by graduate students in school psychology and special education, on a daily basis to select a daily goal and practice the goal through modeling and role playing. Rewards were administered for successful demonstration of daily goal behaviors. Outcome measures included a standardized social skills improvement measure and an intervention rating profile. In this study, boys exhibited improvement on outcome measures while girls did not.

These three studies were all based on our coaching model. Studies that employ coaching without following our model explicitly, as well as those that include all the elements of our model without calling it "coaching," have also supported the efficacy of the process.

Anderson, Munk, Young, Conley, and Caldarella (2008) described in some detail a process for teaching organizational skills to junior high school students that employed most of the elements of coaching, including direct instruction of organizational skills, data collection, individualized adult support, positive reinforcement, goal setting, and behavioral contracting. Students in a life skills class were shown how to organize their notebooks and were taught to use a daily checklist to help them come to class prepared, write down assignments, complete and turn in assignments, and track their performance on assignments. As the year went along, they added two features, goal setting and behavioral contracting. Three of the four students featured in that study significantly improved report card grades in the subjects in which they employed the process, one student improving from a D– to a B– in science and two other students improving to A's from C and C– grades.

In an extensive review, Devine, Meyers, and Houssemand (2013) reported on outcomes for student coaching from the United Kingdom and Australia. In the United Kingdom, outcomes included improved examination performance and increased hope for student participants. In Australia, outcomes for senior high school coaching participants included the following: development of personal learning goals and study skills that led to improved performance; increased resilience, coping skills, and a sense of well-being; and decreased levels of depression, among other positive changes.

Coaching has also been employed effectively at the college level. Swartz, Prevatt, and Proctor (2005) described a coaching intervention for students with ADHD that included an initial goal meeting at which the coaching process was explained and long-term goals were established. At this meeting, decisions were also made regarding rewards and consequences for meeting or failing to meet goals as well as the frequency and nature of the ongoing coaching contacts, with participants choosing weekly or biweekly face-to-face contact at the campus assessment center, phone calls, and/or emails. Weekly objectives (interim steps to be followed to achieve the long-term goals) were also developed at the initial session and reviewed and revised at each subsequent coaching session. The authors provided a case study of a single student, a senior majoring in nursing, who participated in the coaching process in order to address problems with procrastination, concentration in class, and time management issues. A comparison of pre- and posttest data showed that the student improved on a majority of the goals she selected to work on, showed improvement in her study time, and achieved her goal of earning a B in the course.

More recently, controlled studies with academically at-risk college students have confirmed the benefits of coaching for this population. Capstick, Harrell-Williams, Cockrum, and West (2019) reported on a study involving archival data for 1,434 undergraduates. Students who participated in academic coaching evidenced significant increases in GPA and were more likely to earn a GPA of at least 2.0 during their intervention semester than were students who did not engage in coaching. Grassley (2019) reported an increase of 0.4 points in GPAs of coached students whose prior GPAs ranged from 1.0 to 2.0. Grassley also reported that these students were about 10% more likely to enroll in the following semester and earned on average two more credits than noncoached students.

While coaching has not been extensively researched in controlled studies, what is encouraging about the research to date is that coaching has shown that it can be an effective intervention with students ranging from elementary age to college age and it can be used to address both academic and social goals. What follows in subsequent chapters is a how-to manual for establishing coaching interventions either for individual students or more programmatically to address the needs of groups of underperforming students at all ages.

OUR COACHING MODEL

CHAPTER 3

Introduction

WHO BENEFITS FROM COACHING?

When we first developed our coaching model, our target population was teenagers with ADHD and the behaviors we focused on were those associated with academic underachievement. Over the years, though, as we've coached students and trained others to coach students, we've realized that coaching is a highly versatile strategy that can be easily adapted to meet a wide range of students with a variety of learning and behavioral needs. There *are* students for whom coaching is not an appropriate intervention, but this is less determined by age, disability category, or cognitive capacity and more by the student's receptivity to the process.

ESSENTIAL FEATURES OF OUR COACHING MODEL

Here are the features we consider to be essential for coaching to be successful:

• Coaching must be voluntary. The student has to willingly engage in the process—which means they have permission *not* to engage in coaching as well. There may be exceptions to this in the case of classwide coaching models, which is discussed in Chapter 14, but with all other models—individual coaching, peer coaching, reciprocal coaching, or small-group coaching— the expectation is that the process will be clearly explained to the student, and they can choose to opt in or out. This stipulation can be a source of frustration to parents, who may think this is *exactly* what their child needs, or to teachers, who may view coaching as an intervention perfectly designed for an unmotivated student. In our experience, though, students who feel they have been forced into the process will find ways to ensure that it fails. This isn't to say we don't spend some time explaining coaching to a reluctant participant to try to bring them on board. That's where motivational interviewing comes in. But ultimately, we respect a student's right to choose not to work with a coach.

• It is the *student* who's responsible for choosing the goals they want to work on. This again can be a source of frustration to parents or teachers, who often feel that they can see clearly what the student needs to be working on to be successful in school. But a key piece of the coaching process is teaching students how to set goals and develop plans for achieving those goals. If someone else is creating the goals and the action plans, then the student does not have the opportunity to learn these key skills. We think of our coaching process as being *student-centered*. The role of the coach is to collaborate with the student to help them meet their goals.

• Coaches and students have frequent contact. Counseling and tutoring sessions often take place weekly. More frequent contact, especially in the early stages of coaching, is almost always necessary. Since our coaching process focuses on strengthening executive skills that are weak, the practice required ideally occurs on a daily basis (even if the practice sessions are short). If a student is only reporting back to a coach once a week, it increases the likelihood that the student will either procrastinate or forget altogether. In a school setting, the contact could be face-to-face (and once the process is up and running it may be no more than a 5-minute daily check-in). For coaches working independently, face-to-face contact on a daily basis is not feasible—but texts, phone calls, or emails between sessions can be ways to stay connected. The frequency of contact is reduced as coaching continues, but in the beginning we recommend that coach and student touch base at least a few additional times a week until the coach is comfortable that the student is keeping pace with their plan.

• Progress monitoring takes place throughout the coaching process. Giving students objective feedback—preferably using some kind of visual display such as a chart or a graph—is part of the appeal of coaching. Helping students set realistic goals and then showing them that they are reaching those goals is, in our experience, as powerful a motivator as any other, to keep students doing the hard work needed to strengthen skills and build habits. Since data collection can be cumbersome, we've focused on finding progress monitoring measures that do not require a lot of work. In fact, some of the most effective progress monitoring methods involve capturing data that's already available and converting it into a self-explanatory visual display. More about that in Chapter 11.

COACHING ELEMENTARY STUDENTS VERSUS SECONDARY STUDENTS

The first edition of this manual focused on coaching secondary (middle/high school) students. Since its publication we have adapted our model for use with coaches who want to work with elementary students. All of the elements described above are common to both age groups, but there are some distinctions—primarily in terms of the role that parents or teachers (or both) play in the coaching process. Table 3.1 lists the distinctions.

TABLE 3.1. Differences between Coaching Elementary Students and Secondary Students

Secondary	Elementary
Coaching must be voluntary	Parent or teacher can initiate, but student buy-in is necessary for success
Student selects goals	Student selects goals (but may need suggestions from parents or teachers)
Student is helped to identify the strategies that work best for them	Coach suggests strategies; lets child choose one to try
Can work well virtually using technology for progress monitoring	Works best face-to-face, and for some children pencil-and-paper progress monitoring works better
Parents/teachers have limited role in the coaching process	Either a parent or a teacher will need to facilitate the process
Coaching sessions or check-ins are frequent to begin with, but can move from daily to weekly in time	Daily check-ins are needed for most children

WHO CAN BE A COACH?

Coaches are either employed by school districts or they come from the private sector. If they work in schools, here are the people we've seen make good coaches:

- A school psychologist
- A special education teacher
- A favorite teacher
- A school counselor
- An intern (teacher, counselor, school psychology)
- A paraprofessional (classroom or personal aide)
- A volunteer who's been trained
- Another school employee (secretary, custodian, nurse, assistant principal, or sports coach) that the student feels well connected to

In the private sector, we have trained people from a wide variety of backgrounds to work as executive skills coaches. These include:

- Tutors
- Speech pathologists
- Occupational therapists

- Social workers or other counselors
- Educational therapists
- Retired educators/school professionals

For those training as coaches coming from different professional fields, an understanding of the distinction between their other professional roles and coaching is essential. In most cases, as they learn and practice the coaching process, that distinction becomes clear.

WHAT QUALITIES DEFINE A GOOD COACH?

When we ask coaches to define the factors that made a particular coaching experience a success for the student, the number one answer we get is this: the relationship between the coach and the student. Good coaches focus first on building relationships with the students they work with before jumping into goal setting, problem solving, and action planning. Relationships are built on trust, and students need to feel that the person coaching them understands and likes them—will support them when they struggle and won't judge them harshly. Atul Gawande (2011), in an article on coaching published several years ago in *The New Yorker* magazine, noted that coaching can be "tricky." As he wrote so eloquently, "Human beings resist exposure and critique; our brains are well defended. So coaches use a variety of approaches—showing what other, respected colleagues do, for instance, or reviewing videos of the subject's performance. The most common, however, is just conversation" (p. 49).

Figure 3.1 summarizes the attributes of good coaches. Good coaches need to be reliable: They need to be able to make plans and keep schedules. Clear thinking helps. When a student describes a goal that is vague or grandiose, a coach needs to be able to help translate it into something practical. Good coaches need to be good problem-solvers, but more importantly, they need to know how to empower students to solve their own problems. Good coaches don't lecture or instruct; rather, through using a Socratic method, they primarily ask questions that lead students to identify for themselves solutions for the problems they present. A coach also needs to be enthusiastic and supportive—someone who can find the silver lining in the cloud. When plans don't work, coaches need to be able to highlight the positive, bring students back to the long-term plan, remind them how far they've come. Finally, good coaches are invested in their students without taking setbacks or disappointments personally.

- They like kids and relate to them in a natural way.
- They are empathic and good listeners.
- They're reliable, organized, and have good planning skills.
- They teach more through questions than lectures.
- They have training in coaching.

FIGURE 3.1. Characteristics of good coaches.

CHAPTER 4

Coaching Secondary Students

AN OVERVIEW OF THE COACHING STEPS

Students and coaches connect through a variety of means. Very often, parents recognize that their youngsters would benefit from coaching and seek out services on their own. Psychologists or neuropsychologists who uncover executive skills challenges in the course of conducting evaluations often recommend coaching. In a school setting, coaching may be recommended by a teacher, a special education teacher, a school counselor, or a school psychologist. Not all students referred for coaching are good candidates for coaching, and this issue is explored early in the coaching process. The rest of this chapter outlines the steps in the coaching process, with the steps previewed in Table 4.1.

Step 1. Gather Background Information on the Student

The first session (or several) between the coach and the student is intended to achieve several aims. First of all, it is an opportunity for them to get to know and feel comfortable with each other. When we've asked experienced coaches what's the most important ingredient for successful coaching, the answer we get is, "The relationship between the coach and the student." This means the coach should allow enough time for the rapport building to unfold naturally. This can be combined with information gathering that will inform the coaching process, but it may work best when it's conducted in an informal, casual way, particularly early on in the conversation. Finding out what the student's nonacademic interests and passions are is a good place to start, and if it brings to light some common interests between the coach and the student, all the better.

Motivational interviewing is the best vehicle for conducting the early conversations around coaching. This process is described in detail in Chapter 7. Some students may state definitively

TABLE 4.1. Steps in the Coaching Process

Step	Description
1	Gather background information on the student.
2	Conduct readiness assessment to determine if the student is a good fit for coaching.
3	Make a go/no-go decision.
4	Communicate with parents about the nature of coaching and clarify the parents' role in the process.
5	Conduct goal-setting interview.
6	Decide on a meeting schedule.
7	Conduct coaching sessions using REAP (review, evaluate, anticipate, plan).
8	Collect progress monitoring data and share with the student.
9	Review with the student an appropriate timeline to end coaching.
10	End coaching.

at this point that they have no interest in coaching, at which point the coach should respect their wishes. Many students may continue to be unsure of the process, but they may be willing to continue with the information-gathering phase to help them understand coaching better before making a decision about whether they want to continue.

Having the student complete the Getting to Know You Survey (Appendix 1; pp. 141–142) is a good entry point into the information-gathering phase. The survey does not focus on problems but asks about the student's preferred leisure activities and their talents and personal strengths. One question on this survey that we've found particularly helpful is *What areas of skill or knowledge would you like to become an expert in?* Nonacademic examples are included in the question to help students think more broadly, and we've often been surprised by the wide range of interests students report. The answer to this question can be particularly useful when trying to determine potential motivators than can be used during the coaching process to entice students to work on building skills and habits or changing behaviors. This survey also asks questions about learning style, favorite study locations, and preferred classroom activities—good information to have as the coaching process proceeds.

Coaches also have available a number of informal surveys that focus on executive skills. These include pencil-and-paper measures, such as the Executive Skills Questionnaire and the Executive Skills Problem Checklist, as well as the Executive Skills Semistructured Interview.

Coaches should not feel obligated to use all these options, but we recommend that they elicit information in a couple of different formats. Each option is briefly described here.

Executive Skills Questionnaire (ESQ)

The student version of this tool (Appendix 2; pp. 143–146) allows students to quickly assess their executive skills. It is not norm-referenced, but it captures a student's view of stronger and weaker skills. Because students tend to underreport problems, we encourage coaches to read the instructions for completing the ESQ with the student, so that they understand the frame of mind they should be bringing to the task. When the student has completed the questionnaire, we recommend that the coach talks with them about the results. We also recommend talking about the student's strengths before discussing weaknesses. This discussion might sound like this:

> "I want to start by talking about what you're good at. You have a high score on flexibility, which means you adjust easily to change and can 'think outside the box' when something requires creativity. You also scored high on metacognition, which means you're good at making connections between ideas and you're probably a good problem-solver. On the other hand, your low scores on task initiation and sustained attention tell me that you have issues with procrastination, and you often stop working before the task is done. Does this make sense to you?"

One of the messages that coaches give students that is particularly valuable is that *all* of us have executive skills strengths and challenges. It is the rare adult who has strong executive skills across the board, and we encourage coaches both to let students know this and, as appropriate, to share their own profile of executive skills strengths and challenges by way of example. Sharing the coping strategies coaches have developed to address their challenges as well as admitting that they are still working on some of these skills even as adults lets students know that it is *normal* to have stronger and weaker skills. Coaches can find the adult ESQ in Appendix 3 (pp. 147–149).

Executive Skills Problem Checklist (ESPC)

This checklist (Appendix 4; pp. 150–153) identifies a range of specific study behaviors associated with each executive skill. The behavioral descriptors are more precise than the ESQ, and students are asked to complete the checklist in two steps. The first pass-through, they are asked to check off any behaviors that "significantly interfere with effective studying." They are then asked to review all the items they checked off and choose three that "cause the greatest problems." These can be used during the goal-setting phase of coaching to help a student select a goal to work on.

Sometimes we ask parents to complete the ESPC on their child as well. Although we advise parents that the student is the coaching client and the goal will come from them, having the parent complete the ESPC gives them an opportunity to share their perspective with the coach. Although in our experience parents tend to check off many more items than students do, we've also found that they frequently agree on a fair number of them, and even if they select three different priorities, they often agree on which executive skill the biggest problems are associated with.

Executive Skills Semistructured Interview

This interview template (Appendix 5; pp. 154–159) offers an alternative way of collecting information about a student's executive skills strengths and weaknesses. Although it takes longer than the ESQ or the ESPC, it has a number of advantages. It's a way to learn about a student by means of conversation and may feel less burdensome to some students than completing written forms. It also gives the coach the opportunity to follow up with additional questions when more detail would be helpful—or to skip questions that don't seem to be germane. Questions are arranged by topic areas, such as homework, long-term projects, and study skills, rather than by executive skills. Each question, however, is tagged to specific executive skills, so as the interview progresses, patterns may emerge. Some questions address nonschool topics, such as chores and work/leisure time activities, which allows the coach to see how executive skills strengths and challenges may affect the student's life outside of school.

When the information-gathering phase of the coaching process is completed, the coach should offer the student a summary of what they have learned about the student. Here's an example of what that summary might sound like:

> "I really appreciate you talking with me and completing the surveys I gave you. Let me see if I can capture some of the things I have learned about you. I've learned that you like to hang out with friends and play online video games. You also enjoy playing on the school soccer team. You see yourself as having talents in writing and communication skills, and the personal qualities that are most important to you include empathy, creativity, and problem solving. You also have a good sense of humor. In terms of executive skills, your stronger skills include emotional control and goal-directed persistence. Your weaker skills include task initiation and time management, and this gets you in trouble in terms of handing in homework on time and completing long-term assignments by the deadlines. On the Executive Skills Problem Checklist, you identified three study behaviors that you think get in the way of being a more effective student: You have trouble making yourself do homework when there are more fun things to do, you tend to procrastinate, especially when the assignment is tedious or boring, and you have trouble estimating how long it takes to do assignments. Have I got that about right, or is there something you'd like to correct or add to what I've said?"

Step 2. Conduct a Readiness Assessment to Determine If the Student Is a Good Fit for Coaching

This may be a relatively simple matter of determining whether the student's agreement to continue with coaching is voluntary on their part. When parents set up the meeting with the coach, it's important that the coach determine whether the student is going along with the process willingly or only because they feel pressured to do so by the parent. As part of the intake process, the coach should meet alone with the student to gauge the student's independent interest in pursuing coaching. If the coach has some doubts that the process is truly voluntary on the part of the student, they may want to raise the issue directly. "I know your parents are eager for you to work with a coach, but I can't tell whether this is something you want to do or if you just feel the need to please your parents." If the student admits that they're mostly there to please their parents, that doesn't mean that coaching is out of the question, but it does mean that the coach may want to pursue the topic a little further to determine what level of resistance the student might have. "It sounds like you're kind of hesitant about this. Are you willing to give it a go for a few weeks, or should we figure out how to tell your parents that you don't think this is for you?"

A helpful tool in considering whether coaching will be appropriate comes from the readiness-for-change literature (Prochaska, Norcross, & DiClemente, 1994). Prochaska and colleagues (1994) outlined five stages of change and proposed that an individual's ability to do the hard work required to change behavior depends on the stage they are at. Table 4.2 briefly describes the five stages. The coach may find it helpful to share this table with a potential student client and ask them which stage best fits them. Typical students at the precontemplation stage may deny that they have a problem or attribute the cause of the problem to something outside themselves. Or they may feel demoralized—"I've tried a lot of things, and nothing has worked, so it's not worth my time to work on this." If the student is committed to this stage, then the coach should be willing to walk away, while leaving the door open for engagement down the road.

At the contemplation stage, the student recognizes that there are things to work on, but they're not sure they are ready to begin the work. As Prochaska and colleagues (1994) stated it, "You know your destination, and even know how to get there, but you are not quite ready to go yet" (p. 42). At this stage, motivational interviewing can be particularly effective. The coach can elicit "change talk" from the student to help them see the benefits of working on change.

Students (or anybody for that matter) can be stuck at the contemplation stage for a long time. Signs that they are getting ready for the preparation phase include instead of focusing on problems they start focusing on the solution, and they begin to think more about the future than the past.

When people reach the preparation phase, they are ready to take action in the near future. At this stage, having them make a public commitment to acting helps solidify the intent. Once they begin to follow through on that commitment, they are at the action phase.

TABLE 4.2. Five Stages of Change

1. Precontemplation	Student doesn't feel change is needed.
2. Contemplation	Student knows change may be necessary and is weighing pros and cons.
3. Preparation	Student decides change is necessary and is making a plan to do so.
4. Action	Student enacts plan/strategies for change.
5. Maintenance	Student puts out effort to maintain the achieved change.

Very often, coaching involves toggling back and forth between preparation and action. We ask students to set goals, create action plans, and follow through on those action plans. For students who are fearful of making a commitment to coaching, we let them know that we've found that in the early stages of coaching the goals should be small and the action plans easy to follow through on. We explain that the main purpose of coaching is to build goal-directed persistence, and the best way to do this is to practice by setting small goals to build a cushion of success before taking on goals that may take more effort.

Step 3. Make a Go/No-Go Decision

If the first two steps have gone smoothly, the decision to enter a coaching relationship should be straightforward. If the coach believes the student is not committed to the process, then they should explain to the parent, or the referring party, why they don't think coaching is a good fit for this student.

If the student is hesitant, the coach may suggest they try it for a time and then revisit the decision. At a minimum, we recommend that the student commit to a 5- to 6-week trial period before taking a status check. With this amount of time, the student will have some experience setting goals, making plans, and following through on plans and will have a track record that the coach can use to determine if the process is going well.

When it is parents who are contracting for coaching services—and the student is a willing participant—communicating realistic timelines is important. Parents have unrealistic expectations about how quickly success can be achieved. At a minimum we recommend that coaching continue for at least a marking period, but many students work with coaches for a year or more, and some may continue to work with a coach throughout high school, setting new goals as their skill set changes due to past successes.

Step 4. Communicate with Parents about the Nature of Coaching and Clarify the Parents' Role in the Process

Many parents who seek coaches for their teenagers have played a management (maybe even a micromanagement) role for many years prior to enlisting the help of a coach. Ceding this role to a coach is often uncomfortable for them. Explaining to parents both how coaching works and the role they can play in supporting the process can alleviate problems down the road if the communication is clear at the beginning. To facilitate this discussion, the coach may want to share the Parent Handout in Appendix 6 (pp. 160–162). Ask the parents to read the handout and ask any questions they may have.

Coaches who are engaged in an independent practice generally ask a parent to sign a contract before coaching begins. The contract should specify (1) the duration of coaching, (2) the kind and frequency of contact between the coach and the student, (3) the nature and frequency of the feedback parents will be given about the process, (4) how missed appointments will be handled, and (5) the extent and limits of confidentiality between the coach and the student. Two model coaching contracts are included in the Appendices. The first is a school-based contract (Appendix 7; pp. 163–165), and the second is one developed by a coach with an independent coaching practice (Appendix 8; pp. 166–167).

Step 5. Conduct Goal-Setting Interview

When the student has made the decision to work with a coach, the first step in the coaching process is to help the student select a goal, or a couple of goals, they want to work on. It's helpful for the coach to start by reviewing with the student what they've learned about the student from the information-gathering phase. This may be a reiteration of the summary provided at the end of that phase, followed by asking the student if they've given some thought as to the goal they might want to focus on first. Parents and teachers may have communicated to the coach what *they* think the emphasis should be, and perhaps the coach has identified what they think is most important. All of this should be set aside if the student has a very clear idea of what they want to work on. If the student seems at a loss, the coach can highlight areas of concern they picked up from the information-gathering phase, but the primary focus should be on the student's input rather than parent, teacher, or coach input.

A form that can be used to facilitate goal setting is included in Appendix 9 (pp. 168–170). The specific process to follow in the goal-setting interview is outlined in Chapter 10. When this phase is completed, the student should have identified a goal they want to work on, converting it to a SMART goal (i.e., a goal that is specific, measurable, attainable, relevant, and time-bound) where appropriate. They should also begin the action-planning process, including what the student will do before the next coaching session.

Step 6. Decide on a Meeting Schedule

In the beginning, we recommend that the coach and student check in daily with each other or at least several times a week. When coaching is conducted in a school setting, daily contact is often feasible. When coaching is taking place outside of school, daily check-ins may not be realistic. The nature of the contact can be a mix of face-to-face sessions and electronic contact (typically texts, but it could also include emails or FaceTime).

People who come to coaching from a background in counseling or tutoring often assume that because counseling and tutoring can be effective with once-a-week meetings, then coaching can, too. We would caution against making this assumption, at least if the focus is on helping students strengthen executive skills to meet goals. Students with weak working memory often forget that they are supposed to be working on something before the next coaching session. Students who struggle with task initiation typically procrastinate, leaving the task until the last minute. If they are working on performing a daily task with consistency, this kind of procrastination defeats the purpose. Students with weak sustained attention may start their action plan, but they run out of steam and may convince themselves they can get back to it "later" and have plenty of time to accomplish the task before the next coaching session. Students who struggle with time management tend to have more difficulty managing tasks with long time horizons (e.g., a week) than they do managing tasks with short time horizons (e.g., tomorrow). And finally, students who struggle with planning and prioritizing find the task of planning out a week's worth of action steps daunting—if they could do that, they wouldn't need coaching! For all these reasons, the experienced coaches we work with stress the benefits of connecting with students more than once a week, even if that connection is brief and via electronic methods.

Step 7. *Conduct Coaching Sessions*

Coaching sessions benefit from following a format or a step-by-step process. This makes it easier to run the sessions efficiently and alleviates some of the guesswork for both the coach and the student, since both parties know roughly how the session will progress.

The main goal of any coaching session is to help students make short-term plans that are consistent with the goal they set during the goal-setting session. Once the coaching process is up and running, the bulk of the coaching session follows the acronym REAP. We ask students to *review* the plans they made in the last session and *evaluate* how well they followed their plan. Then we ask them to *anticipate* what is coming next so that they can *plan* what they need to accomplish before the next coaching session.

A form that either the student or the coach could complete to guide the session can be found in Appendix 10 (pp. 171–172). It includes the following elements:

- *Student's current goal.* This can be condensed into a couple of words or symbols (e.g., higher science grade, good night's sleep, follow test study plan). The point is to start with the reminder that the student is working on a specific goal.
- *Snapshot.* This is a way to take a "temperature check." This section asks the student to use a 7-point scale to rate how things are going. Students can also identify any topics they would like to talk about. Since many students see completing forms as burdensome, the coach may find the session goes better if the coach uses the form as an interview and fills in each section themselves. When the session is over, the coach may want to photocopy the plan or scan it and send it to the student, so they'll have a copy on their laptop to refer to.
- *The big picture.* Prior to making a daily plan, it's helpful to create a bigger picture of things other than nightly homework assignments that the student has to keep track of, including upcoming tests and quizzes, long-term assignments, and other responsibilities (such as extracurricular activities, jobs, or family responsibilities).
- *Today's plans.* This is where the student identifies what they plan to accomplish before the next coaching session. Two questions need to be answered: What are you going to do? and When will you do it? At the next coaching session, the coach and student review the plan made at the previous session and determine whether the plan was followed (or how much of the plan was followed) and how the student felt it went by answering the other two questions in this section: Did you do it? and How did it go?

While some coaches we've trained use the Daily Coaching Form as is, many coaches create a more personalized form adapted to the needs of the individual students with whom they're working. The form as we've designed it, though, allows you to capture some important information that can be used for progress monitoring. The 7-point scale included in the Snapshot is a quick measure of overall well-being that may change for the better as the student makes progress on their goal or gets on top of their schoolwork. Another metric that is easy to track is the percentage of daily tasks completed. As students learn to manage their time better or become more realistic about what they can accomplish on any given day, the percentage of tasks completed should increase. This by itself can be a good measure of coaching efficacy.

Step 8. *Collect Progress Monitoring Data and Share with the Student*

This step builds in accountability for both the student and the coach. Unless we're collecting data, we won't know either whether the student is meeting the goals they're setting for themselves or if coaching is helping them do this. Our emphasis is on collecting quantitative data to help answer these questions. In Step 7 above, we described how the Daily Coaching Form can be used for progress monitoring. Chapter 11 covers a variety of progress monitoring tools and methods, and the reader should review that chapter to select the most appropriate tools for each of the students they are working with.

Whenever possible, the data we're collecting are such that they can be presented in a visual form to the student so that they can see the progress they are making. This visual display by itself can be a powerful motivator. While we sometimes build external reinforcers into our coaching process, more often than not we find that the clear evidence that the student is progressing toward their goal is as effective as anything else—and it gets closer to helping the student find intrinsic motivation in what they're doing.

We caution students, however, that progress with dips or regressions along the way is more realistic than thinking that the trajectory is always upward. Sometimes we help students draw "trend lines" so that they can see that while there may have been some backslides, the improvement is still pretty steady. Drawing trendlines is explained in Chapter 11.

Progress monitoring is also a way to communicate with parents that coaching is helping their child, especially since progress can feel elusive to parents. We worked with a student once who wanted to improve overall academic performance, so we tracked the grades they were earning on assignments, tests, or quizzes on a weekly basis. The student's parents were tracking his class averages on a weekly basis through the school's web portal. Since the contact began partway through the semester and the student was struggling in a number of classes, parents weren't seeing the average change very quickly. However, we were tracking any grades higher than a C+, and we were able to point out that in the first couple of weeks, very few grades hit that threshold, but after that the student was earning many grades ranging from B– to A. With this evidence, the parents were reassured that their son was on the right track.

Step 9. *Review with the Student the Appropriate Timeline to End Coaching*

Coaching reaches a logical conclusion when the student has achieved the goals they set for themselves and has achieved some stability in terms of the level of academic performance they want to achieve. We generally recommend tapering the process by gradually increasing the time between coaching sessions and decreasing the length of the coaching sessions. When coaching is done at school on a daily basis, the fading process might follow a schedule of reducing the sessions from daily to every other day to twice a week, to once a week, to once every other week. If at any point the student hits a bump in the road or regresses, the contact can be increased to get them back on track.

Another way to fade coaching is to decrease face-to-face meetings and replace them with electronic check-ins. One coach we know moves students from individual coaching to group coaching as way to decrease supports but still provide a safety net.

Whatever approach is taken, it's important that the student (and their parents) understand that the long-term goal of the coach is to work themselves out of a job by helping the student become more independent. If a student—or their parents—have become dependent on the coach, it will be particularly important to remind them gently that the ultimate outcome of coaching is that the student will no longer need a coach.

Step 10. End Coaching

Coaching should conclude with an exit interview that gives both the coach and the student a chance to reflect on the process. This should include highlighting successes and celebrating victories. Teenagers tend to live in the present, so reminding them where they started and how far they've come can help empower them by reminding them of the work they did to achieve their goals.

To facilitate this conversation, both the coach and the student may want to complete the Coach Feedback Forms found in Appendices 11 and 12 (pp. 173–174, 175–176). These include scales for collecting quantitative data as well as open-ended questions to capture qualitative information.

Even if—maybe *especially* if—the coach feels that coaching is being discontinued prematurely, the student should be encouraged to participate in an exit interview and/or complete the Coach Feedback Form, since this allows the coach to better understand the process and why it may not have worked in the present case. In all cases, the coach should communicate to the student that their door is always open should the need arise in the future.

A NOTE ABOUT COACHING COLLEGE STUDENTS

The coaching process we have outlined for high school students can also work effectively with college students. Unfortunately, while colleges provide services to students with disabilities that include tutoring, scheduling help (e.g., finding the best classes for students with disabilities), and classroom accommodations (such as note-takers and testing modifications), most colleges do not recognize that executive skills weaknesses often account for students failing classes and dropping out of school. Nor do they understand that an intervention such as coaching is ideally suited to address this cause of college dropout.

Coaching college students follows the same basic outline for coaching high school students:

1. Collect background information regarding executive skills strengths and weaknesses.
2. Establish long-term goals (in this case, what the student hopes to achieve by the time they graduate and what they hope to do following college graduation).
3. Arrange for regular coaching sessions (in the case of college students, coaching sessions may not occur daily, and they may not be face-to-face).

In our experience coaching college students, the issue of verification is as important at this level as it is with high school students. We once set up a coaching program for a college student in which he met daily with someone from the school's center for students with disabilities for the purpose of drawing up a study plan. The plan was quite precise, and the student assured his coach every day that he was following the plan as drawn up. It wasn't until the student walked out of his first mid-term exam without completing it that it came to light that while he had stated that he was studying in the library every night for several hours, he was, in fact, spending most of that time surfing the internet.

College coaches are generally unable to check in with professors to make sure students are staying on top of their work. However, they can obtain from students a commitment to demonstrate to them that they are doing what they say they are doing. For instance, they can be asked to bring their laptops with them to the coaching session to demonstrate that they have begun to write a term paper, or they can be asked to bring reading assignments with them to show that they have used a highlighter when reading.

This has to be done carefully and should be arranged as one of the ground rules for coaching. The coach may want to introduce this by saying something like the following:

> "I've found that when working with college students, time sometimes gets away from them and they do not always follow the plans they make. And then they feel bad and want to cover up the fact that they've not followed their plans. What I'd like to do in the beginning is for you to bring to our coaching session the stuff you've been working on. This will let me know that the plans we're making are realistic. I'm not here to critique your work (unless you want me to), but it will help you avoid the temptation of telling me that you're following your plans when something got in the way. If it turns out you're having trouble carrying out your plans, then we can troubleshoot and figure out what needs to change—the plans or the strategies for following them."

For additional information about how to coach college students, with lots of suggestions for handling the kinds of pressures that college students typically face, we recommend the book *Coaching College Students with Executive Function Problems* (Kennedy, 2017).

CHAPTER 5

Coaching Elementary Students

As we've noted, coaching in all its forms is built around goal setting. We've also cited research showing that goal setting is effective with elementary-age students and can lead to improvements in academics and behaviors related to executive skills. At the same time, coaching procedures at these age levels require adjustments in the goal-setting process, the management of day-to-day objectives, and coaching strategies. Specifically, in this chapter, we are focused on lower elementary students in grades K–3.

REFERRAL SOURCES

In our experience with K–3 students, more often than not teachers are the primary referral source. The reason for this is that the majority of issues that initiate a referral involve some aspect of classroom work or behavior such as work completion/quality or behavior that interferes with classroom instruction or peer relationships. That said, we have also seen referrals from recess and lunch monitors related to behavioral issues in these settings, school counselors/psychologists for issues that children have discussed with them, and administrators concerned with discipline issues. While parents are not a frequent referral source for this age group, occasionally parents will contact the school about an issue at school that their child has spoken to them about. While this range of referrals can involve a wide array of school issues, we believe that coaching is a viable intervention strategy and have utilized it in our work with schools.

WHO CAN BE THE COACH?

If, as we have indicated, most issues will involve some aspect of classroom performance or behavior, the classroom teacher, by virtue of experience and knowledge of the child, is well positioned to be the coach. The caveat is time. Teachers are confronted with a myriad and growing list of responsibilities, and coaching may not be feasible. At the same time, some teachers conference with students on a regular basis and if the target behavior is specific and the context is part of the daily classroom schedule and limited to a specific situation or time period, the teacher may be comfortable acting as the coach. As another option, teachers can partner with a school counselor, school psychologist, or behavioral specialist to help with the design, implementation, and check-ins of the coaching plan. One of us (Richard) has used this approach, which has the advantage of reducing the workload for the teacher and providing a backup if the teacher is not available due to meetings or illness. If the behavior of concern is outside of the classroom, in our experience the coach is more likely to be a counselor, psychologist, or behavioral specialist working in conjunction with the staff who monitors the child in that setting. Given that most referrals involve school-based issues, and the age of the children necessitates close monitoring and frequent check-ins, we assume that coaches for K–3 students will be school based.

THE GOAL-SETTING PROCESS

Prior to beginning coaching with elementary-age children, especially those in the younger grades, it is important to consider how children at this age differ from their older peers. Two aspects of their cognitive development are particularly important. One of these involves a difference in time horizons. In this case, time horizon refers to how long a child can plan into the future. The time horizons of elementary-age students, particularly those in the early grades, are markedly shorter than those of teenagers. Whereas with teens we typically think of goals in terms of days, weeks, and months, with elementary-age students plans and goals are more likely to fit into a time frame of minutes, hours, and days. This has implications for how long a child can be expected to persist in an activity related to a goal, for example, completion of work or engaging in a specific behavior. In our coaching with elementary students, we've followed the principle that, from the child's perspective, at the beginning of the task the end should be in sight.

The second issue involves specificity of the task behavior as the child moves toward their goal. The objective is that the behavior that the child executes is sufficiently concrete that the child is able to evaluate their performance in comparison to an already established baseline. There are two reasons for this. As we've noted elsewhere in this book, self-monitoring has been shown to improve academic performance in students. This has more recently been confirmed in studies by Lower and colleagues (2016) and Wells, Sheehey, and Sheehey (2017), among others, involving improvements in academics and behavior. In addition, experience in self-evaluating behavior can aid in the development of metacognition and give children a sense of control over their behavior.

A third consideration involves goal setting, specifically how goals are set and who sets them. Throughout this book we have advocated for the active involvement of children in their own problem solving and goal setting. Research supports this position. Bruhn, McDaniel, Fernando, and Troughton (2016), in a review of studies involving over 1,300 mostly elementary-age children, noted that allowing students to engage in the goal-setting process improved student outcomes and increased social validity. Social validity reflects student opinions about the acceptability of and satisfaction with interventions. Sutherland, Conroy, McLeod, Kunemund, and McKnight (2019) identified choice among a set of practices important for improving social, emotional, and behavioral outcomes for young children. In the following sections we discuss how to actively involve children in planning and goal selection.

COACHING STEPS

In the first edition of this book, we described a six-step process that encompasses the coaching process. In this edition we have modified this process to incorporate evidence-based practices suggested in research by Wells and colleagues (2017) and Kumm and Maggin (2021), among others. Table 5.1 lists the steps in the coaching process.

Step 1. *Notify and Obtain Permission from the Parents*

If coaching is outside the scope of the usual classroom procedure and the classroom teacher's typical interaction with students, and the coach is not the teacher, parents should be notified and their permission should be obtained in advance of implementation. It is important to explain the coaching process, who will be involved, how the procedure will be conducted, and how/when the child's performance will be reported to the parent. It should also be noted that if the child is reluctant or refuses, coaching will not be implemented.

If, on the other hand, coaching takes place by the teacher within the classroom and represents a type of intervention that the teacher routinely uses with students to address performance issues, parental permission is not necessary. This assumes that no supports or personnel outside

TABLE 5.1. Steps in the Elementary Coaching Process

Step	Description
1	Notify and obtain permission from the parents.
2	Gather background information on the student.
3	Set the stage for coaching.
4	Identify and define the target behavior that the student will work on.
5	Brainstorm with the student strategies to help the student successfully perform the behavior.
6	Rehearse the procedure with the student.
7	Implement the procedure.
8	Monitor progress.
9	Review progress with the student to decide next steps.

the classroom are involved. Having said this, if the child has recurring issues, we encourage teachers to discuss this with parents.

Step 2. Gather Background Information on the Student

For younger elementary-age students, both the process of information gathering and the type of information gathered differ from those with older students. Whereas with older students the process relies in good part on student self-report tools, with younger children the process is more informal, occurring in casual conversations, interactions, and observations. As noted, the reason for this is that we see the need for coaching with younger elementary students as based on issues that are occurring in the school setting and the coaching itself as based primarily in school with school staff.

Nonetheless, the reasons for information gathering remain similar. Chief among these is the relationship between the coach and the student, which is built on trust and a sense of collaboration. The coach accomplishes this through conversations with the child to understand their interests and activities, their likes and dislikes, their perceived strengths and challenges, and their feelings, both in and beyond their school life. The desired outcome is a relationship where student and coach feel like they know each other and are comfortable interacting.

While rapport between student and coach is a key element in the process, it is not the sole reason for information gathering. The objective of coaching is performance improvement. For the purposes of coaching, we assume that performance challenges or problems are not the result of weaknesses in academic skills. If they are, then instruction rather than coaching is the intervention of choice. We assume that performance issues are related to executive skills challenges such as sustained attention, task initiation, time management, or goal-directed persistence, among others. In younger students, these skills are most easily assessed through the observation of adults who see students on a regular basis across a variety of school situations, such as classroom teachers. For this purpose we have developed several executive skills questionnaires that can be used with children of different ages (see Appendices 13–17; pp. 177–188).

While the ESQs are not a necessity for coaching, they provide the coach with information about a student's strengths that can be used to develop possible intervention strategies. In addition, the coach can use the information to anticipate tasks/situations that are challenging for the student and to consider modifications.

Step 3. Set the Stage for Coaching

Regardless of the student's age, at its heart successful coaching is a collaborative relationship that is built on cooperation and trust. Rapport is built by the adult attending to and showing interest in the child, their personal characteristics, and their likes and dislikes. Although the focus of coaching will eventually be an issue or problem that the child is having, it is important that the coach attend to the interests and skill strengths of the child in building their relationship. This ensures that the child will not associate the coach's attention only with a problem. Knowledge of the child's interests and strengths will also allow the coach to discuss how the child might use these to improve performance.

Once it has been decided to engage the coaching process, the coach arranges a private conference with the child. The purpose of the conference is to determine if the child would like help through coaching. The coach offers a brief explanation of the coaching process, emphasizing that they would work together to decide what to work on, what check-ins and strategies the child would like to use, how they would collect data and monitor progress, and when they might like to begin. The coach gives the child the opportunity to ask any questions, and then asks if the child if they would be okay with trying coaching. This first step in establishing a cooperative, trusting relationship is key to the student's success in the process.

The content of the initial meeting depends on who the coach is. If it is the classroom teacher, presumably they know the child reasonably well and already have a relationship. If not, then the teacher takes some time to get to know the interests, likes, and dislikes of the child. If the teacher already has a comfortable relationship with the child, the purpose of the conference is to discuss the coaching process and the issue of concern. The coach opens the meeting with some examples of the child's strengths that the coach has observed. The coach then moves on to the issue of concern and describes the coaching process and how it might help the child.

If the coach is not the classroom teacher and the issue involves some aspect of classroom performance/behavior, we have found it helpful, although not a necessity, that teacher and coach meet together with the child. The purpose of this meeting is first about coach and child getting to know each other, so the discussion can focus on favorite things to do in and outside of school, favorite foods and games, any pets, and so forth. The coach can also note some of the child's strengths in school. The coach then describes the coaching process and the issue that the child is having some difficulty with. As above, the coach describes in some detail how the process would work and asks if the student would be okay with trying coaching.

Step 4. Identify and Define the Target Behavior That the Student Will Work On

If the initial concern is broad—for example, work completion—there is an opportunity for the coach to offer a choice to the child on where to begin, such as math (number of problems completed) or language arts (number of words written). If the issue is specific (amount of math completed during independent work time, frequency of hand raising at morning meeting), the coach can describe the child's current level of performance and give the child a choice of saying what they think they could do to improve their performance. In our experience, it is preferable if the coach offers two specific options for the child to choose from. This ensures that the target performance is within the child's capability and increases the likelihood of building on success. The coach may offer additional choice options, such as when the child would like to begin the process.

To establish the target behavior, three components are necessary. The first is collection of baseline data about the child's present level of performance, for example, how many math problems completed in a specific period of time in a specific context. Baseline data is important because it is the measure against which progress will be determined. In addition, it is used to determine realistic expectations for initial and ongoing performance. Baseline data should be collected over a few days to ensure that it reflects accurate and consistent current performance. This is also the time to determine how and on what schedule data collection during coaching will be done.

The second component is to ensure that the target behavior is within the child's already existing skill set. That means that the child has been observed independently performing the behavior that the goal is based on. If the target behavioral skill is not secure in the child's current repertoire, the skill weakness may be the reason for the child performance difficulty. In this case, instruction in the skill rather than coaching is the first intervention. Once the child has demonstrated independent, correct execution of the skill, if performance still lags then coaching should be considered.

The third component is the specific definition of the behavior. This means that the child, the coach, and any other involved adult understand exactly what is expected and in what context, and it is written down and/or pictured in some fashion. The goal or target behavior should be specific, measurable, and within a designated time frame. The goal should be a positively stated, replacement behavior (e.g., "Tara will raise her hand in morning meeting when she wants to ask a question or share something," as opposed to, "Tara will not talk out during morning meeting").

Step 5. Brainstorm with the Student Strategies to Help the Student Successfully Perform the Behavior

In our experience, brainstorm sessions often involve prompts or cues from an adult about what the child will be working on prior to beginning the task or entering the situation. This includes when and how often the child will be prompted and how the prompts will be provided. Other examples include modifying the task (reducing the number of problems on a page) or situation (letting the child sit next to the teacher in circle). If the child does not have specific strategies to offer, the teacher can provide options and let the child choose which are preferable. They also decide together what the initial target level of performance will be.

The final component in this step is presenting options to the student for self-monitoring. Examples include a rating scale tied to specific behaviors or a frequency count (e.g., number of problems completed). We also recommend giving students the opportunity to graph their performance, since this is an easy way to see changes. If graphs have already been introduced to the class, the child can choose the one they are most comfortable with. If not, the child can be taught to complete a graph based on a rating or frequency count, and then they can decide how often this data will be collected. The components of the process will be written in the sequence that they occur and also provided to the child in a written or picture format.

Step 6. Rehearse the Procedure with the Student

We have found it particularly valuable to do a "walk-through" of how the procedure will work with the child. More often than not, the setting will be the child's classroom, but it could also be the gym, cafeteria, or playground depending on the target behavior and goal. The coach accompanies the child to the specific setting. For the rehearsal, it is preferable that other children are not present so as to avoid any embarrassment the child might feel. The coach can offer the child the options of the coach first modeling the procedure, combining actions with a verbal description, or providing verbal directions that the child listens to.

If the child chooses the coach-modeling option, once this is completed, the child will carry out the modeled actions. The objective is to rehearse each step exactly as it will occur during the "live" procedure. Thus, the child will be in the same location and the same prompts and task/situation modifications will be given and the child will carry out the target behaviors. This will also include what happens at the end of the time period, what data will be recorded, and when the coach check-in will be. If the coach will be supervising the overall procedure but will not be present daily during the procedure, whoever will be conducting the procedure (e.g., classroom teacher, paraprofessional) should be present and actively participating in the rehearsal.

We have found this practice to be particularly helpful in determining if there are any aspects that need to be modified or if the child or other adults have any questions or concerns. Once the coach is satisfied that the child and any adults involved understand and can implement the procedure, the child is asked if they are comfortable and on what day, out of two options, they would like to start.

Step 7. Implement the Procedure

If, as noted above, the coach is not implementing the procedure, we recommend that the coach at least twice observe the procedure when it is implemented to ensure fidelity to the process. If the coach is implementing the procedure, this is an opportunity to provide any corrective feedback to the child. It is also the time to check the student's data and compare this with independent adult data to determine degree of agreement. Kumm and Maggin (2021) noted that fidelity checklists are an effective means for assessing both whether the coaching plan contains the key elements for success and whether the procedure is being followed as designed. We have provided examples of both below.

Step 8. Monitor Progress

The coach meets one-on-one with the student to review the data and discuss performance. They discuss how the student felt about the plan and whether they accomplished the target they set. They also discuss any questions or concerns the child has and make any adjustments in the procedure based on the data. For students in the lower elementary grades (K–3), we recommend daily check-ins for at least 2 weeks.

If the student continues to make good progress, there are two options. If the initial procedure was designed to gradually increase performance (e.g., from a baseline of 10 out of 20 arithmetic problems to 13 out of 20), the coach and student can discuss a new target number and continue with daily check-ins. If there was a single target goal and the child is reaching it, they can move to every other day with continued check-in reductions as long as progress is maintained. For older students, coach and student can discuss what check-in schedule the student is comfortable with and maintain this if the student is progressing. If there is a decline in progress, the coach observes the procedure to ensure fidelity and makes adjustments as necessary, including modifying the procedure and check-in frequency.

Step 9. Review Progress with the Student to Decide Next Steps

If the performance issue they are working on involves a specific skill in a specific situation only, and the child continues to make good progress with infrequent check-ins, they can discuss when to end coaching. The coach asks the child if they would be okay with the coach checking with the teacher from time to time about continued progress. Another possibility is that the initial target performance (e.g., work completion) applies to more than one situation and the issue has been addressed only in one situation. In this case, after reviewing and reinforcing the success that the child has had in the first situation, the coach discusses with the child if they would be okay with trying coaching in the new situation. While some of the elements of the original procedure can remain, new information, including baseline performance, skill proficiency, target performance, and process of data collection, will be needed.

SAMPLE COACH DIALOGUE

Dakota is a 7-year-old second-grade student. She is familiar with her potential coach, who is also the school counselor, through the classwide social skills group that the counselor conducts on a twice-weekly basis. Her teacher reports that Dakota has struggled with completion of math work during independent work time, which has recently been introduced as part of the math period. Her teacher wondered if this might be a skill issue but after conducting an assessment and sitting with her while she works independently, the teacher is satisfied that Dakota has good command of the skills needed to complete her work without help. The teacher and school counselor have discussed this, and the counselor has agreed to be a coach for Dakota if she is agreeable to this in order to help her with math completion. Her teacher and coach arrange a private meeting with Dakota to discuss this.

> TEACHER: Dakota, I've noticed that you seem to be having some difficulty completing your math during independent work time. Can you tell us why that might be happening?
>
> DAKOTA: I don't know. I know how to do the work.
>
> COACH: So the work isn't too hard for you?
>
> DAKOTA: No, sometimes I just forget to keep working on it.
>
> COACH: Well, I'd like to help you. Would it be okay if we work together on this?
>
> DAKOTA: I guess so.
>
> COACH: Your teacher told me that in the last couple of days, you usually get about 10 out of 20 problems done. If we make a plan, how many problems do you think you could get done when we start?
>
> DAKOTA: I think I could do 14.
>
> COACH: Okay, that sounds like a good place to start. And if you decide you want to do more, that's okay, too. When would you like to start?
>
> DAKOTA: Maybe tomorrow?
>
> COACH: Sure, that sounds good. How would you like your teacher to remind you about this?
>
> DAKOTA: I'm not sure.
>
> COACH: Can I suggest some choices?
>
> DAKOTA: Yeah, okay.
>
> COACH: Well, your teacher could say at the beginning of math, "Remember what you're working on," or she could walk by your desk and give you a thumbs-up, or the teacher could remind the whole class what they are working on.

DAKOTA: Remind the whole class, I like that.

COACH: Would it help to know when to start and how much time is left?

DAKOTA: Yeah, maybe.

TEACHER: You know that big timer we have in front of the room?

DAKOTA: Yeah.

TEACHER: How about if I remind the whole class when to begin, I'll set the timer, and then every 5 minutes let everyone know how much time is left.

DAKOTA: Okay.

COACH: How might you keep track of how many problems you finish each day?

DAKOTA: I could count the number of problems I did and write the number at the top.

COACH: Counting the number of problems is a great idea. Can I make a suggestion?

DAKOTA: Yeah, okay.

COACH: Remember you did bar graphs like this in class (*shows example*)?

DAKOTA: Yeah, I remember.

COACH: Suppose we made a bar graph so you could fill in what you did each day for the whole week, would that be okay?

DAKOTA: Yeah, I'd like that.

COACH: What else might help you?

DAKOTA: I can't think of anything right now.

COACH: How about I check in with you each day just before lunch to see how your plan went?

DAKOTA: Okay.

ADDITIONAL CONSIDERATIONS IN THE COACHING PROCESS

Incentives

The coaching process can be combined with incentive systems for those students who do not respond to coaching alone or who are reluctant to engage in the process. Data such as rating scales or frequency counts can be tied to point systems, with different rewards available according to the number of points earned. Typical rewards include activities such as games or choice of an object from a prize box. While incentives can be very effective for some children, coaching by itself, especially self-monitoring of progress and task mastery, can also be a powerful incentive. We typically begin the coaching process without using an extrinsic reinforcement system, since this promotes the self-reinforcement value of learning and self-regulation.

Coaching Students on Home Issues

Although more typical at the middle school level, parents sometimes seek help from coaches to work with elementary-age children. Educational issues might include homework completion, studying for tests, organization of school materials (notebooks, backpacks), writing papers, and completing projects. Home-based issues might include morning and bedtime schedules and routines, completing chores, organization of belongings, and maintaining practice schedules (sports, music lessons, etc.). We have previously addressed these issues for parents in *Smart but Scattered* (Dawson & Guare, 2009, chap. 10) and refer coaches to this as a potential resource for parents.

In terms of the coaching component, we think that coaches who come from an education background (teachers, case managers, school counselors, school psychologists) and who are knowledgeable about executive skills are well equipped to address the educational issues. If they have been working in a coaching capacity with students, they likely have encountered most, if not all, of these topics already. The steps of the coaching process outlined previously are equally applicable to home educational issues, including the coach establishing a trusting relationship with the child. The key difference is that instead of teachers or other classroom-based staff initiating and monitoring day-to-day implementation, parents will now fill that role. That means that prior to final design and implementation, the coach will need to have met with the parents and child to explain the coaching process and what general role each of the parties will play.

If parents and child are comfortable with continuing, the coach, with input from the child and parents, designs a plan to include specific target behaviors, prompts, and any task modifications, as well as a self-monitoring system. The plan will also include the specific expectations for the child, parents, and coach, including method and frequency of monitoring and contact. As the final step before implementation, the coach seeks assurances from the child and parents that they are comfortable with and agree to follow the plan as designed.

For home-based issues unrelated to school performance, the process is essentially the same as above. The difference may be in the background of the coach. In our experience as psychologists and behavioral specialists, home-based issues tend to be more within the purview of coaches with a mental health background (counselors, social workers, behavioral analysts, psychologists). By virtue of their work, coaches from these disciplines are more likely to have been sought out by parents for help in these areas, especially if parents have been unsuccessful in attempts to go it alone. Hence, coaches from these disciplines may be more comfortable and have more of an experience base to draw from in addressing these issues.

CHAPTER 6

Case Examples

The following case examples illustrate in narrative form the coaching process with elementary- and secondary-age students. Although names have been changed, the examples are real. We have selected them because we feel they are authentic depictions of how coaching works. They illustrate both the creativity and flexibility that exemplifies good coaching. As coaching progresses, circumstances change, and students often decide to change their focus. The coaches who provided these case examples always respected the students they were working with and often let them steer the process. Even at the preschool level, the coach let the child make important contributions and determine how and in what setting they wanted to practice the skills they were learning.

Many thanks to coaches Andrea Kreckler, Lisa Kubrin, and Maura Sabatos-DeVito for providing these examples.

ELEMENTARY CASE EXAMPLE 1

James is a 10-year-old fourth grader whose parents felt that he would benefit from being enrolled in Executive Functioning Coaching sessions due to their observations at home and school. During the intake process, the coach noted that James's parents listed a variety of skills that they thought James could work to develop over the course of the sessions.

Together, the coach and parents spoke about James's hobbies and the material he was learning at school. In the initial intake session, James mentioned that he loved his old school and missed his friends. Over the past year, he had changed schools and was struggling to find his bearings. Due to the COVID-19 pandemic, James felt that his learning was constantly stopping and starting. Switching between online and in-person classes felt overwhelming to him, disrupted his learning flow, and disadvantaged him socially. James felt that he did not have an opportunity to acclimatize to the new social landscape at the new school and solidify new friendships with his peers and make connections with the teachers.

At first, James told the coach that he was doing well in school and did not feel that he needed any support. Later, when chatting with James, he reevaluated and mentioned that he could do better when listening in French. As a goal, James decided he wanted to try to raise his grade in his French class. His coach asked him if he had any ideas for workable strategies to achieve this goal, and James said that he needed to pay more attention in class. That way, he would understand what was happening as lessons progressed and he would perform better on in-class tests. He disclosed that he often became distracted by classmates. James settled on the goal of "listening in French." James worked toward this goal over the course of a month before meeting back on Zoom with the coach to discuss how he was progressing toward this goal. Together, James and his coach co-constructed a checklist with a yes/no framework for James to use to see how often he was able to listen during class.

The following session, when James was asked about how he was managing in French class, he told the coach that he did not need strategies to listen because he felt he was not learning much since the classes moved back online. The coach and student agreed to resume coaching when in-person learning started up again.

During the next meeting, James and the coach discussed how he was managing with in-person learning again. James felt that he was once again distracted because he needed some catch-up time with his peers. The coach and James brainstormed strategies that would help him focus in class. James suggested that he could ask the teacher for a few minutes to chat with his peers before the onset of the lesson; that way, he would not be distracted by his friends. When the coach asked if he had any other suggestions, James mentioned that he could use a fidget tool when he felt that he was getting distracted and possibly draw on a piece of paper at his desk. The coach suggested he could ask his teacher for a break to get a drink or take a walk. James was reluctant to go for a walk because he said that does not really work for him. They again together cocreated a yes/no checklist to help keep track of his listening skills over the course of a 2-week period.

The next time they met, James shared his checklist, which was partially complete. When asked about why he did not complete the checklist for the full 2 weeks, James said that school was online again, and he did not feel that it was necessary until he went back to in-person learning. When asked how he was doing in class, he said that he was doing well and did not need support anymore, although he did mention that he still was talking a little bit in class. Together, James and his coach decided to cocreate a rubric to keep him accountable:

4—Listened the entire time

3—Talked a little

2—Talked a lot

1—Did not listen at all

At the next meeting, James told his coach he was doing really well in his French class and his marks had improved significantly. His teacher was giving the class more time to chat at the beginning of class and James felt that he was able to use his social energy before the lesson began. He told his coach that he could use some support in another subject area with the same skill: listening. Together, James and his coach discussed the new goal and the coach reviewed how James could use some of the same strategies to achieve this new goal. By setting a new goal that utilized some of James's previous strategies, James will be able to develop transferrable skills that he can employ in a variety of circumstances. In addition to improving his marks, setting small, achievable goals and co-constructing the strategies and checklist will improve James's confidence in his listening skills, allowing him to improve his ability to sustain attention and listen attentively when those strategies are used.

ELEMENTARY CASE EXAMPLE 2

[*Note:* This is an example of a coach working with a 5-year old, primarily addressing behavioral issues in the home. However, the child exhibited the same issues at school, and the coach included a classroom modification to help the child in that setting as well. Coaching children this young can be difficult—and is not for everyone—but we've included this example because Ryan's coach used some very clever techniques to engage Ryan in the coaching process and to help him practice the coping strategies that helped him get control over his feelings.]

Ryan is a 5-year-old in a PreK program. His parents told the coach that he was typically shy but once he was comfortable, he didn't stop talking. His parents called upon the coach to help him learn strategies to manage emotional outbursts when he became frustrated. Ryan's parents explained that when Ryan got frustrated at home, he would throw things, get really angry, and stomp his feet. This type of episode could last more than an hour. Ryan's parents told the coach that when this type of outburst occurred, they typically gave him a warning first followed by a time-out if the behavior persisted.

In addition, Ryan's teachers had been starting to witness similar behavior during the school day, especially during small-group games where the game concludes with a winner. His parents told the coach that when Ryan won the game he was very happy but if he did not come in first place, he lost emotional control and was very hard to calm down.

Outside of the home, Ryan's teacher told his parents that when he got frustrated at school, he would not talk or interact with anyone for a long period of time. If pressed to talk, he would frequently burst into tears and would not participate until the game had been over for a while. The same occurred in sports as well.

Ryan and the coach met with a special guest, a puppet, coincidentally named Ryan. The coach used the same name as the child as a tool to open up communication. The coach explained that the special guest was very shy and usually would come out when a special song was sung. Ryan happily joined in. When the "puppet Ryan" came out, Ryan excitedly told the puppet that they had the same name! The coach used the puppet as a tool for fostering communication between the coach and Ryan. The coach learned that Ryan liked soccer, loved art, and loved to play with cars.

The next time the coach met Ryan with the puppet, he was eager to show the coach how he remembered the song. He also remembered that the puppet was a little shy to come out. The puppet shared that he had a problem and was hoping Ryan could help solve it. The puppet explained that he got so angry when he was not chosen to be the line leader in his class. He told Ryan that he broke his pencils and threw them on the floor, which did not make his teachers happy. At this point, Ryan opened up and explained what happened when he got upset.

The coach explained to both Ryan and the puppet what coaching was and both the puppet and Ryan said they wanted to try to do things to help them when they got upset. The coach taught Ryan a calm-down strategy, which Ryan then taught the puppet. The silly puppet kept forgetting the calm-down strategy and Ryan had to run through it again and again. Eventually, Ryan was making up his own scenarios for the puppet to practice. This gave him ownership and a feeling of self-worth.

The following sessions involved creating make-and-take projects, which were based on Ryan's interests. The coach used these opportunities to induce a little frustration to give Ryan a chance to practice his strategies. The projects included making a worry pet, a visual reminder of steps to take a break, and a sign that said "I need a break," which had a Velcro piece on his door and on his sign. He was eventually able to grab the sign on his own and put it on his door, and his mom and dad were instructed to not come in until he came out. He used a visual timer or a sand timer and came out when the time passed. If he needed more time, he told his parents but at least by that time he was no longer emotional and could actually be spoken to without any outbursts.

The coach also worked with Ryan's teacher to create a cozy corner in the classroom that Ryan could use when he needed a break in that setting. He was able to teach his classmates how to use it as well.

After 6 months, Ryan was using strategies to calm down on his own, and he learned to identify the feelings in his body that happen before he became emotional. He also continued to teach the puppet, who always seemed to forget what to do. Ryan's mom and dad were so happy with his progress that he taught them what to do when *they* got upset.

SECONDARY CASE EXAMPLE 1

Elizabeth was a 16-year-old honors student in her junior year of high school. Her parents reached out for coaching services in order to help Elizabeth figure out what was getting in her way of succeeding in certain classes. During the initial meeting with Elizabeth, she shared her love for dance, musical theater, and singing. She told the coach that she was usually in one or two local musicals during the school year.

After explaining the coaching process, Elizabeth told the coach that in some of her classes, she understood the topics and concepts but still did not do well on her exams. She also told the coach that she found it difficult to pay attention during class because she got bored easily.

Elizabeth was most concerned with her grades in her AP U.S. History class. She revealed to the coach that she had failed all of her exams and was concerned she would fail the class. The coach asked Elizabeth how she typically studied for her exams. Elizabeth said that she usually reread class notes, went to get extra help, and watched YouTube videos on the subject. She admitted to the coach that she found it difficult to study because it was so boring. Since this was the class Elizabeth was struggling in, she chose to set a goal to improve her grade in AP U.S. History by the next marking period.

Drawing on her acting experience, the coach asked Elizabeth how she learned her lines for the plays she was in. Elizabeth described a multistep process that included highlighting her lines, recording scenes with the lines of others in the scene, and leaving enough time on the recording for her to fill in her own lines, practicing several times while looking at the script, and then practicing without the script. It was evident that Elizabeth had good strategies for memorizing material when it was important to her.

The coach wondered if she could help Elizabeth use her interest in theater to help her meet her goal of improving her U.S. History grade. Together, the coach and Elizabeth came up with the idea of making a study guide out of a playbill. Since her teacher divided U.S. History into "periods," they decided to turn each period into a play and created a playbill to summarize the important information from each period. They identified the actors (the key historical figures), the scene breakdown (the historical timeline), and the plot summary (the critical events of the period). For each period they created a mock playbill that she then used as a study guide.

When the marking period ended, Elizabeth's grade had increased from a 78 to a 92. Elizabeth had met her goal. She told the coach that she was going to try to use the playbill template to make a study guide in another subject.

SECONDARY CASE EXAMPLE 2

Sarah was a 14-year-old high school freshman who was academically engaged, was motivated to succeed and challenge herself, and loved running and music. She was a member of her school's track and cross-country team. Her long-term goal for high school was to enroll in the International Baccalaureate program to prepare herself for college.

During the intake process, both Sarah and her parent independently rated Sarah's executive skills and identified time management and goal-directed persistence as relative strengths, and organization and response inhibition as challenges. However, they differed in their view on one domain of executive skills: planning/prioritizing. Whereas Sarah viewed planning/prioritizing as a relative strength, her parent reported it to be a challenge; instead, Sarah noted that task initiation was difficult for her. Her parent also noted that metacognition was a relative weakness for Sarah.

Sarah explained that she wanted to use coaching sessions to work toward her running and music goals; however, because it was her first semester of high school, she first wanted to focus on her academic goals. Although she did have a grade goal for each class for the fall semester, she did not reveal that to the coach until the semester was over and she knew how she had performed. Instead, Sarah stated that her goal was to get assignments completed ahead of the due dates so that she would have time to ask questions and get help, particularly for math.

Coaching sessions started with a focus on planning out how many math assignments Sarah needed to do each day to get them completed ahead of time. Sarah and the coach talked about how long each assignment might take and discussed potential obstacles and planned for them. When she and her coach met the following week, Sarah reported that she had not done the assignments as planned and had not met her goal. Sarah and the coach realized that she had a lot of competing and more immediate priorities that week that had taken precedence over the goal of getting ahead with her math work. This demonstrated Sarah's ability to be flexible and prioritize, which are strengths, but also revealed a weakness in planning a goal with the whole picture of competing demands in mind.

So, Sarah and the coach broadened the scope of their planning, by using coaching sessions to talk through and write up a more comprehensive plan for each week. During coaching sessions, Sarah would explain the work and exams she had to address for the week and would include in her plans other obligations that took time, such as track, extracurricular activities, and family responsibilities. At the start of each coaching session, they would then reflect on the degree to which Sarah was able to follow the plan:

How well did I follow the plan for week?

Not at all (0/total days)

Once (1/total days)

Somewhat (2–3/total days)

Mostly (3–4/total days)

100% (all of total days)

Over time, with this approach, Sarah was able to achieve more of the tasks and goals that she included in her plan each week.

Sarah and the coach talked about Sarah trying to build some independence around writing down her priorities for the week. She agreed to start using her agenda rather than the form the coach had created. She did do that for a few weeks, but then lost that momentum with a fall break period and an increasing workload after the break. It felt too overwhelming to Sarah to write it independently and see it all, but she responded well to having her coach write it out for her each week, and then share it in an email. So, they made the goal toward independent planning smaller by having her try to update her work plan for just one day of the week. Although they checked in on this each week, this too was not something Sarah was able to do.

The coach noticed that Sarah was reporting more stress as the semester wore on, perhaps due to a heavy workload and busy schedule. So, the coach continued with the role of writing out Sarah's plans for each week. However, the coach also started asking Sarah to reflect on and rate her stress level each week so they could track it.

On average, how stressed did I feel this week?

What made it hard to follow the plan or update the plan?

1: Not stressed at all

2: A little bit stressed

3: Somewhat stressed

4: Very stressed

5: Extremely stressed

Overall, while Sarah showed progress in her ability to plan her work for the week and follow through on most of it, she maintained a feeling of stress and was not able to take on the role of writing or updating her own plan in her agenda or in the form her coach used. However, Sarah did achieve her overall grade goal in three of her four classes and came extremely close to her grade goal in her math class.

Having met her grade goals and gotten through the first semester of high school, Sarah seemed to have a new level of confidence and was ready to shift focus to her personal goals, including music, running, and a morning routine. This time she was able to state specific goals, such as "I want to practice music 10 minutes every day"; "I want to run 20 to 30 miles a week"; "I want to wake up by 6:30 A.M. each morning to have more time to myself"; and "By the start of the summer, I want to have purchased a guitar so I can be ready to learn to play." The first few coaching sessions for these goals continued as they had the previous semester with the coach writing the plans that Sarah set for herself, and then reflecting on them together in the next session.

However, after 2 weeks of that approach, Sarah came up with her own rating system for how she felt about each goal:

1: Dreading/stressed
2: Annoyance/annoyed
3: Mediocre/okay
4: At peace

Then, Sarah also started taking the initiative to update the document herself with her stress ratings and to update what items she did and did not accomplish. During coaching sessions, she started updating her weekly planning sheet with goals each week with the coach just present and listening. Sarah also started addressing her long-term goal of learning to play the guitar by breaking down that goal into small actionable steps. She has also maintained and stated her goal of achieving A-level grades in each of her classes, and feels she is on track to do so this semester but is willing to pivot to academic planning and goals with her coach if she needs that support.

Sarah has shown tremendous growth in developing her independence toward naming her goals, determining what steps she needs to take toward them and when, and then reflecting on them.

UNIT III

COACHING TECHNIQUES

CHAPTER 7

Motivational Interviewing

This chapter is an introduction to motivational interviewing (MI) and to our rationale for including it in the coaching process. It is not intended to provide detailed instruction in motivational interviewing. In Appendix 20 (p. 191), we have listed training opportunities and books for readers interested in learning more about motivational interviewing and further developing their skills in this area. While each of us has had training in MI, we are not certified as trainers and would recommend that coaches who are interested in learning this process seek training with individuals who are certified through the Motivational Interviewing Network of Trainers (MINT).

As noted in Chapter 2, the goal of our coaching model is student self-determination. Through coaching, students identify their goals and develop strategies for reaching these goals that are based on the best fit for their skills and life circumstances. In so doing, they increase their self-knowledge and develop a template for planning and decision making that they can use going forward. Research demonstrates that self-determination, autonomy, a sense of purpose, and feelings of competency in at-risk high school students are strong predictors of academic achievement (Dike, 2012). MI has been shown to be effective in improving the academic achievement of middle school students (Terry, Smith, Strait, & McQuillin, 2013; Terry, Strait, McQuillin, & Smith, 2014). Gutierrez, Foxx, and Kondili (2018) demonstrated the effectiveness of MI in comparison to wait-list control and study skills conditions in improving academic motivation in at-risk high school students.

To help students attain a sense of competence or agency requires a particular communication style on the part of the coach—one that promotes student self-control, a sense of competence, and a relationship of trust. MI embodies this style. As Naar-King and Suarez (2011) explained, the job of the coach "is not to take responsibility for change, but rather to support and guide while seeking to elicit the young person's own ideas for change" (p. 17). The coach is able to accomplish this by providing a menu of choices and information, by enquiring about the student's perspectives, and by encouraging personal choice and responsibility. The goal is to create an environment of "supportive autonomy" (Williams, 2002). Thus, we see MI as a nonjudgmental, student-centered approach to coaching that seeks to establish "a collaborative conversation style for strengthening a person's own motivation and commitment to change" (Miller & Rollnick, 2012, p. 12).

Our coaching model assumes that change depends on the motivation of the student to seek change. As coaches, we cannot *make* the students whom we work with change. This is especially true in working with adolescents, since one of the primary tasks of adolescence is the development of autonomy. We also assume that the most powerful and sustained motivation for change emanates from personal choice. In the coaching relationship, the stance or mindset of the coach is a key component in creating an environment for the student that facilitates personal choice. This mindset is captured in a description provided by Stephen Andrew (2015), our MI trainer, in his training handout:

> [Working with students] in a way that is collaborative rather than prescriptive, honors the [student's] autonomy and self-direction, and is more about evoking than installing. This involves at least a willingness to suspend an authoritarian or directive role, and to explore [student] capacity rather than incapacity, with a genuine interest in the [student's] experience and perspective.

SETTING THE STAGE FOR COLLABORATION AND STUDENT SELF-DETERMINATION

As North (2017) pointed out, much of the educational experience of students consists of adults either telling them what is expected of them or telling them what they need to do. MI takes a distinctly different approach: The job of the coach is to collaborate with students to elicit and support the goals that the student has. Since this is not the typical experience of students with adults in the educational setting, we believe it is important that the coach explicitly communicates this stance at the outset of the relationship. We paraphrase the approach suggested by Naar-King and Suarez (2011): "In our coaching sessions I'm not going to tell you what goals you need to set or how to manage them. We'll talk about what's important to you in your education and I'll help you to accomplish the changes you want to make." While this statement might not completely eliminate the skepticism of some students, you have set the stage for your work together. The types of conversations you will use going forward, outlined below, will reinforce your intent.

There is one other strategy in MI that we recommend coaches make part of their encounters with students: asking permission before you engage in a task or offer a suggestion. Asking permission demonstrates your respect for the student's autonomy and increases the likelihood of participation since, if the student gives permission, they have agreed to engage.

Here are a few examples:

- "Is it okay with you if we talk about some ways we could track progress toward your goals?"
- "Would it be all right if I get you some more information about your homework?"
- "Can we explore some strategies that you might use to help you remember everything you have to do?"

Another situation where asking permission is important is whenever the coach offers suggestions or guidance. In our student-centered approach, the coach's stance is nondirective. The coach does not independently set the coaching agenda or give unsolicited advice or directions to the student. This does not mean that the coach is barred from offering suggestions or options. Coaches with years of personal and professional experience can use their skills to serve as a sounding board and source of information. The keys for the coach are asking permission and limiting suggestions or advice to those situations where the student is genuinely stuck. To separate themselves from a directive stance, we recommend the following guidelines:

1. Coaches *always* ask the student's permission to offer guidance or suggestions.
2. If the student gives permission, the coach can move forward. If the student declines permission, the coach accepts this without judgment or protest and goes no further.
3. If the student gives permission, the coach offers *multiple* options for the student to choose from. Options reinforce student choice and selection of the best-fit option.
4. If the student asks the coach what *they* would do, the coach defers, saying that they would always select the answer that suits *them*, which may not be the right answer for the student.

COMMUNICATION AND RELATIONSHIP BUILDING

To realize the outcome of student self-determination in the coaching relationship, the coach engages in four actions:

1. Building a relationship of understanding and acceptance of the student's perspective based on communication of empathy.
2. Focusing on the student and what they want—supporting them to articulate their wishes, desires, and goals.
3. Discovering the student's internal motivation for change. Listening for examples of "change talk" (moving ahead) versus "sustain talk" (maintaining status quo) and encouraging the former while minimizing the latter.
4. Approaching commitment and planning. The frequency and strength of change talk in the context of diminishing sustain talk is a sign of growing motivation for change on the part of the student. Planning only begins when there is evidence of strong commitment.

We believe that the development of the coaching mindset depends on a particular style of communication. That style is at the heart of the MI process and is characterized by the acronym OARS, which stands for the following:

Open-ended questions	These are the kind of questions that open the door to more words from the student than from you, as opposed to yes/no questions used to collect information or data.
Affirmations	Affirmations comment favorably on a specific positive trait, attribute, or strength of the student that endures over time.

| **R**eflections | Accurate empathic reflections involve listening not only to what the student *says,* but also for what the student *means.* |
| **S**ummaries | This is a special form of empathic reflection where you collect statements from a part of or the whole of the conversation. (adapted from Andrew, 2015) |

The OARS acronym describes the essential conversational components of MI, but it is not a prescription for the order in which these components occur in the development of the coaching relationship.

Reflections

The strength of the coaching relationship is that it is built on a foundation of trust. That trust is developed through the coach's demonstration of an empathetic understanding and acceptance of the student's experience and perspective. How does the student know that they are being heard and accepted by the coach? The student learns this over time by virtue of the coach's accurate reflections of what the student says and means.

Think of the process in this way. When a student speaks to a coach about their thoughts and feelings, they are constructing a story about or picture of themself. When the coach reflects back what the student has said, the student can process this thought or feeling. Hearing their words gives them the opportunity to affirm and expand on this story or edit it so the coach has a clearer picture of who they are. Thus, reflections by the coach play a key role in demonstrating to the student that they are being heard, as well as helping the coach understand the direction in which the student wants to move.

If you are not used to making reflections, they can seem awkward or contrived at first. Like any skill, it will improve with practice. Students like to know they are being listened to and reflections confirm that you are listening. Simple reflections are easiest to start with and they are basically a paraphrase of what the student has said. Here are some examples:

- If the student says, "I hate doing homework," a reflection might be, "You really don't like having to do homework."
- If the student says, "My science teacher wants me to attend a study session after school, but I've already made plans to go to the mall with a friend," a reflection might be, "You're torn between going to the study session and your promise to your friend."
- If the student says, "My mom wants me to work with a coach, but I don't think I need to," a reflection might be, "Your mom thinks coaching is a good idea, but you think you can do fine without it."

If the student doesn't immediately respond, resist the urge to fill in the silence and instead wait for them to offer more. Your objective is to capture the essential meaning of the student's statement in your reflection.

After you've had a chance to practice simple reflections for a while, you can move on to more complex reflections. Complex reflections capture the real meaning of the student's statement. For example, if the student says, "My parents are constantly asking about my homework," a complex reflection might be, "You're tired of your parents nagging you about your work" or "It's annoying to have your parents always questioning you about your performance." Here you are reflecting the feelings of the student.

Complex reflections go beneath the surface by tapping into the student's feelings, goals, or values. Here are other examples of complex reflections.

Example 1

Student: "My teacher yelled at me 2 days in a row for forgetting to bring a pen to class!"

Complex reflection: "You're mad at your teacher for embarrassing you in front of the class" or "You're mad at your teacher because it just reminds you how you keep forgetting things."

Student's response: "It was such a small thing that she turned into something major—it happens all the time!" or "I'm so tired of being so absent-minded!"

Complex reflection: "You're mad at your teacher for constantly getting on your case" or "You're pretty discouraged about how hard it is for you to remember everything you need to remember."

Example 2

Student: "I have a group of friends that I like but they keep suggesting things that make me uncomfortable, like smoking weed or staying out past my curfew."

Complex reflection: "A goal of yours is to stay out of that kind of trouble."

Example 3

Student: "I forgot that I had set up a test review session with my chemistry teacher. Now he thinks I've just blown him off and that I don't really care about how I'm doing in the class."

Complex reflection: "It's important to you that your teacher sees you as wanting to do well in his class."

Naar-King and Suarez (2011), among others, offered two specific tips for practitioners. First, they noted that when initially learning to use reflections, it is not uncommon for people to preface a reflection with one or another stem, such as "What I hear you saying . . ." or "It sounds like. . . ." If it feels more comfortable to begin this way, we prefer the latter since it sounds less like what a therapist might say. However, over time, as you develop the skill, it is preferable to drop the stem.

Their second recommendation is to guard against turning reflections into questions. Suppose, for example, the student says, "Play practice ran late and I didn't get to my homework." Your reflection might be, "A school activity interfered with your homework plan." This is a straightforward statement and lets the student know you heard them, and it is judgment free. However, if you change your inflection at the end of the reflection by asking, "A school activity interfered with your homework plan?" this could suggest that you are not listening. It could also suggest a judgment on your part, for example that the statement is just an excuse for avoiding homework. Since the point of a reflection is accurate perception and acceptance of what the student says, a question undermines this objective.

Open-Ended Questions

While we prioritize reflections in the coach's communication with the student, we understand that there are other components of communication that will take place throughout the coaching relationship. Questions, while not as effective as reflections in communicating empathy and understanding, can open the door to the student's thoughts and feelings, provided that they are open-ended. Open-ended questions present the student with the opportunity to elaborate thoughts and feelings and provide the coach with the opportunity to further reflect what the student offers. In other words, they are conversation facilitators. For example, the coach might ask, "Can you tell me about how homework affects your grades?" The response gives the coach an opportunity for reflection as well as information that the coach can later refer to when exploring change talk.

In contrast, closed-ended questions are conversation stoppers, since they typically call for a yes/no or a specific, brief answer (e.g., "Did you go to class today?" or "What was your grade on the test?") Thus, open-ended are clearly preferable to closed-ended questions. Nonetheless, if open-ended questions constitute the bulk of the coach's conversation, they can seem like an interrogation and undermine communication of empathetic understanding. Ideally, a response by the student to an open-ended question is always followed by one or more reflections by the coach.

We are not suggesting that closed-ended questions are never to be used. There are times when a coach has to have specific, factual information (e.g., a grade on a test, number of classes and study periods). What we are suggesting is that they be used sparingly.

Affirmations

Affirmations are the coach's opportunity to comment positively on a student's words, actions, or characteristics. Affirmations are most effective when they reflect the coach's honest appraisal of the student's action and when they refer specifically to what the student has said or done. Generic positive statements (e.g., "That's great," "Nice work," "Good job"), especially if used routinely by a coach, can ring hollow or false to the student. On the other hand, when the coach's comment references something specific the student has done (e.g., "Nice job following through on your study plan; that shows good persistence") the student is encouraged and recognizes that they are being heard by the coach.

We also note a caution about affirmations. It is natural for some students to be ambivalent about making a change or about their ability to reach a stated goal, especially in the early stages of the coaching process. If a coach offers effusive or overly enthusiastic affirmations at this stage (e.g., "I think it's wonderful that you've decided to improve your grades!"), the student may well pull back since the coach has moved much faster than the student is ready for. Refraining from "I" statements and giving a more tentative appraisal (e.g., "It's good that you're thinking about improving your grades as an option") mitigates this risk. As is the case with reflections, the coach's goal is to understand the feeling state of the student and match their affirmations to the student's readiness for change. As you will see below, affirmations play an important role in encouraging change talk.

Summaries

Summaries, the last component of OARS, are a collection of reflections made by the coach of what the student has talked about during the session. Summaries are an opportunity for the coach to periodically capture the essential features of the student's discussion and to connect these features and present them back to the student. They let the student know that the coach has been listening and give the student the chance to hear back what they have said as well as to edit or further elaborate on the picture that the coach has presented. Thus, they are a way of ensuring that the coach has understood correctly what the student is saying.

If possible, summaries end with a statement of motivation, that is, something that indicates a consideration of change from the student's current behavior. However, in summarizing, the coach neither selectively edits out reasons that the student has given not to change nor cherry picks only statements of change. If a relationship of trust is to be maintained, summaries need to be accurate reflections of the student's words, including their ambivalence about change.

For example, if a student has spent some time talking about their conflict over how they want to spend their time over the weekend, the coach might offer this summary:

> "You've said that all your friends are getting together to go to a concert on Saturday. You really want to join them. At the same time, you know that would mean getting home late. You have a term paper due on Monday that you've only worked on a little, and you're worried that you might be too tired on Sunday to spend the time you'll need in order to finish the paper by the deadline."

CHANGE TALK AND AMBIVALENCE

The goal of coaching is performance improvement. Presumably then, students enter the coaching process because there is discrepancy between their current behavior and some performance goal that they have, and they believe that the coach can help them. In our coaching model, student participation is voluntary. Given that, as coaches we may assume that students who seek coaching are motivated to change their behavior; that is, they are motivated to achieve their goals. However, we have determined that if a goal is to be a source of motivation, three conditions need to be present:

- The goal has been chosen by the student and the student has determined that the goal is relevant to the current context of their life.
- The student is confident that they have the skills and resources necessary to achieve the goal.
- The student believes that the goal is of sufficient importance or value to enable the effort and energy needed to change their behavior and reach the goal.

While coaching is a voluntary process from our perspective, more often than not coaching has been recommended to the student by someone else, such as a teacher, parent, or school counselor. The fact that the student is willing to meet with the coach ensures that at least that act is voluntary, but it tells little else about the student's desire to be there or about any goals they have.

The task of the coach then is twofold. The first is to clarify how/why the student is there. This information will give the coach some insight into the student's desire or motivation to engage in coaching. For example, the student might say, "My parents think I should be getting better grades and a coach will help." Using the communication strategies outlined above, especially reflections and open-ended questions, the coach can begin to clarify if the student shares the goal of better grades and thinks a coach can be of help. The second task for the coach is to let the student know that the coach is there to listen to the student and help them with whatever changes they want to make and not to make decisions for or direct the student's actions.

In MI, ambivalence is viewed as a natural part of the behavioral change process, and the degree of ambivalence is a clue to readiness for change. Changing a behavior means giving up a routine or habit that one is familiar with and that provides some perceived benefit. Hence, it is natural that people feel some ambivalence about change.

Let's take our student from above who finds homework aversive and has been referred to coaching by her parents. The benefit of homework avoidance is that it frees up time to engage in other pursuits that are more pleasurable and less effortful. While the student might indicate that she'd like better grades, she may not be sure that the potential benefit of improved grades is worth the effort required for homework completion.

In MI, ambivalence is identified by the presence of *sustain talk* and *change talk*. *Sustain talk* occurs when the student talks about why they can't change, why change isn't worth the effort, or the benefits of the current behavior. *Change talk* is the opposite of sustain talk and occurs when the student talks about the benefits of changing their behavior. More change talk increases the likelihood of a change in behavior while more sustain talk decreases this likelihood.

The coach's goal in MI is to increase change talk and diminish sustain talk. There are a variety of strategies in MI for responding to ambivalence and increasing change talk. Here's one example.

Returning to our student who has expressed possible interest in improving grades but is concerned about the effortfulness of homework, the coach can demonstrate an understanding and acceptance of the student's ambivalence with what is called a *double-sided reflection*. The coach, for example, might say, "On the one hand, you don't like doing homework and, on the other hand, you would like to get better grades." Miller and Rollnick (2002) recommended using "and" rather than "but" to suggest that it is normal to simultaneously hold two different feelings. Naar-King and Suarez (2011, p. 31) suggested that the reflection should end with positive change to increase the likelihood that student will respond to that side of the change.

Once the coach has recognized and accepted that the student is at best ambivalent about making a change, the next step is to explore the cons and pros of changing a behavior, which is an extension of the double-sided reflection (Naar-King & Suarez, 2011, p. 43). For example, the coach could say, "Tell me about the disadvantages of doing homework" (the cons of change). Although the natural inclination of the coach might be to ask about the advantages of doing homework, to do so risks the student feeling that the coach is trying to move them in that direction before they are ready. Starting with the disadvantages of change acknowledges the student's ambivalence.

After the student has had a chance to state the downside of homework, the coach can follow this with a question about the possible pros of change, "So on the other side, what might be some reasons for doing homework?" If the student is able to offer some reasons for doing homework—for example, improved grades—the coach can reflect what the student has said and thus reinforce change talk without leaving the student feeling that they are being pushed in that direction.

For the student and coach, the next step to continuing the journey toward change involves elaborating change talk while at the same time recognizing that ambivalence has not necessarily resolved. The coach's conversation with the student can acknowledge that some ambivalence remains while at the same time encouraging additional thinking about change. For example, the coach might say, "You're giving some thought to improving your grades but you're not sure if you are ready. If you decided that you wanted to have better grades, how you might go about it?" In this approach, the coach does not presume that the student is ready and poses a hypothetical question that does not involve a commitment by the student.

As an additional strategy to encourage change talk, rulers are often used in MI (Naar-King & Suarez, 2011, pp. 60–61). The ruler is a scaling technique designed to gauge how important a change is to the student. The coach describes the ruler as a scale of 1 to 10, with 1 representing "not at all" and 10, "very important." Taking our student who wants to improve their grades, for example, the coach might first reflect, "You said you've given some thought to improving your grades. Is it okay if I ask you a question about that?" If the student says it is, the coach describes or presents a visual of the ruler and says, "On a scale of 1 to 10, with 1 representing not important at all and 10 representing very important, where would you rate how important it is to improve your grades?"

Considering that the student has expressed some interest in better grades, a rating of 1 is unlikely. In our experience, students presented with the ruler strategy will offer a rating between 4 and 6, which gives the coach some insight into their level of ambivalence. Whatever number the student gives (other than 1), the coach next says, for example, "Why are you at 5 rather than 3?" By making the second number lower than the first, the question increases the likelihood of change talk since the student will offer reasons for the higher rating.

The ruler strategy also can be used to inquire what it would take to get to a higher number than the student's current rating.

> COACH: You've given some good reasons why you are a 5 rather than a 3. What do you think it would take to get to a higher number, like 6 or 7?
>
> STUDENT: Well, I suppose I could start with homework in subjects that are more interesting to me, like biology. Some of the labs are really fun.
>
> COACH: So you like some subjects and doing homework for those would be easier. Any others?
>
> STUDENT: Yeah, social studies, I guess. We talk about different points of view and get to write about our opinions.

Having this information gives student and coach a potential starting point for change, and down the line this might be the basis for beginning a plan.

CHANGE TALK AND COMMITMENT

As we noted above, the student's motivation for change is signaled by the presence of increased change talk in the context of diminishing sustain talk. The coach, using OARS, opens the door for this by recognizing change talk and selectively encouraging it while minimizing attention to sustain talk. Miller and Rollnick (2012) proposed the acronym DARNCAT to recognize different types and qualities of change talk. Other practitioners (e.g., Andrew, 2015) have offered an abbreviated form, DARN-C. For our purposes here, we use DARN-C, which stands for desire, ability, reason, need, and commitment. The DARN component in the following example signals preparatory change talk.

Desire to change—wishes, wants, hopes	"I want to get better grades." "It would be nice if I could get better grades."
Ability to change—confidence	"If I try I know I can do it." "I think maybe I can do it."
Reasons to change—motive, rationale	"I've got to get better grades for admission to college." "Better grades might improve my college chances."
Need to change—necessity	"I've got to start doing my homework." "I should start doing more homework."

In each of the categories, the first change talk statement by the student indicates a stronger level of motivation and commitment to change. In listening for change talk, particularly before moving on to the commitment component of DARN-C, it is important for the coach to be aware of the quality of the student's change talk. In each of the second statements above, the student is more tentative about change, suggesting some continuing ambivalence. Strength in the student's change talk and diminished sustain talk is thus the indicator of readiness for change.

Before moving on to commitment and planning, there are some cautions to keep in mind. As a coach, all of the work you have done to this point has been in the service of the student making a change. It is natural to be excited about this and anxious to move the process forward. North (2017) suggested that this is a time for the coach to step back and slow down. The step from talk to action is not a small one. If the coach, who up until this time has followed the student's lead, suddenly takes the lead in an effort to pull the student across the finish line, the student may well pull back. Naar-King and Suarez (2011) suggested that this is a good time for "testing the water" (p. 67), particularly if the coach senses some lingering ambivalence. The authors suggest these types of coach questions:

- "You're thinking about making a change. Where might you go from here?"
- "Why do you feel that this is the time to make a change?"
- "If you did decide to take the next step, what might that look like?"

If the student indicates that they're not sure how to proceed, the coach could offer some assistance. The coach could say, "Sometimes if students are not sure what to do next it can be helpful to think about different options. If you're okay with this, we can talk about some different plans and see if any of them feel like a good fit for you." With the student's permission, the coach can present some different options. For example, in the case of our student who wants to improve grades, options might include starting with a preferred subject or preferred type of assignment, setting aside a set amount of time, or selecting a specific setting.

The options discussed will depend in part on how much information the coach has about the student's current homework habits. If the student is unable to settle on any plan, the coach returns to OARS for additional work with the student on change talk and resolution of ambivalence. If the student is able to select a plan, the coach can again ask if the student is open to using the ruler once more to get the student's estimate of their confidence in the success of the plan. We believe that this needs to be a 7 or higher in order to proceed. Less than that signals ambivalence in the commitment and decreased likelihood of success. If the student is confident in the plan, they can proceed with setting goals and action steps. We have described in detail the strategies for how to accomplish this in other chapters of this book.

FINAL THOUGHTS: DOS AND DON'TS

Do . . .	Don't . . .
Develop a relationship of supportive autonomy through empathetic reflection and collaboration	Enter the relationship with your own agenda and assume that you are the expert and know what's best for the student and therefore should take control
Evoke, elicit, and accept the student's reasons for and ambivalence about change	Engage in the *righting reflex*, the tendency to correct some statement/behavior of the student in order to put them on what you think is the right path to success
Ask permission before offering suggestions or requests that they engage in a task	Offer unsolicited advice, suggestions, or directions about how you think the student should proceed

CHAPTER 8

Communication Techniques for Elementary School Coaches

The MI literature, while extensive, primarily focuses on work with teens and adults. Many of the techniques that are central to MI can be used with younger children as well, but in this chapter, we focus on the communication tools that we feel are most useful to incorporate into a coaching practice that centers on working with elementary-age students. There will be some redundancy with the previous chapter, but we use terminology that will be familiar to teachers or counselors working with this age group, and we provide developmentally appropriate examples.

As with MI, the purposes of these communication techniques are to:

- Let the child know that you heard what they said and understand their point of view.
- Reflect back their thoughts and feelings so that the child knows that you not only heard their words but you understand the feelings they're expressing.
- Give the child positive feedback about aspects of their behavior or performance in such a way that it illuminates for the child strengths or skills that they may not have recognized on their own.
- Help the child engage in problem solving in such a way that the coach avoids being prescriptive but encourages the child to arrive at a solution that works for them.

While there are adaptations made in some MI techniques, one technique that we use without modification is asking permission before we make suggestions or try to influence the coaching process. Even to elementary-age children, coaches say things like:

68

- "Would it be okay if I make a suggestion about something you might try?"
- "I have some ideas for that. Would you like me to share them with you?"
- "I have a couple of strategies I think might work. Can I run them by you and see what you think?"

When we make suggestions, we're careful to offer children more than one option. When we only give children one choice, then we box them in to two choices: yes or no. When we make suggestions, we frequently say to children, "These are my ideas—but they may help you think of something that would work better for you."

The communication skills that are most in demand in the coaching process include reflective listening, providing effective praise, and asking open-ended questions. Each of these is defined below, with examples.

REFLECTIVE LISTENING

This skill involves two components, listening carefully and responding reflectively. Reflective listeners work to understand in an empathic way whatever the person is saying from the speaker's viewpoint or internal frame of reference. Beyond empathy, however, the listener *accepts* what the speaker is saying without agreeing or disagreeing with them. There are two types of reflections: simple and complex.

Simple Reflections

Simple reflections mean capturing the essence of the words and ideas of what someone has just said and stating it back to them succinctly. Reflecting serves several purposes: (1) It shows you've listened carefully; (2) it allows you to check the accuracy of what you heard; and (3) it allows the speaker to hear what they've said so that the statement can be revised if it was not what they intended to convey.

Example 1

Student: "I was going to do my homework last night, but then my mom asked me to play with my little brother so she could do a Zoom meeting. And by the time that ended, it was almost bedtime, and I was too tired to do any work!"

Reflection: "You were set to do your homework but then your mom asked you to spend time with your little brother while she did a Zoom meeting. That took almost until bedtime, and then you were too exhausted to work."

Example 2

Student: "Mrs. Dobson got mad at me at recess because she thought I was bossing other kids around. But she didn't see that the kids I was talking to were picking on a younger kid and I was just trying to stick up for him."

Reflection: "You felt like you were protecting a smaller child and when your teacher got mad at you, you felt she didn't have the full picture."

Complex Reflections

Complex reflections mean capturing the essence of the idea that someone has expressed, as well as what motivates them, and their emotions, values, and goals. It means zeroing in on the feeling elements of the speaker's statements and responding with acceptance and empathy rather than indifference or judgment.

Example 1

Student: "My group is supposed to present our project to the class tomorrow. I *hate* getting up in front of the whole class. I always forget what I'm supposed to say and then I make a fool of myself."

Reflection: "Getting up in front of the class makes you nervous and then you feel embarrassed because you forget what you were going to say."

Example 2

Student: "My soccer coach never plays me. I go to every single practice, and I work really hard. If I'm lucky, he'll put me in for 2 minutes at the end of the game if our team is ahead and he knows we're going to win. It's not like we're a professional team—I'm only in fifth grade!" [*Note:* This is not an academically relevant comment, but when students form relationships with academic coaches, they often bring up other topics. It is obvious that this student is preoccupied with this event and, by reflecting the student's feelings, the coach may help the student to move on from that experience and focus on the coaching session.]

Reflection: "You really want to improve. You're pretty angry at your soccer coach for only playing you for such a short time, especially since you never miss a practice and work hard while you're there."

SPECIFIC PRAISE

Praise is a powerful way to shape behavior, but there is a sharp distinction between effective and ineffective (or even damaging) praise. When we praise children for traits over which they feel they have no control ("You're so smart!" "What a pretty girl you are!"), the information we're giving them is not particularly useful because they don't know what they have to do to stay that way. On top of that, particularly in the case of telling someone how smart they are, we run the risk of them avoiding challenging tasks in the future for fear they won't succeed and therefore will stop being smart. The best kind of praise is the kind that specifies what the student has done that's praiseworthy.

When praise is used effectively it (1) is delivered immediately after the display of positive behavior; (2) specifies the particulars of the accomplishment (e.g., "You got out your assignment book without me having to ask you"); (3) provides information to the student about the value of the accomplishment (e.g., "I can see you're learning to remember to use the strategies we've been talking about"); (4) lets the student know that they worked hard to accomplish the task (e.g., "I can see you put a lot of time and thought into this writing assignment"); and (5) orients the student to better appreciate their own task-related behavior and thinking about problem solving (e.g., "I like the way you used brainstorming to think of a lot of ideas before zeroing in on the best one").

A general rule of thumb is that for every critical or corrective statement directed toward a student, they should receive three positive statements. In fact, there's substantial research to show that just using praise in this way can by itself lead to significant positive behavior change. This is often difficult to accomplish with students who seem to be bent on just trying to "get by." For this reason, we often recommend reinforcing *improvement* or approximations of desired behavior (e.g., "It looks like you hung in there a little longer with your math homework last night than you did with the last math assignment you had").

Coaching lends itself to lots of opportunities for genuine praise. Furthermore, by praising executive skills, we're increasing the likelihood that students will continue to practice these effortful skills. Here are some examples:

- "Hey, you got here right on time. Good time management skills!"
- "It looks like you were able to use that checklist to help you remember everything you needed to bring home from school."
- "I can see you were angry at me, but it looked like you worked hard to control your emotions."
- "For the last three nights, you've followed your homework schedule just the way you wrote it out. I think your task initiation skills are really coming along."

OPEN-ENDED QUESTIONS VERSUS CLOSED-ENDED QUESTIONS

Open-ended questions are designed to gather more information about something a student is talking about. They help students use their executive skills, whether we're talking about working memory ("Tell me everything you have to do for homework tonight") or other skills such as planning ("What steps are you going to follow to complete your science project?") or organization ("How do you think you could set up your work area so that you can find everything you need?"). Open-ended questions encourage students to think more deeply about how they approach learning and academic tasks.

Closed-ended questions are yes/no questions or any other question designed to "pin down" a student to a precise answer. Coaches use both kinds of questions and need to know when to use which kind.

It should be noted that there are some populations coaches may be working with who have difficulty with open-ended questions. Younger children as well as students who are cognitively inflexible, such as those with autism spectrum disorder or nonverbal learning disabilities, may find these questions more difficult to answer. When working with these students, coaches may need to alter the way they ask questions to suit their students' style. This usually means asking more closed-ended questions and then, with permission, giving students choices (e.g., "Let me describe a couple of different ways you might do this assignment and you tell me which one might work best"). Coaching with these populations may work best when the focus is narrower—helping students make plans, helping them create checklists for things they have to do or remember, and so forth.

With more typical underachievers, coaching employs a mix of open-ended and closed-ended questions. Here are some examples of how each kind of question is used in the coaching process.

Examples of Open-Ended Questions

- "What is your study plan for the weekend?"
- "How are you going to study for your social studies test?"
- "How are you going to work around your practice for the school play given the homework load you have?"
- "I've noticed you have a hard time estimating how long it takes you to do your English homework. What do you think you could do to fix that?"
- "What will you say to your science teacher if she gets on your case about forgetting your homework?"
- "It seems like studying in your bedroom doesn't work out for you because there are too many distractions. Do you have ideas for other places you could work?"

The purpose of all these questions is to encourage students to come up with strategies on their own or to generate their own solutions to problems. Very often, these kinds of open-ended questions are lead-ins that enable the coach to offer suggestions.

Examples of Closed-Ended Questions

- "What time do you plan to do your math homework today?"
- "What's the first step you have to do for your social studies project?"
- "How much time do you plan on studying for your science test?"
- "Did you remember to hand in your English essay?"

Since part of coaching involves having students make a commitment to carrying out a plan or working on a goal, closed-ended questions enable them to develop the plan with adequate specificity. Consider the following:

COACH: So what time do you plan to do your math homework today?

STUDENT: I think I'll do it just before dinner.

COACH: Can you paint a picture for me of how you spend your time once you get home from school? I want to see how math homework fits into the larger schedule.

STUDENT: Okay, usually I get a snack. And then I either play video games or I go outside with my friend who lives next door.

COACH: And then what?

STUDENT: Well, if I'm playing video games, my mom won't let me play for more than half an hour. So then I just kind of kill time until dinner.

COACH: It sounds like starting math homework before dinner would be something new for you.

STUDENT: Yeah, mostly I do homework after dinner.

COACH: If you're making a new plan, do you have some ideas about how you'll remember to start your homework before dinner?

That old phrase *The devil is in the details* should hang in a frame on the office wall of every coach. The coach in the example above used a closed-ended question to help the student decide on a time, then followed this with open-ended questions and a reflection to refine the plan. Students with executive skills deficits can be walked through a planning process so that when they leave the coach's office they have a detailed schedule for what they plan on accomplishing that day. But if they don't remember to follow their plan, the planning is for naught. *How will you remember to . . . ?* is a common question for coaches to use, particularly in the early stages of coaching.

With MI, it's generally recommended that coaches use reflections more than they use open-ended questions. The same guideline applies to communicating with elementary-age students as well. Because students at this age do not have the metacognitive skills of older students, however, they are less likely to "connect the dots" when coaches are helping them develop plans or solve problems. Coaches can help them do this by starting with a closed-ended question or an open-ended question and then following up with more specificity if the student is not making connections on their own.

With a teenager, a coach might use a reflection such as, "You're mad at yourself for leaving that paper until the last minute and having to hand in an assignment that you knew could have been better." The student might respond, "Yeah, next time I'm going to do a better job of following the plan I made for spreading out the work over several days." With a younger student, a statement such as that from a coach may not produce the same result. In this case, a coach might follow up with, "How might you handle it differently the next time? I have some ideas I'd be happy to run by you, if you'd like to hear them."

Similarly, a coach working with a teenager might say, "What are your ideas for how you could manage your time differently the next time you get a long-term assignment?" Teenagers are often able to answer those kinds of questions, but this same kind of question might stump a younger child. If a younger child can't answer a question such as "What do you think you might do to avoid getting in trouble at recess?" the coach might ask permission to offer suggestions and then turn it into a "multiple choice"—for example, "Here are some ideas: You could join the supervised activity during recess; you could invite a friend to join you in an activity; or you could decide to play in a different part of the playground than the kid who bugs you and leads you to lose your temper. Would any of those work for you—or do you have a different idea?"

All of these communication techniques are designed to build trust between the coach and the student, let the student know that they are heard and understood, and help the child set goals and solve problems without doing the work for the child.

CHAPTER 9

Self-Assessment as a Tool for Honing Coaching Skills

Coaching incorporates a range of skills. Many education professionals begin coaching without training and experience in MI. Applying these skills in your coaching conversations with children may involve a learning curve as you experiment, practice, and refine these techniques with the students you're coaching. It will likely feel awkward and maybe even uncomfortable in the beginning. As you practice, it will start to feel more natural, and you will no doubt see changes in how your students talk in sessions and respond to the approach overall.

The sense that "things are going better" is gratifying, and probably means you're on the right track as you work on improving your coaching skills. This chapter spells out a self-evaluation process you can use to collect more precise and objective data about your skill development.

We offer two levels for self-assessment—basic and advanced. We suggest you start with the basic level. As you acquire some experience with this level, we suspect that (1) you'll find value in doing this kind of self-reflection as a way to improve your skills and (2) you'll be eager to use the more advanced approach as a way of honing your skills even further.

Our goals for this chapter are for you to emerge with some basic techniques for self-assessment, along with the rationale for the style of assessment. Although knowing the "why" of our assessments is not strictly necessary to perform them, comfort with the rationale will improve any coach's interpretation and future use of the results.

Assessing performance of a nondirective coaching style is tricky. In the abstract, student outcomes are the most logical measure. What could be a better metric than a uniform criterion stating how much of what kind of progress a student should make, and in how much time, for the coach's performance to be deemed successful? Our initial answer was, nothing could be better! So we got out our whiteboards, gathered references, and set to researching and defining some uniform criteria of student success. And we made a lot of progress.

However, it also became apparent that a student outcome criterion alone wouldn't be sufficient. Which speaks to the distinguishing component of this approach; if the coaching stance is nondirective, if we ask coaches to ride shotgun instead of drive, then assessing only based on student outcome will overemphasize the coach's role in the outcome, while also failing to account for some pretty important contributions a coach does make in service of student goal setting and attainment. Therefore, although we certainly hold improved student outcomes as the overall benchmark for successful coaching programs, you will notice that a fair portion of this chapter is devoted to assessing how coaches make use of the coaching techniques and to what degree their coaching "fits" the model.

Our self-assessments entail both quantitative and qualitative measures. The quantitative portions allow us to transform elements of a session into a visual that can be counted, manipulated, and inspected. These measures are a foundation for analysis; they give a broad look at what occurred where in the session.

In our experience, good and less-good coaching sessions come in many different shapes and sizes. The quantitative data are a box score or sheet music, an objective account of what techniques the coach used and where they occurred during a session. But we know that two musicians can follow the same sheet music and come out with very different-sounding results. Likewise, examining the quality of the coaching elements—the language, tone, timing, and sequence of the statements—is an important component of assessing the overall coaching performance.

The quantitative and qualitative work in concert. A hypothetical session may show very few open-ended questions and many closed-ended questions, which typically indicates a coaching deficit. This information, provided by the quantitative side, is reason to dig further and likely to seek ways to replace the closed-ended questions with open-ended ones or reflections. Conversely, a coach may record a session they feel should have gone better than it did. The quantitative data show a lot of good techniques being used, but at a much higher rate than usual. In this case, the quantitative data might reassure the coach that their skills are strong and the coach might look deeper at the why of the change in rate (perhaps the student was tired, or distracted, leading the coach simply to talk more than usual).

BASIC SELF-ASSESSMENT

The checklist for basic self-assessment serves two purposes. For those new to MI and this coaching style, it is a simple way to begin self-review of sessions. For all coaches, it is a straightforward, quick process that can be used frequently without added time.

The basic assessment can be found in Appendix 18 (p. 189). It is a template of self-reflective questions we most often ask ourselves right after a session has occurred.

Remember, this is not a graded test. These questions do have yes or no answers, but the real value of the exercise is in remembering the session and thinking specifically about instances where you used a technique. You may even write it down, as an added rehearsal. To put it another way, answering "yes" and recalling one specific example, especially one you're proud of, is more desirable than answering "Yes, I used many reflections throughout." By recalling one example you're reinforcing not only the specific language that made this successful for you but also the context, and in future sessions you're more likely to spot similar patterns that are good places for this technique.

We recommend keeping the number of closed-ended questions or directive statements to a minimum. For this item on the checklist, recall one you used (writing it down may help), and consider these questions: "Could I have rephrased this?"; "Could I have asked permission?"; or "Did I really need to make this point at all?" Over time, answering these questions will give you a range of examples of how to "open a closed question," when to ask for permission, and what kinds of statements you can get rid of altogether, and you will start applying these rules proactively in sessions.

We finish our self-review with two takeaways:

- "What was my best moment during the session?"
- "Next session, I would like to . . ."

For the second question, the more specific and simpler the answer, the easier it will be to approach. For example, we might say, "Next session, I would like to ask for permission one time" or "Next session, I'd like to use one reflection where I label the *emotion* of what the student is communicating."

ADVANCED SELF-ASSESSMENT

The heart of the quantitative aspect in this coaching method is the score sheet (see Figure 9.1). Pictured is a partially filled-in sheet we use when reviewing coaching sessions. The blank score sheet can also be found in Appendix 19 (p. 190). A link to directions for creating an online spreadsheet (*www.dropbox.com/s/hjb3tyt5mmimkw9/Session%20Call%20Template.pdf?dl=0*) performs the same function using buttons that can be clicked when one of the target coach statements occurs. Once a coach is comfortable with identifying the elements, this score sheet can be used to effectively and efficiently diagram the elements of a session.

1 min	2	3	4	5	6	7	8	9	10	11	12	13	14	15
O, R, A, S	P, R, C, O	R, R, O, P												
16	17	18	19	20	21	22	23	24	25	26	27	28	29	30
31	32	33	34	35	36	37	38	39	40	41	42	43	44	45
46	47	48	49	50	51	52	53	54	55	56	57	58	59	60

O = Open-Ended Question	C = Closed-Ended Question	P = Permission	DS = Directive Statement
CR = Cognitive Rehearsal	R = Reflection	A = Affirmation	S = Summary

FIGURE 9.1. Advanced self-assessment score sheet. Copyright © Colin Guare, Executive Skills LLC. Reprinted by permission.

It may be a surprise to learn that, aside from one element (cognitive rehearsal), the score sheet does not measure any student behavior in alignment with a nondirective model, as measuring student behaviors would likely encourage attempts by coaches to direct or influence student behaviors. However, when a student is speaking for several consecutive minutes, we typically note this on the sheet to account for blank space. A coach may also want to look qualitatively at student behavior if the score sheet looks unusual. By focusing exclusively on coach behavior during this stage, we keep the process as efficient as possible and record things we can control.

What Gets Recorded

The first items to record are OARS (see Chapter 7). For simplicity, we identify open-ended questions and open-ended statements the same. Definitions and abbreviations for all the techniques included on the score sheet can be found in Table 9.1.

TABLE 9.1. Advanced Self-Assessment Elements

Technique (abbreviation)	Brief description
Open-ended question/ statement (O)	A question or statement that invites variety and depth of response from participants—for example: "How did _____ [experience] go for you?"; "Tell me more about _____" (the "O" in OARS).
Affirmation (A)	A genuine, substantive, positive comment by a coach, often focused on a desirable attribute or strength the participant exhibited in a circumstance (the "A" in OARS).
Reflection (R)	A statement by a coach attempting to paraphrase the meaning of a participant statement, not just its content. Accurate reflections of meaning are quintessential examples of coach empathy (the "R" in OARS).
Summary (S)	Similar to a reflection but drawing together several parts of a conversation and attempting to capture the sum of their meaning (the "S" in OARS).
Asking permission (P)	A coach asking for denial or consent prior to offering a resource, direction, or opinion.
Cognitive rehearsal (CR)	A period of the meeting in which the participant vocally figures out or rehearses the steps to reach a desired goal, with great detail and as little support from the coach as needed to be successful.
Closed-ended question (C)	A question that is narrow or has limited possible responses. Yes/no questions are prototypical closed-ended questions.
Directive statement (DS)	A statement made by the coach about what the participant should do, say, or think. Rhetorical questions are almost always a directive statement in disguise.

"C" is recorded for closed-ended questions. Closed-ended questions are closed because the question allows for few possible answers. Yes/no questions—questions seeking short, factual answers—are examples of closed-ended questions. Closed-ended questions are not inherently bad and are a necessary component of coaching. How, when, and how often they are used is our concern. Perhaps the largest structural difference between directive and nondirective models is the degree to which closed-ended or open-ended questions are used. A sheet peppered with C's isn't automatically a bad session but would be a reason to (1) look closely at the qualitative elicits of the session and (2) refer to other sheets of other sessions to see if a pattern emerges. If it does, the coach should be even more apt to look into these sessions, suspecting that a number of these C's could be O's and that there is an opportunity to improve this coaching component.

We use "P" for instances where a coach asked permission before sharing and presenting a choice or offering help in "some way." "DS" denotes a directive statement. Directive statements are instances in which a coach gave unsolicited advice or critiqued a student statement without asking permission. Directive statements also include chastising—for example, a rhetorical question in the style of "Shouldn't you have known better?" Directive statements prioritize the coach's opinion of what the student should be doing, rather than reflecting, amplifying, supporting, and, if necessary, exploring the potential obstacles of the student's goal.

The last element included in the sheet is cognitive rehearsal (CR). This is the only element that is not able to be broken down into a single phrase or sentence. During a coaching session, an instance of CR may last for several minutes and be made up of many reflections, open-ended questions, affirmations, and summaries. We highlight CR because it is something of significant importance to the coaching process. Not always, but quite often, a CR in a session signifies a shift from MI to coaching. DARN-C and other MI elements will help the coach identify and amplify a student's motivation to change. The CR marks a time when the discussion moves from a "What is my goal?" question to a "How do I get there?" question. CRs consist of a student, with the assistance of a coach using OARS, walking through the steps to achieve a goal.

Although it will vary from person to person, a coach's goal is for the student to walk through the steps in as great detail as possible (we would not at this point pull out a worksheet with "SMART goal" written across the top but keeping those criteria in mind can be helpful for coaches when figuring out how to guide their reflections and open-ended questions). CRs are incredibly valuable to coaching because they are practice sessions, chances for a student to lay out the steps to a goal and identify and account for any obstacles. The more specific to their own lives that a rehearsal can be, the closer to "real" this practice session gets.

How and When to Record a Session

Student permission should always be sought prior to recording any exchange, and our rule of thumb is to approach the subject in advance of the session the coach would like to record. If a student declines to be recorded, a coach should immediately defer to this decision and move on. In most cases our primary assurance to students rests on preexisting policies on privacy and confidentiality. If these are not in place, then a supplemental agreement to neither reveal any identifying information nor share or reproduce any content of the session without express prior permission should be considered.

Here is a sample statement:

"John, part of my work as a coach involves reviewing and analyzing my own performance. One way coaches do this is by recording a session with a student. I'd like to ask your permission to record one of our sessions for this purpose. As with everything we do, this recording and any private information it might contain is confidential and will not be shared with anyone. I review the session using a process that involves labeling my portions of the conversation. I will be the only person that listens to this recording, and the data I collect from it will contain no mention of your name, no statements you make, and no other identifying information. Nothing about our sessions will change, regardless of whether you accept or decline."

Recording audio is the predominant method of gathering data sufficient for this type of review. Video conferencing services like Zoom and Google Meet now provide real-time captioning and transcription functions. These can be quite helpful at times and are often a reliable way to gather accurate timestamp information (i.e., the start and stop times and durations of utterances by each party). The content of the transcription itself can vary widely in quality depending on the speed of the conversation, audio recording quality, and internet connection, so we avoid relying solely on computer transcriptions when analyzing sessions. Given the recent proliferation of virtual sessions, it may in fact be possible to make a recording that consists *only* of the coach's side of the conversation. This can add an extra layer of privacy and confidentiality, with the downside that identifying cognitive rehearsals (instances when a child vocally rehearses the steps of a plan, with coach support) is much more difficult without any student statements to use.

Whether to use a paper score sheet, or to record data on a phone or computer, is mostly a matter of personal preference. We do find that when using a phone or computer, we like to have pen and paper handy, or to open a blank Word document, to record any points of personal interest or particularly important parts of the session that are not marked on the sheet (e.g., "From 4 min 35 sec to 8 min 40 sec student on phone with parent"). We use a stopwatch or timer app and start it the first time someone speaks (even if there are greetings or nonpertinent conversation, syncing the start time with the first utterance eliminates confusion about when the "real" beginning of the session occurs).

When recording using the score sheet, it is helpful to (1) keep the timer in your peripheral vision, or use an interval beep, to know when to switch to the next box and (2) bias your listening toward your *own* statements. Remember, other than cognitive rehearsals, the score sheet records *coach statements only*; staying focused on them will mean speedier reviews and fewer times stopping and rewinding. If a particular statement by a coach doesn't seem to fit any category you can mark it with a "?" and return to it later.

Any data you can gather and review have the potential to help your coaching. However, we have developed several habits in our own practice that we recommend.

- Aim to record entire sessions. They do not need to conform to a particular length, but having the entire session recorded and scored is the only way to visualize not just the total numbers of techniques you used but how they relate to one another. If you have recorded and scored an entire session, the context and relative placement of the elements will greatly amplify the information you get back (as opposed to say a 3-minute clip from the middle of a conversation, which may speak to the technique in that exact span, but the technique cannot be contextualized). Imagine watching a 3-minute clip taken from the middle of a car race. It may contain relevant examples of skilled and unskilled driving, but there is a cap on its usefulness. The same clip, examined both individually and in the context of the whole race, has exponentially greater value. The same is true for recording and reviewing coaching sessions.

- Determining how often to review a session is heavily dependent on a coach's caseload, their experience with the model, how students in the caseload are responding to the coach, and importantly a coach's day-to-day perception of their own performance. The broad suggestions we have are:
  o Create a schedule for regular recordings. Once or twice per week, once or twice per month, one out of every five sessions, one out of every 10 or 20 sessions, all are within an acceptable range of options. For coaches with less experience, we think a goal of one to two sessions per month is enough to make an impact without becoming burdensome.
  o The greater variety of students a coach can record sessions with, the better. Children have incredibly varied backgrounds and experiences and approach coaching services in unique ways. Recording and reviewing calls with a range of children can help a coach see through the noise of variation and get a clearer picture of their role and impact as a coach.
  o On the flip side, recording sessions with the same student at different stages of the relationship can also be insightful, and rewarding! It is a chance to see how coaching sessions change in style as students progress, and a chance for a coach to celebrate the evolution of the relationship and growth of their own skills.

Analyzing the Score Sheet

Table 9.2 presents patterns we frequently see and that often (but not always) indicate a place in the session that should be reviewed.

Good Indicators: Quantitative

Reflections are used the most compared to any other technique.

Closed-ended questions are used rarely. When we do see them, they typically are more palatable when used at the end of a session, for example when a student is setting a SMART goal. Using more reflections and open-ended questions at the beginning of a session is a key part of establishing nondirectiveness and creating a supportive environment.

"Plus" patterns—an open-ended question followed by two to four reflections—involve a student talking a lot.

Qualitative Assessment

As stated earlier, the range of "successful" (consistent with a nondirective, MI-based approach) statements a coach can make is infinite. A skilled coach can create novel questions and phrases during a conversation. The following are suggestions based on our experience and observa-

TABLE 9.2. Communication Patterns

Appearance	What to do
Tightly bunched or consecutive closed-ended questions	Review segment. Could you rephrase with an open-ended question and some reflections that would have gathered the same information?
Consecutive open-ended questions	An occasional two in a row is fine. A pattern of back-to-back, or three-plus in a row, should be checked. Most likely one or more could be changed to reflections.
High rate of permission asking	Asking permission is a good thing. Asking permission all the time (more than once every 5–7 minutes of session time) can indicate a directive coaching stance in disguise.
Directive statements	Listen back, identify alternatives, and imagine how it may have affected the conversation. Would an open-ended question, reflection, or permission have been better? Or it may be something that was better left unsaid altogether.

tions and cover the types of things we most often hear from coaches who are new to this approach.

FILLING "DEAD AIR"

Questions and statements from coaches that aim to elicit exploration and contemplation often do just that! A side effect can be pauses in speaking that are not necessarily part of everyday conversation. Often, being greeted with silence after a statement or question, we feel the urge to restate, clarify, even narrow the scope of what we just said—for example, "You mentioned that a teacher 'called you out' yesterday. Tell me more about that." A perfectly fine open-ended statement, and it gets you . . . crickets. We think, *Maybe they didn't understand, maybe I've been too broad.* So, after a few seconds, we say, "Did you feel embarrassed? Was it about missing homework? Or about being on your phone?" These add-ons are not the end of the world, but they do turn the statement from open to closed, and (maybe unintentionally) reframe the conversation. We started with (1) whatever the student wanted to say about the situation and moved to (2) the coach orienting the discussion toward a particular emotion or cause.

The best thing to do is breathe, stay present, project open and supportive body language, and wait. Anticipating that pauses are an expected part of every session can also help. Accepting them as a part of the process, and projecting that acceptance, will dissipate discomfort, often in the course of a single session.

CLOSING OPEN-ENDED QUESTIONS

Closely related to the above, closing an open-ended question is common, and (we think) stems from concern that a question is so open that it is too vague to be answered. "So, you had a lot going on this week. How are things going?" (open) . . . "Did you meet with the guidance counselor?" (turned closed). In this case, the coach starts with a perfectly acceptable open-ended question, then closes it with the follow-up. The intent of the coach is likely benign, even attempting to help. However, there is a detrimental effect, even if it is slight. The first part, paraphrased, is "I am interested in any information, opinion, or feeling about this topic." The follow-up risks conveying "I am interested in a specific piece of information, which I identified." This is a subtle, but often palpable, shift in the dynamic of the conversation, from a mutual understanding that the student's perspective drives the conversation, to one where the coach selects the topic by the types of questions. Again, one here and there will not sink the whole enterprise, but a repeated pattern can.

If necessary, some of these instances can be worked around by including more contextual information prior to the ending phrase (provided this was a topic already spoken about). So, the above becomes "So, you had a busy week! Last time you mentioned reaching out to the guidance counselor. How did that go?" Using an open-ended question to ask about something already mentioned by the student is no problem at all, if it precedes the ending phrase that creates the question.

"STALLING OUT" OPEN-ENDED QUESTIONS

"Stalling out" refers to the repetition or rephrasing of an open-ended question. Sometimes a student will respond that they don't understand an open-ended question. With less experienced coaches, we most typically observe this is because the question is too vague (e.g., "How are you feeling about this?") for the context, or when a student feels they've already answered and are confused by a follow-up. Listen back to see if either of these seemed like the issue. Revise the first by using a noun instead of a preposition (i.e., "this"). With the second, it may be that a coach is relying on an open-ended question to continue the conversation, fill space, or seek clarity when a simple reflection would often do those things, while also leaving open the possibility for a few seconds of silence, since the student isn't under an obligation to answer.

Fixing Phrasing

We often see MI described as a stance or style or attitude; we frequently rely on the stance description ourselves. These words are shorthand, cue words, referring to the ethos of MI, that the sum of the speech, body language, techniques, and mindset creates something greater than the whole. The practitioner's goal is learning to occupy and be comfortable in that intersection of elements, and at times it can feel like a nebulous target.

In our experience, there is much ground to be gained in observing and practicing the differences in language between MI and a "traditional" conversation about change and goals. In Table 9.3, there are pairs of questions or statements, one that is consistent with the MI stance and another that is more conventional. Go ahead and select which one you think best fits the MI style, and consider the pair together, noting the differences in structure, word use, and the effect on the overall tone.

Table 9.4 (on p. 84) depicts the same statements, with our rating of those we see as more consistent with the MI stance.

TABLE 9.3. MI versus Traditional Conversation

"Do you like math class?"	"Tell me about your math class."
"You mentioned your lab notebook going missing again, and that it frustrated you. Tell me more about what's happening."	"Is organization a strength or weakness for you?"
"Do you think your reasons for being late to class are legitimate?"	"What concerns or thoughts do you have about your class schedule this year?"
"On a scale of 1 to 10, how important is homework to you? Why did you choose number _____?"	"Do you think you do enough homework?"
"Assuming school is important to you, what are some things you could do to improve?"	"You said that the day-to-day of school feels pointless and that getting good grades is important to you. What kinds of things during the day do you find enjoyable or exciting?"
"You seem to spend very little time on chemistry. Do you think it's enough?"	"You ranked chemistry as a 3-out-of-10 priority for you; what made you choose 3 instead of 1 or 2?"
"What are your thoughts on the obligations in your life? How important are they to you, compared to other things?"	"Shouldn't obligations have some importance, even if they don't mean anything to you personally?"
"You mentioned being excited for the end of the year and summer. What are you looking forward to?"	"Are you excited for the summer? Do you have plans?"

There is no "best" or "apex" in the practice of MI. There is no universal starting line and no single, step-by-step recipe that will lead to the perfect session time after time. Self-assessment in this coaching model is as much a part of coaching development itself as it is a record of growth. We offer that the "best" use of these tools is to seek gradual, steady change by identifying specific habits, phrases, or points in a session; consulting this and other literature for recommendations; practicing; and applying changes in a steady, stable manner. In other words, coach yourself in MI by applying the same principles and techniques that you do with your students.

TABLE 9.4. MI versus Traditional Conversation: Explained

MI stance	Directive/closed stance	Reasoning
"Do you like math class?"	"Tell me about your math class."	MI statement allows student to share whatever they want and expand beyond the yes/no of the closed stance.
"You mentioned your lab notebook going missing again, and that it frustrated you. Tell me more about what's happening."	"Is organization a strength or weakness for you?"	MI statement invites student to describe their personal experience. Directive asks them to ascribe a broad label.
"What concerns or thoughts do you have about your class schedule this year?"	"Do you think your reasons for being late to class are legitimate?"	A coach's goal is to understand and empathize with the student's experience. The closed question is only asking whether they agree or disagree with an outside assessment.
"On a scale of 1 to 10, how important is homework to you? Why did you choose number _____?"	"Do you think you do enough homework?"	Conventional statement is usually interpreted as a rhetorical question, that is, phrasing the question this way creates the impression that regardless of the student, the coach thinks the answer is no. MI is not here, or ever, about the coach's opinion of what the student should do or think.
"You said that the day-to-day of school feels pointless and that getting good grades is important to you. What kinds of things during the day do you find enjoyable or exciting?"	"Assuming school is important to you, what are some things you could do to improve?"	Avoid assuming, especially when it reflects a societal norm.
"You ranked chemistry as a 3-out-of-10 priority for you; what made you choose 3 instead of 1 or 2?"	"You seem to spend very little time on chemistry. Do you think it's enough?"	Similar to above, coach assumes judge role and uses rhetorical question. Instead, seek student's thoughts on the matter and look to evoke details on strengths.
"What are your thoughts on the obligations in your life? How important are they to you, compared to other things?"	"Shouldn't obligations have some importance, even if they don't mean anything to you personally?"	Again, the directive question is rhetorical, "shouldn't" is often a giveaway that what follows it is a judgment or opinion disguised as a question.
"You mentioned being excited for the end of the year and summer. What are you looking forward to?"	"Are you excited for the summer? Do you have plans?"	Changes two yes/no questions into a simple reflection and an open-ended question.

CHAPTER 10

Goal Setting and Action Planning

Our coaching model is built on the understanding that the person being coached wants to get better at something and they think that a coach can help them do that. Working toward a goal is implicit in the process. With teenagers, in particular, we've found that the process of setting a goal can sometimes be tricky. By the time kids hit adolescence, many have had some prior experience with goal setting, and in the case of students struggling in school, that experience may not have been positive. We keep this in mind as we conduct the goal-setting interview, treading lightly at times or exploring further when we sense resistance. At the end of the interview the coach has reached one of two possibilities: (1) either the coach helped the student identify something they want to work on and the student has at least identified the initial steps they need to take to making that "something" a reality or (2) the coach recognizes that the student is not ready to set a goal and further exploration will take place through MI. We discuss this in more detail at the end of this chapter.

If the student has some semblance of a goal in mind, we have a template that the coach can use to guide the student through the goal-setting process (Appendix 9, pp. 168–170). While the template includes the steps that need to be covered, we recommend that coaches use it as an outline to guide the conversation rather than a form to be filled out. The steps in the goal-setting interview, listed in Table 10.1 and outlined below, follow this template, but coaches should feel comfortable adjusting the steps to match the student they're working with.

STEPS IN THE GOAL-SETTING INTERVIEW

Step 1. Discuss Possible Goals

The goal-setting interview takes place after the coach has collected background information on the student and has established some rapport. When coaching is contracted for by parents, some agreement has been reached about the nature and terms of coaching. The coach has reaffirmed

TABLE 10.1. Steps in the Goal-Setting Process

Step	Description
1	Discuss possible goals.
2	Narrow down the options to select a single goal to work on.
3	Refine the goal.
4	Identify what the student needs to do to achieve the goal.
5	Discuss potential obstacles that might get in the way and strategies to overcome the obstacles.
6	Talk about what resources the student might draw on to help them reach their goal.
7	Turn the goal into a SMART goal.
8	Create an action plan for achieving the SMART goal.

with the student that they are a willing participant in the process. Now the time has come to establish what it is the student wants to work on.

We recommend beginning the goal-setting process by asking an open-ended question. Here are some possibilities:

- "Is there something in particular you would like to work on?"
- "Have you thought about something you'd like to get better at?"
- "Students who work with coaches select a wide variety of goals to work on. Is there something that jumps out at you that you'd like to use this process for?"

If the student struggles to answer that question, the coach might refer to some of the background information they've collected. For instance, the coach might look at the ESQ and ask the student if there's a particular executive skill they'd like to focus on. Or the coach might look at the starred items the student has selected on the ESPC. Alternatively, the coach might consider what the student wrote in response to the question on the Getting to Know You Survey in which they were asked to describe "an area of skill or knowledge that you would like to become an expert in." Since the response to that question may not be directly related to why the student has been referred for coaching (which is usually associated with an academic challenge), the coach may want to avoid this question unless they are searching for a "hook" to help the student see the benefits of goal setting. A skilled coach can help the student make a connection between the skills they need to work on a personal goal that they're passionate about and the skills they need to improve their academic performance.

We've said this before, but we want to emphasize that the person who selects the goal is the student themselves. Parents often want to influence this process. Parents often believe that they have a clearer picture both of their child's challenges and of the road that the child is traveling on toward school completion or adulthood. While they may be right, we have never seen coaching be a successful experience for teenagers when it was a parent who selected the child's goal. This hit home in one of the early coach training seminars we taught several years ago. Although most of the trainees shared success stories about the students they were coaching, one trainee commented that it hadn't gone as well as she'd hoped. When we explored with her where the breakdown occurred, she remarked that "the mom changed the goal." Coaching went south after that. We have seen situations where student and parent agree on a goal because the student has discussed the goal with the parent and they support the student's choice. While not the usual presentation, as long as the parent is on board with the student's decision making, including what goal they pursue and how, unequivocal parent support is a bonus.

Step 2. Narrow Down the Options to Select a Single Goal to Work On

In Step 1, we often encourage students to brainstorm several goals they'd like to work on. Having several to choose from sometimes makes it easier for a student to land on a single goal because they can weigh how each of their options feels to them—which is the best fit for their interests and energies. If the student does have more than one goal, the coach asks the student to prioritize or rank the goals in order of importance to them. The objective is to establish one goal as a starting point as they work through the early stages of the coaching process.

Working toward a goal requires behavior change, and since changing one's behavior is often hard, the coach encourages the student to select a goal that they care about and they feel they can achieve. The goal they settle on might not be the one that the coach would choose as a priority, but working on any goal, no matter how inconsequential, helps the student build goal-directed persistence, and therefore should be considered a valuable experience. Some students, especially those who've had a negative experience with goal setting in the past, benefit from building a cushion of success before moving on to more challenging goals.

Step 3. Refine the Goal

This step may be necessary when the goal the student has identified is vague, entails multiple goals, or exceeds what seems achievable given the student's starting point. A vague goal is one that can't be operationalized. A highly ambitious goal is one that may be very challenging for the student to achieve, given their starting point.

Here are some examples of vague goals:

- "I want to do better in school."
- "I want to use my time more wisely."
- "I need to learn to study more efficiently."
- "I want to become a better writer."

The coach's first response to any of these stated goals might be to use an MI technique such as a reflection. For example, the coach could say, "You are not satisfied with your current school performance and you would like to improve it." If the reflection does not elicit specifics, the coach could follow up with "Tell me more about that" or "Tell me what that would look like." If the student offered that they wanted to get better grades in multiple subjects, the coach might ask them to prioritize or rank-order the subjects starting with the most important. Again, the coach could reflect this and follow this with an open-ended question about what the student thinks they might need to do to achieve a better grade in their priority subject. The objective, through a series of reflections and questions, is to help the student decide on a specific plan of their choosing.

Occasionally, a student may set a goal that, considering their current performance, may be difficult to achieve. For example, let us suppose an extreme case where the student is failing two classes, earning C's and D's in the remaining ones, and sets a goal of making the honor roll when the marking period is half over. Coaches do not want their students to fail. In this situation the natural inclination of the coach may be to try to advise the student to walk back their goal to one that the coach feels is more realistic. In MI, this is known as the "righting reflex" (see Chapter 7). The dilemma here is that this inclination is antithetical to a student-centered, nondirective coaching stance.

An alternative approach, similar to that described for vague goals above, is to lead the student to specificity and, hopefully, a recognition of the demanding nature of their proposed goal. The coach might begin with a reflection and affirmation: "You really want to improve your grades in school and your commitment to that goal is impressive." Depending on the student's response, the coach asks, "What steps do you think you might need to take to accomplish your goal?" Since multiple subjects are involved, the coach can also follow up with asking the student if they would prioritize their subjects and decide which one they would like to start with immediately. If the student is not inclined to do this, the coach accepts the decision and moves on to what needs to be done to achieve the goal (Step 4 below). Specificity in the SMART goals and action plans are key here so that the student is able to see what is needed in what time frame to accomplish the goal. If the student is not deterred, the coach can ask, "Would it be okay if I made a suggestion?" If the student gives permission, the coach asks, "Would you consider us trying this for 1 week and then deciding whether to make any adjustments from there?" If the student agrees, then they may be open to modifying the goal once they have some experience. If not, the coach accepts the student's decision, offers whatever help they can, and affirms any success they have.

Step 4. *Identify What the Student Needs to Do to Achieve the Goal*

This part of the goal-setting interview might begin with an open-ended question: "Okay, now we've settled on what you want to work toward. What do you think you need to do to be successful?" It may help to ask the student to think about what they need to do differently than they've done in the past. For those who want to improve their grades, this might include things like doing homework more consistently, handing homework in on time, bringing test grades up (e.g., by changing how or how much they study), starting assignments early enough so that they'll have time to proofread or revise them, keeping track of assignments better, taking notes in class, keeping notebooks better organized, making and following a plan for long-term assignments, getting more help with difficult subjects, or figuring out how to avoid temptations that get in the way of reaching the goal. The end point of this portion of the interview would be for the student to be able to finish this sentence: *I am likely to meet my goal if I* _____.

Step 5. Discuss Potential Obstacles That Might Get in the Way and Brainstorm Strategies to Overcome the Obstacles

Just because the coach has helped the student select a goal they care about, refine it to make it specific and realistic, and create a vision of what success looks like, smooth sailing is not guaranteed after that. Barriers, obstacles, and setbacks crop up all the time that make goal attainment difficult. If we anticipate what those barriers might be and generate at the outset strategies for avoiding or overcoming them, then the likelihood of success increases.

At this stage, encouraging the student to be creative in their thinking is recommended. We recommend infusing humor into coaching all along the way, but at this stage it can be particularly valuable. One of the rules of brainstorming is to "think outside the box" and to consider some far-fetched ideas. The reason for this is that the student is more likely to anticipate a greater array of obstacles—and the far-fetched ideas might translate into a more likely obstacle the student might not have otherwise thought of. For example, if a student has established a goal of handing in their English essays on time, an obstacle they might suggest is "A meteor would hit my bedroom the night before the paper is due." That's not going to happen—but it might lead them to think about more realistic things that might get in the way of meeting the deadline (such as their computer crashing or being asked at the last minute to babysit a younger sibling).

Once obstacles have been identified, then the student should be asked to think about how those obstacles might be removed or addressed. If the student comes up with several strategies, then the coach should ask them to select the best one(s) to try and to envision how that would work. A helpful approach at this point is to have them generate an *if–then* self-talk strategy. Here are some examples of if–then statements:

- "If my friend asks me to play Fortnite with him after school, I will tell them I have to do my homework first."
- "If I feel tempted to check my phone when I'm supposed to be studying for my test, then I will set a timer for 5 minutes and get back to work as soon as the time is up."
- "If I'm too tired right after school to start writing my essay, then I will shoot baskets for 15 minutes and then get down to work."

Step 6. Talk about What Resources the Student Might Draw On to Help Them Reach Their Goal

At this point, the coach should explore with the student what kinds of supports might help them be successful. Good students often surround themselves with a support system to help them stay on track. This might include a study buddy or a study group (particularly helpful when studying for tests). But supports might also include accessing a tutor, asking a parent to play a specific role (e.g., making sure they get up early enough so they get to school on time), signing up for the school writing lab or for voluntary help sessions after school, or making environmental modifications to reduce temptations or encourage success (e.g., sitting in the front row in a class where focus is a challenge). The message should be that while self-reliance is admirable, there may be external resources that could help the student be successful, and knowing how to access those resources is something that good students do.

Step 7. Turn the Goal into a SMART Goal

SMART is an acronym that defines an effective goal: It is *s*pecific, *m*easurable, *a*ttainable, *r*elevant, and *t*ime-bound. If the previous steps have already been followed, then much of the work for creating a SMART goal has already been done. At this point, the coach can fill in the SMART goal portion of the template, filling in the missing pieces by interviewing the student. Table 10.2 gives an example of a SMART goal that a student might make.

When talking with the student about how attainable or relevant they think the goal is, the coach might ask them to use a 5-point scale to gauge how confident and committed they are to working on the goal. If they rate either question as 3 or less, then it may make sense to revisit the goal with them and to determine if they are open to either revising it to make it easier for them to reach or changing it to a goal that matters more to them.

Step 8. Create an Action Plan for Achieving the SMART Goal

The next step is to help the student develop an action plan for achieving their goal. The action plan may take different forms depending on what the student's goal is.

In some cases, the plan might be a series of steps the student will follow. For instance, if a student has set as a goal getting their driver's license, then the action plan would include all the steps the student needs to follow (e.g., signing up for a driver's education class, obtaining the manual, studying for the written test, completing the mandatory driving hours), with completion dates for each step identified. In other cases, the action plan might list a set of recurring activities the student will do. Table 10.3 gives an example of this kind of action plan based on the student's goal shown in Table 10.2.

TABLE 10.2. Example of a SMART Goal Planner

Specific	What *exactly* do I want to happen?	*Improve my grade in Algebra II*		
Measurable	I will know I have reached my goal when . . .	*I get an 85 or better on my report card*		
Attainable	Can I reach my goal by the deadline?	How confident am I that I can reach my goal?	1······2······3······4······5 Not very So-so Very!	
Relevant	Is this goal important to me?	How important is it to me to reach my goal?	1······2······3······4······5 Not very So-so Very!	
Time-bound	I will reach my goal by . . .	*The end of marking period 2.*		

TABLE 10.3. Action Plan for Achieving SMART Goal

Steps to follow to complete goal	Target completion date	Done!
I will finish all my math homework assignments.	Ongoing	
I will hand them in on time.	Ongoing	
I will study for tests by completing the practice tests and checking my answers.	Ongoing	
I will retake tests with scores below 85 if allowed.	Ongoing	
I will check my class average every Friday to make sure I am on track.	Ongoing	

When the coach meets with the student for their regular coaching sessions, the student and coach should review the action plan to determine if the student was able to follow the plan. The goal-planning template (Appendix 9, pp. 168–170) includes questions that allow the student to reflect on their success and to determine if the plan needs to be changed or the goal changed (either because it's been met or because the plan was not successful).

STUDENTS WHO RESIST GOAL SETTING

The students we see who resist goal setting either have had negative experiences in the past or they have strong perfectionist tendencies that lead them to believe they must set lofty goals that they recognize won't be able to be achieved. As stated previously, avoiding use of the term *goal* and talking instead about things they want to work on, get better at, or do differently may be a better way to handle the goal-setting conversation.

It may also make sense with these students to soft-pedal the whole goal-setting process or to ease into it gradually. It may even mean keeping the goal statement a little vague initially—and focusing on just the first step of an action plan. Here's a sample dialogue for this approach.

STUDENT: You know, I like the idea of working with a coach, but I hate goal setting. It's never worked for me in the past and nothing's changed to make me believe it will work for me now.

COACH: Okay, let's shelve that language. But is there something you'd like to work on or get better at? Is there some aspect of what's happening at school that you're not happy with?

STUDENT: Yeah, my math grade sucks. I know I could do better because math has always come easily to me, but there's something about geometry that's just not working for me.

COACH: So you'd like to be doing better in geometry. What do you think is getting in the way right now?

STUDENT: I have a tendency to leave my math homework until last and by the time I get to it, I'm exhausted so I decide to go to bed instead. I tell myself I'll get up early or use my study hall to do it, but that doesn't happen.

COACH: (*using the MI techniques of reflection and summarizing*) You do all your other homework first and then you run out of steam. You sound kind of mad at yourself.

STUDENT: Yeah, I have a track record of this not working, but I have a hard time making myself do the math homework earlier in the evening.

COACH: Doing your math earlier is hard for you but doing it late hasn't worked for you.

STUDENT: Yeah, my grades still suck. When I don't do the homework, I don't solidify the concepts. And when the teacher reviews the answers in class, I can't really follow the discussion.

COACH: So you feel like you lose the benefits of the homework review in class.

STUDENT: Right. When I think about it, I think that really helps explain why I'm not doing as well in this class as I'd like. Geometry is different from algebra. Algebra was easier for me to understand, which made the homework seem easier, too, so I didn't put it off like I do geometry.

COACH: You're thinking that might help you improve your grade in that class.

STUDENT: Yeah.

COACH: Hmm. It sounds like you're saying that you put off the math homework because you don't always understand the concept you're supposed to be practicing. If you did decide that you wanted to do something different, what might be some options to try?

STUDENT: I could arrange for an extra help session, but I think I want to start by doing my math homework first rather than last and see how that works.

COACH: Can you walk me through what that will look like? You know, roughly when you will start, where you will do your math homework, kind of like create a picture in your head?

At this point, the student has created a vague goal of doing better in geometry and they've committed to a single action step. By asking the student to paint a picture of what that action step looks like, it may be easier for the student to follow through. If the next coaching session isn't the next day, the coach should arrange to text the student to find out how the plan went.

TECHNIQUES TO SUPPORT GOAL SETTING

Three techniques from the behavioral literature that help students translate goals into actions are implementation intentions, mental simulation, and mental contrasting (see Brier, 2015, for a more extensive discussion of these techniques). Building these techniques into the goal-setting and action-planning interview can both help students increase goal specificity and help them make realistic plans for achieving their goal by (1) rehearsing the steps in advance, (2) identifying likely obstacles that might impede success, and (3) generating strategies they can use to overcome those obstacles.

Implementation Intentions

The goal-setting research (e.g., Locke & Latham, 2002) clearly demonstrates that the more precise the goal is, the more it is likely to be attained. While the precision of the goal is important, it's also important to recognize that obstacles often arise that make it difficult to follow through on action steps. Implementation intentions are if–then plans that target potential obstacles in advance and identify a strategy to overcome the obstacles. *If this happens, I will do this* is the most common way that implementation intentions are constructed. This strategy is used in Step 5 and several examples are provided.

For the student described above who wants to work on doing their geometry homework first rather than last, a coach might help the student identify what might prevent them from doing that. The student might admit, "I tell myself, I can quickly polish off my English and then I'll get to math." An if–then statement to resist that temptation might be, "If I catch myself wanting to do my English first, I will immediately open my math book to the homework assignment." The math book open to the homework page then acts as a cue for the student to start doing their homework assignment.

Mental Simulation

Brier (2015) described mental simulation as "a form of cognitive rehearsal and future oriented thinking" (p. 52). With this process the student is helped to visualize the outcome they want to achieve, rehearse in their minds the steps they need to follow to achieve the outcome, anticipate the obstacles they might encounter along the way, and design strategies for overcoming each obstacle.

There are a number of techniques to incorporate into mental simulation that may make the process more appealing or less threatening to a student who may be worried about committing themselves to something they're not sure they can pull off. These include:

- Suggesting the student imagine a third party carrying out the steps: "So, if someone were going to try to follow a timeline for doing a project rather than doing it at the last minute, what do you think that would look like?" This approach allows the student to visualize the process without feeling an immediate pressure to follow through.

- Asking if the student is willing to try out a goal on a very short-term basis as an experiment: "You've told me you typically study for a test for about an hour the night before the test. Since research shows that spaced practice works better, are you willing to try a different approach with one test that you have coming up? What do you think about studying for 30 minutes each night for four nights before the test as an experiment? Is there a subject you'd like to try this with for the next test?"

- Suggesting the student mentally rehearse a plan by visualizing it as a series of scenes in a movie: "Okay, you've been asked to write a script for a movie where the main character is going to write a term paper that's overdue and resist the temptation to go on a camping trip a couple of friends have suggested." Movies have a beginning, middle, and end and involve a sequence of scenes. The student can be asked to take each scene in order and visualize the scene with detailed stage directions that fit the student. For instance, in the first scene the student is asked to describe what their bedroom looks like, where their laptop is, how they typically set up to work when they're writing a term paper, and so forth. In the second scene, they should describe what happens when they get a text or phone call from a friend, how they feel when they get the communication, and how they think about a response. The scene development would continue until the term paper is written, printed out, and handed in.

- Asking the student to imagine how someone they admire might carry out the plan. This could be a friend or classmate that the student thinks follows through consistently, or the student could be asked to imagine a famous person they admire. "So if Tom Brady took this on as a goal, how do you think he'd go about achieving it?" Since the student is unlikely to know Tom Brady (or whoever) personally, this gives the coach and the student the opportunity to endow the student with all the positive traits they imagine the famous person must have that enables them to achieve goals that are important to them.

We refer the reader to Brier (2015) for more detailed examples of these techniques.

Mental Contrasting

With this technique, the student is asked to visualize the best possible outcome they can imagine if they successfully accomplish their goal. They are then asked to visualize with as much detail as they can all the possible obstacles that might hinder their ability to achieve that outcome. Each obstacle is then considered using a problem-solving process:

- What are some options for overcoming the obstacle?
- Of the options, what are the pros and cons for each option?
- What's the best choice?

The student is then asked to mentally rehearse the steps they have chosen for overcoming each of the potential obstacles.

Duckworth and her colleagues (2013) investigated the efficacy of this approach with fifth graders in an urban middle school. The steps in the process are outlined here since it provides helpful suggestions for how to structure the process.

Students were first asked to "think about your most important wish or goal that's related to schoolwork" and to write it down. To ensure the goal was feasible, students were asked to select a goal that was challenging yet achievable "within the next few weeks or months." Students were then instructed to imagine "the one best outcome, the one best thing of fulfilling your wish or reaching your goal."

Following time to reflect, students were then instructed to identify "something that could prevent you from achieving your wish or goal, an obstacle that stands in the way of you achieving your wish." Again, students were given time to think about the question. They were then asked to identify where and when they were likely to encounter the obstacle: "Where does it occur next—in what place? When exactly—what day, what time?" Students were then asked, "What can you do to overcome your obstacle? What action or behavior could you do that would help to overcome the obstacle?" Finally, students completed an if–then template. With this process students created an implementation intention, which they then rehearsed to themselves.

These three techniques—implementation intentions, mental simulations, and mental contrasting—may take time for novice coaches to master, but they help students chart a clearer course toward goal attainment. By helping students turn vague goals into more specific action plans, students who've not had good luck with goal setting in the past can experience a more successful outcome.

CHAPTER 11

Progress Monitoring

Progress monitoring is a means to communicate with the people we are coaching on the progress they are making as they pursue their goals. It also serves to measure the effectiveness of coaching. And related to that, progress monitoring can assist in planning and decision making. If a student or individual is stalled in their efforts to achieve their goals, then we'll know that through progress monitoring, and it can then help the coach and the student decide whether they need to revise the goals the student has set or try a different strategy for pursuing those goals.

That said, progress monitoring should not be complicated or time-consuming. Whenever possible, coaches can use data that is readily available. Data that schools and teachers routinely collect can be harvested and converted into a visual format that is readily understood by the student. We begin our discussion of progress monitoring with this, and then move on to describe other techniques that coaches can use.

MEASUREMENT STRATEGIES

Naturally Occurring Data

Here are some statistics that schools or teachers routinely record:

- School and class attendance
- School and class tardiness
- Homework completion rates
- Homework handed in on time
- Grades on homework assignments
- Quiz and test grades

- Report card grades
- Class participation
- School discipline referrals

All these data are readily available through the school's web portal or from office records.

Here are examples of the kinds of student goals whose progress could be assessed using this information:

- Arrive at school on time
- Get to class before the bell rings
- Complete 90% or more of my math homework
- Hand in my homework on time 4 days out of 5
- Improve my homework grade in English
- Earn grades of 80 or better on biology tests and quizzes
- Pass chemistry
- Participate more in Spanish class [some foreign language teachers track how often students speak in class]
- Remain in biology class for the duration of the period

There are two steps involved in making the best use of this information. First, collect it. Second, convert it to a visual display that is easily understood by the student. Commonly, this involves depicting the data in graphic form. Graphing data on a weekly basis, rather than daily or monthly, is generally the most useful. And because the number of days in a school week varies, due to holidays or early release days, **graph the percentage of days the student meets their goal** rather than number of days. Using the examples above, one might graph on a weekly basis the percentage of days the student arrived on time to school or to class, the percentage of math homework handed in for the week, and the percentage of days the student lasted the entire biology class without getting thrown out. Other ways of graphing behavior are described in the next section.

Case Examples

EXAMPLE 1

A coach was working with a 10th-grade student on the autism spectrum who had set three goals for themselves: (1) Come prepared to class (with all the materials they needed for the class), (2) fill out agenda book every day, and (3) earn more A's. The coach tracked all three goals on one graph. For the first two goals, the total possible number of points per week the student could earn was 5 (one for each day of the week). Figure 11.1 depicts the graph.

EXAMPLE 2

A high school student wanted to work on reducing the number of missing assignments. Figure 11.2 shows the graph the coach generated to show the student's progress.

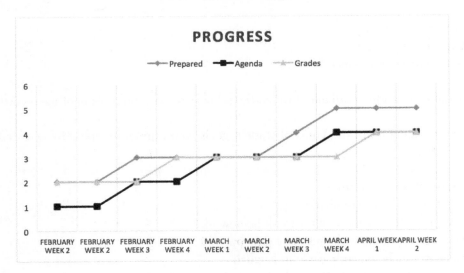

FIGURE 11.1. Graph tracking three goals.

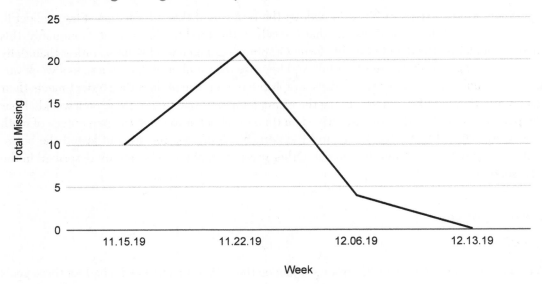

FIGURE 11.2. Graph tracking missing assignments.

Counting and Graphing Behaviors

Not all goals that students set can be assessed using data that schools or teachers are collecting. We then ask the students themselves (or possibly parents or teachers, in the case of elementary-age students) to count and graph behaviors. For this to be reasonable, the behaviors should occur less than five to six times a day; otherwise counting becomes quite burdensome. This may mean that the student should target a particular class or time of day to track the behavior rather than all day long in every setting. For instance, a student who wants to work on increasing raising their hand in class before speaking might decide to work on this in morning meeting (if it's an elementary-age child) or during U.S. history class (if it's a high school student).

Perhaps the most challenging aspect of this form of data collection is remembering to do it. One of our favorite methods is placing a sticky note in an upper corner of the student's workspace. For instance, a fifth-grade teacher we know was working with a student to help them pay attention better. The teacher placed a sticky note on the student's desk and drew a line down the center of the note. The teacher told the child that whenever they were near the child's desk and noticed that they were doing a good job of paying attention, the teacher would

TABLE 11.1. Examples of Behaviors That Can Be Graphed

Behavior	How to graph
"Meltdown" (whining, crying, angry voice) during independent work time	Graph the number per day or per week (depending on frequency)
Write down homework assignments in planner at the end of every class	Graph percentage of classes per day that student wrote down homework
Get to bed no later than 10:30 on school nights	Keep track on index card by bed; graph the number of days per week the goal was met
Spend at least 30 minutes per night on math homework	Either graph the amount of time spent per night or graph the percentage of nights the goal was met
Finish homework by 8:00 P.M.	Graph the time when the homework was completed or graph the percentage of nights the goal was met
Not interrupt others during dinner	Graph the number of interruptions per meal
Take notes during social studies class	Graph the percentage of classes per week when notes were taken
Put homework in backpack when finished	Graph percentage of days per week when homework was placed in backpack
Get through recess with no teacher reprimands	Graph percentage of days per week when recess completed without reprimands

place a slash mark on the left-hand side of the sticky note. But the teacher was also working with them to self-monitor, so the teacher told the child that whenever they themselves noticed that they were doing a good job of paying attention, they should place a slash mark on the right-hand side.

Table 11.1 lists a variety of behaviors that students might decide to work on with a coach, along with a description of how the behaviors might be graphed and counted.

Case Examples

EXAMPLE 1

A coach was working with a middle school student on the autism spectrum who set as a goal managing their emotions better. The coach and the student created a list of coping strategies the student could use to replace "meltdowns," and the coach had the student keep track of the number of meltdowns per week. Figure 11.3 shows the student's progress across a 2-month period.

EXAMPLE 2

A middle school student wanted to reduce the amount of time they spent getting organized before starting their homework. They timed themselves and tracked it on a monthly basis. The results are shown in Figure 11.4.

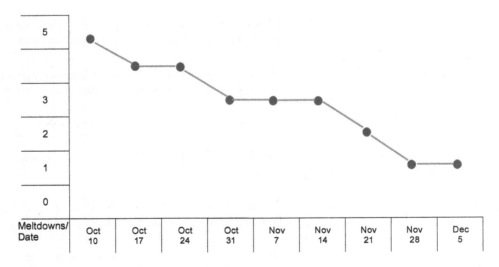

FIGURE 11.3. Graph measuring student meltdowns.

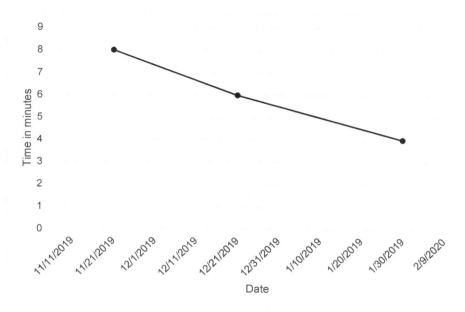

FIGURE 11.4. Graph depicting improved task initiation.

Checklists

Coaches frequently help students create checklists, which are helpful tools for students wanting to improve working memory and planning, among other executive skills. Here are some examples of the kinds of tasks for which checklists may be useful:

- To-do lists (e.g., beginning of the school day routines)
- Multistep assignments (e.g., elements of a chemistry lab report)
- Step-by-step procedures (e.g., proofreading checklist)
- Behavioral strategies (e.g., steps to take to "stay calm" in a crisis)

Checklists are useful not only for helping students complete multistep tasks, but they can be turned into outcome measures and used for progress monitoring. Here are some ways to turn checklists into quantitative measures:

- Keep track of percentage of steps followed or items completed
- Allot points for each item on the checklist and count the total points earned
- Keep track of frequency of handing in the checklist

Case Examples

EXAMPLE 1

First-grade teachers at an elementary school in New Hampshire wanted to help students remember to start sentences with capital letters and end them with periods, so they created

> Place a check (✓) by each item:
>
> _____ All sentences begin with a capital letter.
>
> _____ All sentences end with a period.

FIGURE 11.5. Example of proofreading checklist.

a simple checklist, shown in Figure 11.5. While they didn't track the results, they found that requiring students to hand in the checklist along with each writing assignment they completed led to the desired result. Had they wanted to track the results, they could have graphed the percent of sentences in each writing assignment that began with capitals and ended with periods.

EXAMPLE 2

A teenager wanted to decrease procrastination around tasks that they found boring or unpleasant. The teenager and their coach created a checklist that was completed every day, and the teenager earned a point for each item checked off. Points could then be graphed (on a daily or weekly basis) and traded in for a reward that was attractive to the teenager. The checklist is shown in Figure 11.6.

Direct Behavior Ratings

Direct behavior ratings (DBRs) are a measurement strategy that is a hybrid—lifting elements of traditional behavior rating scales and systematic direct observations of behavior in a naturalistic setting. Succinctly defined, a DBR is "an emerging alternative to systematic direct observation and behavior rating scales which involves *brief rating* of target behavior following a specified observation period" (Riley-Tillman, Christ, Chafouleas, Boice-Mallach, & Briesch, 2011). It is characterized by a diverse and flexible set of procedures and instrumentation. At its core, however, the term *DBR* incorporates three components:

1. *Directness of observation.* According to Briesch and Chafouleas (2009), "the direct feature of DBR means that rating should occur in close proximity to the time and place of a relatively short observational interval" (p. 12).

Date: *Nov. 26–30*					
Item	**Monday**	**Tuesday**	**Wednesday**	**Thursday**	**Friday**
Practice mantra (×3)	✓	✓	✓	✓	✓
Set timer in shower	✓			✓	
Set timer for social media	✓	✓		✓	
Complete daily task sheet	✓	✓	✓	✓	✓

FIGURE 11.6. Example of procrastination checklist.

2. *Observation of specific behaviors.* The focus of the ratings should be on what the individual does in a specific context or setting. Thus, the behavior(s) selected should be seen as situationally specific (as opposed to an underlying trait that presumably persists across situations). By selecting behaviors that are observable and measurable, the need for inferences is avoided.

3. *Rating of behaviors.* DBR is designed to quantify a person's perception of behavior using a numbered rating scale. Rather than relying on behavior counts (e.g., frequency counts or timing the duration of behavior), ratings provide an estimate of the chosen behavior.

Three additional elements make a DBR an attractive measure for progress monitoring: (1) It represents a highly efficient assessment tool that can be completed very quickly by an individual present in the target situation; (2) it has the advantage of being a repeated measure to track behavior change over time; and (3) it is a tool that students can use themselves to rate their own behavior.

Examples of the most commonly used DBRs are shown in Table 11.2.

When coaches use a DBR with a student, they may have the student complete the DBR every day or they may complete it whenever they meet with the student, in which case they do it together. If the student is expected to complete it daily, they sometimes need a text from the coach to remind them to do it. A daily DBR is likely to be more accurate than a weekly

TABLE 11.2. DBR Types

A					B						
1	2	3	4	5	0	1	2	3	4	5	6
Never				Always	Never	Occasionally		Often		Almost Always	

C						D				
0	1	2	3	4	5	0	1	2	3	4
Never					Every Day	Not at all				Very Much

E					F				
1	2	3	4	5	0	1	2	3	4
Not Well				Very Well	None				100%

G						H				
0	1	2	3	4	5	0	1	2	3	4
None	<25%	26–50%	51–75%	76–99%	All of it!	Never	1–2 times	3–4 times	5–6 times	>6 times

☐ YES ☐ NO	☐ ACCOMPLISHED ☐ NOT ACCOMPLISHED

A DBR for tracking grades:								
1	2	3	4	5	6	7	8	9
D	D+	C–	C	C+	B–	B	B+	A–

one, since they may have trouble reconstructing their performance from memory, but there are times when weekly is the only realistic time frame for collecting data.

We also recommend that DBR data be converted into a graph, since this is a clearer way for the student to see how things change over time.

Case Examples

EXAMPLE 1

A coach was working with a middle school student on improving their ability to pay attention in math class. The coach created three separate DBRs, which the student completed at the end of class each day. The DBRs are depicted in Figure 11.7.

EXAMPLE 2

A coach was working with a high school student who wanted to bring their grades up in history class. The student felt that if they wrote down their assignments in their homework planner more reliably, this would help. The coach created two DBRs for the student: one to track how often they completed the planner and a second to track their history grade. These are depicted in Figures 11.8 and 11.9, respectively. The coach converted the second DBR into a graph, depicted in Figure 11.10.

Rubrics

Scoring rubrics are tools that list a set of criteria that describe a piece of work and provide gradations of quality for each criterion from "excellent" to "poor." In this way, rubrics link qualitative assessment to a quantitative rating system that allows one to judge a piece of work more objectively and to measure progress toward improvement. Many teachers, when assigning papers, projects (both group and individual), and demonstrations, include a scoring rubric to guide students in creating the piece of work. In the context of coaching, rubrics are most useful in helping students judge how well they perform a given task that can't be easily quantified.

Eye contact with the teacher						
0	1	2	3	4	5	6
Never		Occasionally		Often		Almost always
Eyes on smartboard						
0	1	2	3	4	5	6
Never		Occasionally		Often		Almost always
Hand raised						
0	1	2	3	4	5	6
Never		Occasionally		Often		Almost always

FIGURE 11.7. DBRs measuring sustained attention.

Week 1

0 Never	1 Once a week	2 Twice a week	3 Three times a week	4 Four times a week

Week 2

0 Never	1 Once a week	2 Twice a week	3 Three times a week	4 Four times a week

Week 3

0 Never	1 Once a week	2 Twice a week	3 Three times a week	4 Four times a week

FIGURE 11.8. DBR assessing homework planner completion.

Key: 1 = D 2 = D+ 3 = C– 4 = C 5 = C+ 6 = B– 7 = B 8 = B+ 9 = A–

1	2	3	4	5	6	7	8	9
1	2	3	4	5	6	7	8	9
1	2	3	4	5	6	7	8	9
1	2	3	4	5	6	7	8	9
1	2	3	4	5	6	7	8	9
1	2	3	4	5	6	7	8	9
1	2	3	4	5	6	7	8	9
1	2	3	4	5	6	7	8	9
1	2	3	4	5	6	7	8	9

FIGURE 11.9. DBR assessing history grades.

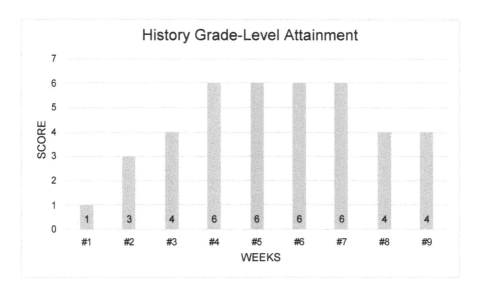

FIGURE 11.10. Graph depicting history grade.

An example of a scoring rubric that might be used to help a student improve how they study for tests is shown in Figure 11.11.

Rubrics could also assist students in working on goals to improve organization (notebooks, desk, backpacks, locker, organization in writing assignments or long-term projects) as well as effort and task persistence. They can also be used to help students learn to control frustration or other emotions that interfere with being a successful student. An example of such a rubric is shown in Figure 11.12.

While rubrics represent a way to capture multifaceted skills or behaviors and quantify them, they are not easy to write. Googling "rubrics" will lead to websites that offer sample rubrics or instructions on how to create rubrics. Most of them focus on rubrics for academic assessment, but one that has some examples that incorporate executive skills (particularly planning and time management) is *http://rubistar.4teachers.org/index.php*.

Case Examples

EXAMPLE 1

A coach developed a rubric to help a middle school student keep their locker clean. The rubric is depicted in Figure 11.13.

EXAMPLE 2

A coach working with a lower elementary school student created a rubric to help the student assess how well they were focusing on work during independent reading time. The rubric is shown in Figure 11.14.

Element	Criteria				Value
	4	**3**	**2**	**1**	
Amount of time spent studying	Met goal of _____ hr. _____ min. spent studying.	Spent at least 75% of committed time studying.	Spent at least 50% of committed time studying.	Spent less than 50% of committed time studying.	
Number of study sessions	4 or more study sessions (1 per day) before exam.	3 study sessions.	1–2 study sessions.	Didn't study.	
Prestudy preparation	Went to extra help sessions with teacher.	Used detailed study guide and/or practice tests.	Skimmed notes to determine what would be on test.	Didn't prepare for studying in advance.	
Variety of study techniques	Used 3 or more different study methods.	Used 2 different study strategies.	Used one study strategy.	Didn't study.	
				Total points earned:	

FIGURE 11.11. Studying for tests rubric.

Element	Criteria				Value
	4	3	2	1	
Getting along with teachers	Did not lose my temper* with any of my teachers. *Losing temper means making an angry, impolite response or comment in class.	Lost my temper in 1–2 classes this week or with one teacher 1–2 times.	Lost my temper in 3–4 classes or with one teacher 3–4 times this week.	Lost my temper 5 times or more this week.	
Completing homework without frustration	Did not "lose my cool"* with any homework assignment. *Losing cool means engaging in an angry rant or refusing to complete assignment.	Lost my cool with 1–2 assignments.	Lost my cool with 3–4 assignments.	Lost my cool with 5 or more assignments.	
Getting along with football coach	Did not lose my temper* with football coach. *Losing temper means making an angry, impolite response or comment; may be nonverbal (e.g., gesture, facial expression).	Lost temper 1–2 times.	Lost temper 3–4 times.	Lost temper 5 or more times.	
				Total points earned:	

FIGURE 11.12. Managing frustration rubric.

EXAMPLE 3

This example shows a rubric for a high school student who wanted to work on diet, study skills, and stress. Although the coach who helped the student create it called it a rubric, the individual items could also be described as DBRs. This example is included because the student and the coach worked out a reward system based on the number of points the student earned each day. Figure 11.15 shows the rubric as well as the point system.

4	3	2	1
No loose papers. Binders, books, notebooks, and writing utensils are all neatly stacked up top. Coat, boots, and PE stuff are stored on the bottom. Only one jacket is stashed in the locker.	A few loose papers. Binders, books, notebooks, and writing utensils are all stored up top, though it is a bit chaotic. Coat, boots, and PE stuff are stored on the bottom. One or two jackets are stashed in the locker.	A number of loose papers. Almost all binders, books, notebooks, and writing utensils are all stored up top. Coat, boots, and PE stuff are stored on the bottom. Three or more jackets are stashed in the locker.	LOTS of loose papers. Binders, notebooks, and pencils are mixed in with coats, PE stuff, and jackets. Four or more jackets are stashed in the locker.

FIGURE 11.13. Clean locker rubric.

Read to Self Rubric

I stayed in one spot.	Yes! 😊	no ☹️
I read the whole time.	Yes! 😊	no ☹️
I kept my eyes on my book.	Yes! 😊	no ☹️
I whisper read to myself.	Yes! 😊	no ☹️

FIGURE 11.14. Focusing during independent reading time.

WHAT IF THE GOAL DOESN'T LEND ITSELF TO PROGRESS MONITORING?

Albert Einstein once said, "Not everything that can be counted counts, and not everything that counts can be counted." Sometimes coaches feel constrained by our recommendation that the coaching process should include measurable outcomes. We believe that the data collection methods we have described above are sufficiently flexible so that some kind of progress monitoring is possible for virtually every goal a student may set. We believe strongly in progress monitoring because without data, how do you know coaching is an effective intervention?

Sometimes coaches we have taught report that the student they are working with keeps changing the goal, which makes it difficult to measure change over time. One coach, for instance, reported that the student they were working with spent each session exploring a different obstacle to effective studying and coming up with a different plan to tackle the obstacle. The coach was concerned that the goal kept changing. But actually, the student was still pursuing their goal of increasing their grade-point average. The student's action plan changed as their understanding of what was getting in the way changed. So we suggested the coach track whether the student followed their action plan—all of it, none of it, or somewhere in between. A DBR could be created for this.

Another relatively easy way to track progress is by using data collected on the Daily Coaching Form (Appendix 10; pp. 171–172). On this form the student and coach outline the tasks the student plans to accomplish before the next coaching session. When the form is reviewed at the next session, the coach can determine the percentage of tasks the student accomplished and keep a graph of that.

HOW TO USE PROGRESS MONITORING DATA

Although we all want to see that students are continuously improving and we'd love for the graph to show only progress from one data point to the next, that is generally not the way behavior change works. When setting goals and progress monitoring methods with students, it's a good idea to warn them that there will be setbacks along the way and they should be prepared for this. Sometimes the fluctuation is enough that the student has trouble seeing that progress is in fact being made. In this case, it may be helpful to draw a trendline by averaging

GOAL	3	2	1	0
Health: 15 lbs. by end of quarter	30 minutes exercise and healthy dinner	15 minutes exercise and 2/3 healthy dinner	5 minutes of exercise and 1/3 healthy dinner	No exercise and unhealthy dinner
Study skills: All B's by end of quarter	Done in 2 hours, preplanning assignments, finishing list	Only half of list completed, waiting until the night before due date	Distracted so takes longer than needed, waiting until the morning of due date	No studying
Stress	In control	OK	Uneasy	Stressed out

HEALTH: Exercise = Elliptical or walking outside
              Healthy dinner = Increase fruits, veggies, good protein (salad, apples, broccoli, lettuce, carrots, grapes, watermelon, shrimp, hamburger), decrease carbs (rice, bread, pasta, sugar), moderate cheese intake. Examples: thin-crust pizza with veggies, fruit, protein (shrimp or BBQ chicken with pineapple)

REWARD: All 9s for one week = Pop figure at Hot Topic
              7 to 9 per day = Play with friend or brother on Nintendo Switch or play mobile games on tablet
              6 to 4 per day = YouTube—no games
              4 to 0 per day = No YouTube, no games

DATE (no Disney days)	Health	Study skills	Stress	TOTAL	REWARD
01/14/19	0	3	3	6	YouTube
01/15/19	0	3	3	6	YouTube
01/16/19	1	3	3	7	Switch!!!!!!
01/17/19	0	3	3	6	YouTube
01/22/19	0	2	3	5	YouTube
01/23/19	1	2	2	5	YouTube
01/24/19	1	2	3	6	YouTube
01/28/19	0	2	3	5	YouTube
01/29/19	0	2	3	5	YouTube

FIGURE 11.15. Rubric with rewards.

the first three data points and the last three data points and connecting those two averages with a line.

When the data shows that progress is not being made, a coach has several options, all of which start with showing the results to the student and asking them to share their thoughts. Talk about whether the student thinks the goal is attainable. If so, then the coach and student should have a discussion about what obstacles are causing the lack of progress and what strategies might be used to overcome the obstacles. The coach and student should then put in place a plan to implement the selected strategies.

Perhaps, however, the student selected a goal that was unrealistic. In this case, it makes sense to revise the goal to make it more attainable. If the student has decided, for instance, that they want to earn all A's and B's for the marking period, and they are currently earning a C in one class and a D in another and there's not enough time to bring those grades up, then the coach and the student may want to revise the goal and create a plan for achieving the revised goal.

The coach may also share the progress monitoring data with the student's parents, but this should be done with the student's knowledge and permission. This process respects the student's autonomy and reinforces the fact that coaching successes are for the benefit of the student more than their parents.

What if the progress monitoring data shows that the goal has been met? Remembering the readiness for change framework outlined in Chapter 4, a single data point that shows the goal has been reached may not mean that the behavior change has been solidified. The coach and the student should talk about how confident the student feels that they are ready to move to the maintenance phase for the goal they've been working on. Does it feel like a habit? Or is it so well embedded in a routine that following the routine feels automatic? We would suggest continuing to do progress monitoring for a few weeks after the goal has been met just to make sure the goal behavior persists over time.

STRATEGIES AND SPECIAL APPLICATIONS

CHAPTER 12

Strategies to Support Executive Skills Coaching

Those who are familiar with our body of work on executive skills know that we emphasize three primary methods to support students with executive skills challenges. Let's review those methods and then describe how they can be incorporated into coaching.

THE ABCs OF EXECUTIVE SKILLS INTERVENTIONS

Modify the Environment

Students with executive skills challenges often struggle because there's a mismatch between environmental demands and their capacity to respond to those demands. By modifying the environment (or altering the <u>A</u>ntecedent, to use a technical term), we reduce that mismatch. When a teacher gives a class multiple oral instructions for an assignment, a student with working memory challenges often fails to hold onto those instructions long enough to complete the task. Some environmental modifications to help the student be more successful might be to suggest giving the student one step at a time, providing a set of written directions (ideally, in a step-by-step format), or pairing the student with another student for guidance on working memory challenges. For an elementary student with response inhibition challenges, getting through an unstructured recess can be full of opportunities to get in trouble. Providing that child with a structured and supervised recess activity might be an appropriate environmental modification. A student with task initiation and time management challenges might leave homework until just before bed and then run out of time or energy before the work is completed. Environmental modifications to support that student might include suggesting setting a recurring alarm to remind them when it's time to start their homework and blocking access to video games and social media for the ensuing two hours.

Environmental modifications fall into three categories: (1) altering the physical or social environment (e.g., providing more structure at recess), (2) modifying the task the student is asked to perform (e.g., cuing a start time for homework and blocking access to distractions), or (3) altering the way adults interact with the student (e.g., providing written task instructions rather than verbal ones). Figure 12.1 provides examples of each. It is also included as a checklist that could be used with a student (see Appendix 21, p. 192).

Enhance the Skill

Here, we focus on helping students *develop* ways to strengthen their executive skills by focusing on the student's **B**ehavior. We don't try to teach the skill in isolation, since generalization from one context or setting to another is difficult to achieve, but we help the student develop the skill by using situations and activities in the student's everyday life where the executive skill is needed. If a student is struggling with organization, for instance, we might suggest that they pick one domain to focus on where their organization issue gets them in trouble (e.g., messy backpack, desk, or locker). If a student has difficulty sustaining attention, we might suggest that they pick a class where they might try out some strategies or, if sticking with homework long

Strategy	Examples (check off choices)
Change the physical or social environment	☐ Remove distractions (e.g., turn off social media) ☐ Create visual reminders ☐ Avoid settings with temptations ☐ Seek out people who support your goal; avoid people who don't ☐ Other: _____
Modify the task	☐ Make task shorter/build in breaks ☐ Use 1–10 scale to adjust effort ☐ Pair unpleasant task with something pleasant ☐ Kill two birds with one stone (pair unpleasant task with another obligation) ☐ Break task into very small pieces and turn into a to-do checklist ☐ Use technology ☐ Turn open-ended tasks into closed-ended tasks ☐ Build in variety or choice (or turn into a game) ☐ Other: _____
Enlist the help of others	☐ Someone to cue you: _____ ☐ Someone to report to: _____ ☐ Someone who will be a cheerleader: _____ ☐ Post goal/progress on social media ☐ Other: _____

FIGURE 12.1. Environmental modifications menu.

enough to get it done is problematic, we might help them develop a plan for getting through the onerous chore. The strategy might be as simple as creating a checklist and figuring out where to post it so the student won't forget about it, or it might be helping the student use techniques such as implementation intentions, mental simulation, and mental contrasting (described in Chapter 10). Key to enhancing the skill, though, is building in ample practice. Ideally, the practice is sustained over time so that eventually it becomes automatic (much as toothbrushing before bed is for most adults).

Provide Incentives

This brings us to the *C* of our ABC model: putting in place a **C**onsequence to reward the student for successfully practicing the skill or following the plan. Whenever possible, we focus on the use of rewards rather than punishments. There are significant amounts of research to show that rewards are more effective, particularly with teenagers. But more than that, in our coaching process, which stresses self-regulation and self-determination, asking a student to punish themselves for failing to follow through with a task or obligation is a big—and unrealistic—ask.

Incentives can take many forms, but they can be divided into two broad categories: simple incentives and elaborate incentive systems.

Here are some of the simple incentives that work well for many students:

- *Alternating between preferred and nonpreferred activities.* This is the "first work, then play" approach. The key to this approach is the amount of time allocated to each. When this approach doesn't work, it's usually because the student is working longer than they can tolerate and they earn a "play" time that is too short for it to feel rewarding. It helps to put the decision in the hands of the student, for example, by asking them, "How long can you go before you need a break?" or "How long do you think the break should be before you get back to work?"
- *Giving the student something to look forward to when the effortful task is done.* This approach works well with people of all ages. If the student has trouble identifying what the rewarding activity might be, look at how they spend their discretionary time. Any one of those activities can become a reward just by delaying access to it until the aversive task is completed.
- *Specific praise.* This is very different from global praise—comments like "Good job," "What a smart kid you are," or "Nice work." Specific praise lets the student know exactly what it is they're being praised for and emphasizes that it was the student's effort that led to the accomplishment. "You really pushed yourself to stick with that math homework until you finished it" is an example of this kind of praise. "You followed through on your plan even though you were tempted to quit and play video games with your brother" is another example. We avoid, when we can, saying things like, "I'm impressed that you . . ." or "I'm proud of you for . . ." because the ultimate goal is to have the student take pride in their own accomplishment rather than pleasing the adult who's praising them.
- *Self-monitoring.* Having students track their own behavior, particularly if they display the tracking in a visual format such as a graph, can act as a very powerful incentive.

Chapter 11 provides numerous examples of behaviors students chose to monitor, along with the graphs that made the results visible.

When we've used elaborate incentive systems, the ones we've found that work best identify a number of tasks or behaviors that the student chooses to work on, attach point values to each task or behavior, and identify the reward(s) for which the points can be used.

The steps involved in setting up a more elaborate system are outlined in Table 12.1. A case example that illustrates a more elaborate system employed with a middle school student is included in Appendix 22 (pp. 193–194).

TABLE 12.1. Steps in Setting up Elaborate Incentive Systems

Step	Description	Additional notes
1	Determine what the student wants to work for.	This might be a larger reward that takes several weeks to earn (such as a piece of tech equipment that the parents are willing to provide) or it could be activity rewards or small tangible rewards that the student could earn on a more frequent basis (e.g., daily). There are reinforcement menus available online (e.g., at *www.pbisworld.com*).
2	List the behaviors or tasks for which the student can earn points.	When used as a part of the coaching process, the items identified should relate directly to the student's goal.
3	Decide on the number of points each item identified in Step 2 will be allotted.	Points are allotted based on how much work the student has to do. This should be from the *student's* perspective, not the coach, teacher, or parent. If a student is good at math but *hates* doing math homework, they might earn more points for math homework than they would for completing other homework assignments that are less aversive to them.
4	Decide on the number of points the student needs to earn the reward.	If the student has identified a number of possible rewards they want to work for, each reward should be given a point value.
5	Create a chart for tracking the points earned.	Examples are provided in Appendix 22 (pp. 193–194).
6	Make a plan for maintaining the chart.	The plan should specify who will log the data and how frequently the chart will be updated. The plan should also specify what method will be used to verify that the student has earned the points.

A NOTE ABOUT SCAFFOLDING

Scaffolding refers to the practice of facilitating a student's ability to solve a problem, carry out a task, or pursue a goal. It involves, through a process of open-ended questions and suggested options, helping students to choose tools and supports that they can use to achieve each step. Scaffolding often involves offering environmental modifications to compensate for executive skills challenges or it allows a student to practice their skills in an environment that facilitates success. The principle of scaffolding is "just enough" support to help the student move forward toward their goal. It is based on Vygotsky's notion of the *zone of proximal development*, which has been defined as "the distance between the actual developmental level as determined by independent problem solving and the level of potential development as determined through problem solving under adult guidance or in collaboration with more capable peers" (1978, p. 86).

Scaffolding is also used for skill enhancement. Scaffolding is provided when we modify the initial demand when beginning a new task or goal. Task demands are greatest when they are new or unfamiliar or if the student does not know, or doubts, they have the resources to complete the task. Breaking the task into small steps can increase the likelihood of success. For example, if a student desires a better grade in a subject, the first step would be to elicit from the student the components that make up a grade. The next step would be to determine the student's strengths and challenges in these components. Coach and student would then develop a graduated improvement plan for the component(s) most likely to result in grade improvement. They would also develop a monitoring and feedback component to enable plan modification.

Scaffolding is designed to be temporary and provide more support in the early stages of skill building, which is gradually faded as the student becomes more experienced and proficient. However, the fading process begins only when the student demonstrates that they are able to independently accomplish the steps that previously received support. Scaffolding also is faded only for the particular task the student is currently working on unless they show transfer of the skill to other tasks. Students fairly new to the goal-setting and achievement process are likely to require more support than a student who has achieved several goals already.

TIPS FOR ADAPTING THESE METHODS TO COACHING

Coaching is, above all, a collaborative process, with the coach and student working side by side to help the student achieve whatever goals they've chosen to work on. All the above methods can be incorporated into coaching by engaging the student in a conversation about what they think might work best for them and by offering suggestions using language that communicates that the student's input is not only sought but vital if the process is to work. Here are some ways a coach might broach these methods and strategies.

- "You've said that when you leave homework until late, you end up too exhausted to finish it. What are some ways you might avoid that?"
- "You've identified organization as a challenge for you and you've described how it leads

to lost assignments and wasted time. If you were going to pick one target to focus on to improve this skill, what might you choose?"

- "I have some thoughts about how you might get better control over your sleep. Would you like me to share them with you?"
- "It sounds like you're getting tired of being sent in from recess. What if we came up with a plan for how you could spend recess that would keep you out of trouble? Is that something you might be interested in working with me on?"
- "What is a small way you can reward yourself each day for following your plan? What might work for you?"
- "What are some options that might remind you to make sure you have all your soccer equipment before you head out for practice?"

Another approach is to present a student with a menu of options and ask them if anything on the list appeals to them. Appendix 23 (pp. 195–197) provides such a menu. None of the items listed are intended to be used prescriptively, but they should be considered a toolbox that a coach can draw on when working with students to find something the student is willing to try. Thus, the coach might say:

- "I have some ideas for ways we could cue you to help you remember to practice your skill or use your strategy. Would it be okay if I make a few suggestions and you can tell me if you think any of them would work for you?"
- "I think I have a strategy that might help you get better at that. Would it be okay if I outline it for you, and you can tell me if you would like to use it?"
- "I have a list of possible strategies for improving time management. Would you like to look at them to see if any appeal to you?"

Note: Some of the strategies on the list are ones that involve the student's teacher (e.g., having the teacher post classroom rules and review them regularly as a way to help a student improve response inhibition). The student should be the one making a choice about which strategy to try. If one or more of the strategies involve the student's teacher, the coach should ask the student if they are comfortable with the coach contacting the teacher. If so, the coach should contact the teacher, explain the coaching situation, and ask if the teacher would be willing to assist the student. Assuming student and teacher are on board, then this is best arranged by setting up a meeting between the coach, the teacher, and the student to come to an agreement about how the intervention will be implemented.

INCORPORATING "MINI-LESSONS" INTO COACHING

During the coaching process, it may become evident that a student lacks knowledge of how to do a variety of school-related tasks, such as note taking, writing essays, planning long-term projects, or studying for tests. If the student expresses an interest in learning those kinds of skills, coaches may be in a good position to help them. One approach is for the coach and student together Google the skill. If you type into Google phrases such as "how to take notes," "how to annotate," or "how to study for tests," you can track down any number of websites with useful information. The coach and the student can view some of those sites and talk about which strategies might be a good fit for the student.

We have also put in the Appendices instructions and templates for a number of study skills (Appendices 24–29; pp. 198–215).

USING SMARTPHONE APPS TO SUPPORT COACHING

Many students who are good candidates for coaching are tech-savvy and see their phones as extensions of themselves. This suggests they may readily take to apps that are designed either to strengthen some executive skills challenges (such as planning) or to provide additional support for managing a skill challenge. Over the years, however, we've discovered that not all students embrace apps and not all apps are created equal in terms of their appeal.

Some words of advice for the use of smartphone apps:

- Simplicity is the rule. One student with ADHD that we know commented that "If an app requires me to move between more than a couple of screens, I'd rather use pencil and paper!" Apps designed to do it all (e.g., act as a planner, a to-do list, a calendar, a reminder program, and a time management device) don't meet the simplicity rule and many students either don't want to take the time to learn the app or abandon it quickly because it takes too much work to maintain.
- For many students, any extra step seems burdensome. Texting between coach and student is one of the best ways we know for them to stay in touch between sessions and to engage in simple progress monitoring. But we recommend streamlining texting, too—making an agreement that the student will respond to a text from their coach with either a "thumbs-up" or a "thumbs-down" emoji may be the best way to use texts.
- Just because a student is "on their phone all the time" doesn't mean they're particularly skilled at using their phone. Be careful to avoid overestimating a student's ability to use their phones with any sophistication.
- An app that works perfectly for one student may be a terrible idea for another student. We've found that putting the choice in the hands of the student is the best way to go. The coach might invite the student to check out a few apps in the app store to see if they find one they like, or they might suggest a short-term experiment: "Would you like to try out app A for the first week and app B for the second week and see if one works better than the other for you?"
- Many, if not most, schools have embraced the idea of using platforms such as Google Classroom or Canvas as a comprehensive management system. Students can monitor their grades, track missing assignments, find out what their homework is in any given subject, keep track of deadlines, and submit written work all through the school's web-based portal. While this offers "one-stop shopping" for students, all too often the complexity of these systems can overwhelm students (and their coaches). Some schools use multiple platforms, but even if every teacher in a school uses the same platform, they tend to use the platform differently, accessing different features or giving students different instructions for where information can be found. In early coaching sessions, the coach and student may want to spend some time familiarizing themselves with how the

Subject	Where are assignments posted?	Where can I find course materials?	How do I turn in assignments?	Who else in my class can I contact?	Teacher contact information	Teacher office hours
	[HOTLINK]	[HOTLINK]	[HOTLINK]	Jane Doe (555) 123-2345	Ms. Hancock l_hancock@highschool.edu	

Other important information or hotlinks: _____

FIGURE 12.2. Sample "cheat sheet."

students' teachers use the platform in their individual classrooms. It may be helpful to create a personalized "cheat sheet" to help a student keep track of how to access information in each of their classes. An example of a such a cheat sheet is shown in Figure 12.2.

Table 12.2 contains a list of apps that students might find helpful. They have been selected for their relative simplicity because they are easy to use and because we think they do a few things well.

Finally, Appendix 23 lists an array of strategies that coaches can draw on to address specific executive skills challenges.

TABLE 12.2. Apps to Support Executive Skills

App/website	Description	Executive skills supported
Best Sand Timer	This is a digitalized hourglass that can be used to time anything up to 60 minutes. For children for whom stopwatches or digital timers cause anxiety, this is a gentler way to keep track of time passing.	Sustained attention, time management
Can Plan	With this app, the user breaks tasks into an easy-to-follow sequence of photos, with optional text or audio as well as timed reminders.	Working memory, task initiation, planning, time management
Choiceworks	This app helps children complete daily routines (morning, day, and night), understand and control their feelings, and improve their waiting skills (taking turns and not interrupting). It includes a "schedule board" for task completion (including an optional timer); a "waiting board" to help children learn to wait, take turns, or not interrupt; and a "feelings board" for helping children understand and express emotions.	Response inhibition, emotional control, task initiation, sustained attention, planning, time management
Goal Streaks	This app lets the user set goals that involve regular activity (e.g., study Spanish 1 hour per day), set a schedule defined by the user (e.g., 4 days a week), and then log on to record the accomplishment. Build up a "streak" by hitting the schedule defined by the user and then try to make the streak as long as possible.	Goal-directed persistence
Mindfulness apps	There are a number of apps that provide guided meditations, meditation chimes, or modules addressing specific problem areas (e.g., managing stress or anxiety, increasing focus, helping with sleep). A couple of popular ones are *Headspace* and *Calm*. Both have many features and require an annual subscription.	Emotional control, sustained attention, flexibility
Original Beeper App	This app sounds tones (selected from a variety of options) at random intervals for specified work periods (e.g., while doing homework or sitting in class). When the tone sounds, the user taps the phone within a few seconds to indicate they were paying attention. At the conclusion of the session, the percentage of time on task is reported.	Sustained attention
Pomodoro Technique	The Pomodoro Technique is a time management system that encourages people to work with the time they have—rather than against it. Using this method, you break your workday into 25-minute chunks separated by 5-minute breaks. After about four pomodoros, you take a longer break of about 15–20 minutes. There are a number of apps that are based on this technique—they also allow you to choose the length of the work sessions and the breaks.	Task initiation, sustained attention, time management

(continued)

TABLE 12.2. *(continued)*

App/website	Description	Executive skills supported
Privilege Points	This app is described as providing a "chore chart and rewards system," but points can be awarded for chore completion as well as for behavior. It's intended for use by parents and can be personalized for each child in the family, with points allotted and rewards defined by parents. It also includes task reminders.	A versatile app than can be adapted to fit a variety of behavioral goals and executive skills
Reminders	This is a free app on all Apple products, with syncing available both between platforms and between users (so coaches and students can add reminders). When a reminder is tagged to a specific time, the reminder appears on the home screen every time it lights up. It can also be used as a to-do list.	Working memory
Study Bunny	This is a timer that enables the user to keep track of how much time they spend studying, but the format is very appealing. The user creates a customized "study bunny" and the more time they spend studying the more points they can earn. They can use the points to buy accessories for the bunny. The app also includes a to-do list and a flashcard maker.	Task initiation, sustained attention, planning, time management, goal-directed persistence
Time Timer	This app offers a visual timer that enables the user to watch time passing.	Response inhibition, task initiation, sustained attention

CHAPTER 13

Adaptations for Coaching Students with Disabilities

We have trained coaches to work with an array of students who are underperforming academically for a variety of reasons. We have found that coaching works particularly well with students with intact cognitive skills and at least adequate academic skills, but who need help honing their executive skills so that they can perform in school at a level that is commensurate with those skills. This is no small feat. When bright students chronically underperform in school, there are long-term negative effects on self-efficacy and self-confidence. Chronic underperformance can also potentially close doors to future opportunities, such as access to higher-level classes, entry to college, or success in training programs that would prepare them for the jobs they want after they finish high school.

Coaching can also be successful for students with disabilities, but for these students, it may work best when it is a supplemental service augmenting other special education services, such as individualized interventions to strengthen academic skills (such as tutoring or resource room support) or social–emotional skills (such as counseling or support from a behavioral specialist). Coaching as a stand-alone service may not be sufficient to meet these students' needs.

Merriman, Codding, Tryon, and Minami (2016), for instance, compared the effects of coaching and more intensive homework support (an after-school homework club) with two groups of middle school students. Both groups were experiencing significant problems with homework completion, but one group consisted of students with documented disabilities (either learning disabilities or other health impairment/ADHD). The results showed that both interventions were effective in improving homework completion, but for students with disabilities, the rate of improvement was faster for the homework club than for coaching.

This chapter offers tips and guidance for coaching students with ADHD, those with autism spectrum disorder (ASD), and students with intellectual disabilities. While the steps outlined in the previous chapters on coaching elementary and secondary students are relevant, the suggestions here are tailored to the more unique needs and characteristics of these populations.

COACHING STUDENTS WITH ADHD

The fifth edition, text revision, of the *Diagnostic and Statistical Manual of Mental Disorders* (American Psychiatric Association, 2022) classifies three categories of ADHD: attention-deficit/hyperactivity disorder, predominantly inattentive presentation; attention-deficit/hyperactivity disorder, predominantly hyperactive/impulsive presentation; and attention-deficit/hyperactivity disorder, combined presentation. Students with the inattentive presentation of ADHD are not as noticeably fidgety, restless, or impulsive as those with the hyperactive/impulsive presentation. The characteristics the first group exhibit that affect school performance are daydreaming, distractibility, and difficulty initiating and completing tasks, as well as disorganization and forgetfulness. Since these symptoms typically impact school performance more than other behavioral or social–emotional difficulties, it is more likely that these students may be referred for coaching. Students with the hyperactive/impulsive presentation tend not to present as candidates for coaching as frequently, because parents and teachers are generally more concerned with the impact of these more disruptive behaviors on classroom discipline and teacher instruction. The combined presentation includes both symptoms of inattention and symptoms of hyperactivity/impulsivity, but it is likely the inattention symptoms that lead parents or teachers to believe these students may benefit from coaching.

The executive skills that are challenging for students with ADHD include, at a minimum, sustained attention, task initiation, and time management, but in our experience, most students with ADHD also have challenges with working memory, planning/prioritizing, organization, and goal-directed persistence. Students who lack goal-directed persistence find it hard to exert the effort to use their other weak executive skills to complete tasks they find aversive. On the other hand, when students *do* have strong goal-directed persistence, they can be shown how to use that skill to overcome some of the other executive skills weaknesses standing between them and the tasks they need to complete.

A number of behaviors seen in students with ADHD can make coaching challenging. Students with ADHD are drawn to novelty, but this can wear off quickly. Thus, they may find the idea of coaching appealing in the beginning, but their engagement in coaching often declines quickly as the novelty fades. This can apply to their enthusiasm for the coaching process as a whole, but it also applies to their commitment to pursuing individual goals. Students with ADHD often tire of pursuing a particular goal before they've attained it, and they may frequently propose changing a goal because in their mind it has lost its urgency or importance. They may propose changing goals frequently because some new issue or problem has grabbed their attention.

We've also found that students with ADHD may overestimate their ability to follow through and underestimate the amount of effort required to persist with the goals they set. As a result, they may set overly ambitious goals and then become quickly discouraged when they realize they won't be able to meet the goals. They may also be reluctant to admit that they're not succeeding and resort to portraying to their coach that all is going according to plan. Unless the coach has a way of independently verifying the student's reports, this not only leads to failure but harms the coach–student relationship when the student's lack of truthfulness eventually becomes apparent.

Our coaching model stresses that progress monitoring is important and this, too, may be challenging for students with ADHD. Coaches often ask students to text them on a daily basis to report whether they followed their plan for the day. Students with ADHD often forget that they've agreed to do this. Coaches compensate for this by sending reminder texts. These students may see the text but if they don't respond right away, they may forget to do so later. They may also decide that responding is too much work and they don't follow through for that reason.

Finally, many students with ADHD either don't recognize that they have a problem or they downplay how much trouble they are in. It is well documented that students with ADHD tend to experience "positive illusory bias" to a greater degree than typical students do (Crisci, Cardillo, & Mammarella, 2022; Emeh, Mikami, & Teachman, 2018). We describe these students as looking at the world "through rose-colored glasses." While this may serve as a protective factor (i.e., preserving an otherwise fragile self-esteem), it can also keep students with ADHD from agreeing to work with a coach in the first place or it may lead them to downplay their academic struggles or their difficulties following through on the plans they commit to in coaching.

Based on the challenges associated with coaching students with ADHD outlined above, here are some suggestions:

- Remind the student of their executive skills strengths as well as any other assets they have. If a student accepts that they have an attention disorder, they frequently dwell on the negative traits associated with the condition. We have seen many teenagers with ADHD who have significant strengths in executive skills, such as flexibility and metacognition, and they fail to recognize the value of these strengths. Any time a coach can point out specific examples where the student uses their strengths and assets successfully, the coach is helping them build a more well-rounded and positive picture of themselves.

- When a student wants to change goals frequently, the coach may want to explore with them their reasons for wanting to do so. Did they decide the goal was unattainable, in which case can it be revised to make it attainable? Did they decide another goal was more important to them? In this case, it may make sense to ask them to explain their thinking and perhaps think about whether they want to continue working on their previous goal while adding a second goal to work on. For students who are constantly shifting goals, the coach may suggest the student shorten the time frame and focus on brief action plans rather than on a longer-term goal ("What would you like to get done between now and our next coaching session?"). Ultimately, the coach respects the student's decision about changing goals. If the coach has reservations, they should ask permission to share their concerns before they speak up.

- If the student sets an overly ambitious goal, there are several steps the coach can take, beginning with affirming the student's desire to focus on improvement. The coach might then ask the student to elaborate on their goal ("Tell me more" or "What would that look like?"). Or they might suggest the student prioritize or outline the steps they think they need to take to achieve their goal. If the coach is still concerned that the student is overreaching, they might ask permission to make a suggestion and then offer an option of working on one piece of their goal for a week and seeing how that goes. Ultimately, though, the student is the owner of whatever goal is chosen and the coach's role is to support them in their efforts. See Chapter 10 for a further elaboration of this process.

• Some students with ADHD falter with the progress monitoring aspect of coaching for the reasons described above. Progress monitoring should be as painless as possible for the student. Many coaches, for instance, spend part of their coaching sessions reviewing with the student information that teachers put in the school's web portal, since a number of goals students set can be tracked that way without any extra work on the part of the student. These include attendance, missing homework assignments, and grades on tests, quizzes, or assignments. When a student sets a daily goal (such as starting homework by 8:00 P.M.), the coach may text the student to see if they've followed through. The coach and the student may agree that all the student has to do is text back with a thumbs-up emoji when the text from the coach comes through. If the student has trouble following through on whatever the communication agreement is, the coach can ask the student at the next coaching session if there's another approach that will work better for the student.

Many teenagers with ADHD think that it's "not normal" to need to use compensating strategies such as checklists and alarms to remember, or to break tasks down into very small manageable pieces in order to overcome problems with task initiation or sustained attention. They may look at high-achieving friends and assume that their friends don't need those "crutches" in order to be successful. When coaches can share examples of the strategies they themselves use to keep track of things and get them done, it may help these students recognize that most people rely on external supports to be successful.

It may help to point out that the research on self-control suggests that those people who are found to have high levels of self-control generally pull this off by limiting their access to temptation. It's not that people with high self-control are great at resisting the ice cream in the freezer—they're just better at not bringing ice cream into the house in the first place. Helping students with ADHD look at their environment and think about how they can redesign that environment to make it easier for them to achieve their goals may work better than talking with them about strengthening their "will power."

COACHING STUDENTS ON THE AUTISM SPECTRUM

The coaching process and strategies detailed throughout this book are applicable to students with executive skills challenges, and those on the autism spectrum are no exception. At the same time, students with ASD may present with some specific executive skills challenges as well as some unique skills and characteristics. Being mindful of these can help coaches to better understand these students and to work with them on strategies and supports that will best suit their needs.

Before proceeding, however, we offer this caveat: ASD covers a wide spectrum of students with a wide spectrum of skills. The success of the coaching process is predicated on an empathetic understanding and acceptance of who the student is and the strengths and challenges they bring to the situation. That means, first and foremost, that the coach comes to the process with an open mind and without any preconceived ideas about students with, or because of, labels that may be attached to them. For any given student, a decision about whether the information below applies or not will only be determined once the coach has a thorough understanding of that student.

In terms of executive skills, Kenworthy and her colleagues (2014) have identified flexibility, planning, and organization as among the most common challenges of these students. The impact of challenges in flexibility can be particularly pronounced. Common everyday events, including changes in routines, situational transitions, unexpected or unwanted events, and management of different viewpoints and opinions can be problematic. Open-ended or ambiguous task demands can also be problematic for students with ASD unless they are subject areas that are familiar and of interest to them. Students with ASD can also have difficulty shifting behavior or generating alternatives when their chosen solution does not work. Problems with planning and organization can further impact problem solving.

In addition to these executive skills, other authors have identified difficulties with working memory (Kercood, Grskovic, Banda, & Begeske, 2014; Rabiee, Vasaghi-Gharamaleki, Samadi, Amiri-Shavaki, & Alaghband-Rad, 2020) and emotion regulation (Mazefsky et al., 2013) in individuals with ASD. It is also noteworthy that anxiety, a frequent co-occurrence with ASD (South & Rogers, 2017), may be related to low tolerance for uncertainty and can adversely impact executive skills.

Because of the unique skills and characteristics that students with ASD bring to the process, familiarity with and trust of the person they work with is particularly important. They value knowing exactly how a process will work, consistency in routines and schedules, and what the expectations are. When a task is import to them, if they have the skills needed and understand specifically what is expected, students with ASD demonstrate good sustained attention, attention to detail, and task initiation. They are effective time managers when they have a specific schedule that they are comfortable with. Students with ASD also tend to be direct in their communication, particularly when it comes to their interests, likes, and dislikes, and they are likely to be more comfortable with direct, unambiguous communication.

With this information in mind, there are several considerations for the coaching process. First, if these students are adolescents, they, like their peers, share the desire for autonomy and an active role in decision making, and they may be direct and emphatic about this. Thus, it is important for the coach to come to the process without a preconceived agenda or expectations. The coach can begin the discussion with a question about how the student arrived at coaching (i.e., if referred by parents or a teacher and how they feel about it). With the student's permission, the coach then can explain the coaching process and emphasize that the role of the coach is to support the student in whatever goals they have for themselves. Since familiarity and trust on the part of the student are keys to success, taking as much time as is needed to get to know the student and responding with understanding and empathy is the priority for the coach. This includes discussing the student's interests, skills, strengths, and preferred methods of learning. The Getting to Know You Survey (Appendix 1; pp. 141–142) covers much of what the coach will want to know. Some students will be comfortable completing it on their own but if not, the coach can use it as a guide to learn about the student. If the student does complete it on their own, it is worthwhile to review it with them so the coach has a clear understanding of the student's situation and perspective.

The same is true of the Executive Skills Questionnaire, since they, like many adolescents, may be unfamiliar with the language or with thinking about behavior in these terms. Using the motivational interviewing approach (Chapter 7), the coach engages the student in a discussion about what they might like to change or work on. If the student indicates that they have a goal or change they would like to work on, regardless of whether this relates to the referral issue, the coach accepts this. The discussions that follow focus on clarifying what the student wants, whether or how they would like to proceed, and whether it seems they have any ambivalence about moving forward.

If the student has a goal and the coach is satisfied that the student is motivated to pursue it, specificity precedes planning. Let's suppose the student wants to improve their grade in a particular subject. The coach determines the following: their current grade, their desired grade, and the time frame for achieving it; the grading components (tests, homework completion, class participation, etc.); the student's confidence in their skill level; and which components are strengths and which are challenges for the student. Coach and student then discuss what the student thinks they need to do to improve their grade. If the student is not sure, with the student's permission, the coach can offer some options to see if any strike a chord with the student.

Assuming the student eventually decides on a goal (e.g., improved homework completion, learning study strategies for tests), they discuss how the student thinks they could achieve that goal. Again, if the student is not sure, with permission the coach offers some suggestions for the student to choose from. Throughout this process, the key for the coach is to accept the student's choices. Since, as noted above, students may have challenges with planning, organization, and working memory, it is important to support them in building a plan with as much specificity as possible. Additionally, it is important that the plan include strategies and tools to promote independence.

Students with ASD are more likely to have had or continue to have educational supports in school and are used to working with adults on a one-to-one basis. This may help the coaching process once a trusting relationship has been established, since these students are accustomed to working with supportive adults. At the same time, as Hume, Loftin, and Lantz (2009) indicated, this extended, ongoing assistance, coupled with executive skills challenges of these students, can lead to overreliance on adult support and can undermine independence. To guard against the student becoming dependent on their support, the coach needs to be mindful of strategies involving task initiation, self-monitoring, and generalization that promote self-reliance. Essentially this means developing a plan with a student with ASD that incorporates strategies and tools that they can use when the coach is not present that will serve as reminders and prompts for them.

Let's suppose a student with ASD has selected on-time completion of homework as a way to improve their grade. The coach and student will first discuss the current completion rate and, based on that, set a completion rate as a first step that the student is confident they can meet. Once that is decided, the coach will ask if the student would be okay discussing some planning questions. If yes, the coach could ask open-ended questions to elicit the following:

- What exactly they will do
- The materials they will need to begin
- The location where they will work
- An approximate time that they plan to begin
- An approximate time that they will work either to complete the task or take a break
- How they will know the task is complete
- What they will do with the completed work

Additionally, they might ask if the student would find any other tools helpful and suggest the following as possible options if the student is not sure:

- An alarm or other auditory/visual cue that will remind them what to do and when to begin
- A timer to let them know how long they have to complete the task or work before a break

The coach and student will then discuss if the student would like to add or change any of the elements and if they are comfortable with the plan. If the student expresses any hesitancy or the coach senses any ambivalence, it is best to put the plan on hold and explore the student's feelings about making or committing to a plan. Students with ASD often need time to feel comfortable with the planning process, particularly if it is new to them. Implementation begins only when the student says they are ready.

While independence is important, it is a skill based on success and confidence. In the early stages of the plan, the coach can provide increased support by helping the student engage in cognitive and behavioral rehearsals of the steps, working with them on the development of picture/text step schedules that match rehearsals, and doing frequent check-ins. Short-term trials of the plan (e.g., trying the homework plan for one or two nights) can be used to troubleshoot or modify the plan based on student feedback. If technology such as apps are part of the plan, the coach and student should work together to ensure the student is proficient in the apps' use. Support is faded as the student demonstrates success with each step.

In summary, we highlight the following:

- Familiarity and trust in the coaching relationship are essential for success.
- The pace and direction of the coaching process is set by the student with the coach in a supportive role.
- Students with ASD are most comfortable when they know specifically what they will be doing. Uncertainty and ambiguity are anxiety provoking.
- Students will be most comfortable with habits and routines they have established. Whenever possible, it is best to build on these.
- Students need time, support, and practice to adjust to procedures and tasks that are new to them.

COACHING STUDENTS WITH INTELLECTUAL DISABILITIES

The term *intellectual disability* is used when a person has limitations in cognitive skills as well as limitations in communication, social, and self-care skills. The American Association on Intellectual and Developmental Disabilities lists three criteria for a designation of intellectual disability: (1) IQ below 70–75, (2) significant limitations in two or more adaptive skills (e.g., communication, self-care, or the ability to function independently in the community), and (3) a manifestation before the age of 18. Students with intellectual disabilities develop and learn more slowly or differently than typically developing peers. In terms of executive skills, flexibility and metacognition are often weaknesses for students with intellectual disabilities, in part because these skills require a level of abstract thinking that they may not be capable of.

Although our coaching model was developed with students with average to high intelligence in mind, we've worked with coaches who have applied the model successfully with students with mild intellectual impairments. They have achieved success by (1) modifying the executive skills definitions and terminology to make the language more accessible; (2) walking students through the data-gathering forms (such as the Executive Skills Questionnaire), both to help the student understand the language and to provide personal examples to help the student make a more accurate assessment of their skills; (3) helping students set short-term goals focused on easily defined behaviors; and (4) simplifying strategies to match the student's capacity to use them.

We reached out to Michael Delman, the founder of Beyond BookSmart, a company that provides executive skills coaching to both young people and adults, to ask about his experience coaching students with intellectual disabilities. He offered some sage advice:

> "We believe that, to a large extent, a coach can be effective with people whose IQ is lower by adjusting their approach to match the needs of the person. Since chronological age may or may not correlate well with intellectual development, it is standard practice for us to choose language, tools, and assessments to fit the intellectual level of the client. As an example, a high school student who has a relatively low IQ would get lost using our 'Fast Break' tool for managing homework because it involves tracking and weighing a number of variables: the urgency and importance of the task, the expected time needed, and the difficulty and sequencing of it given competing demands. A student with a lower IQ would do better with a planning tool that only asks them to list their homework and choose a sequence based on just one variable, such as level of difficulty ('Start with your favorite subject, then do the hardest, then any others after that'). As with all of our tools and approaches, we train and encourage coaches to tailor to the needs and abilities of their clients, documented/tested or not. As a second example, for a client learning to take notes, we'd likely go with graphic organizers or perhaps two-column notes rather than suggesting Cornell notes or four-column guides. We'd also help the client learn self-advocacy skills so they could find the right supports at school by connecting with caregivers, teachers, etc."

To add to this, we would recommend that coaches who are working outside the school system with this population keep an open line of communication with the student's school-based support team in order to facilitate the generalization and transfer of skills in relevant contexts.

To provide a case example to illustrate the process of coaching students with intellectual disabilities, a coach we worked with several years ago was a special education teacher who co-taught in a regular education classroom. The student the coach had selected to coach had cognitive limitations (IQ = 70–75), but the student was willing to work with the special education teacher as the coach. The coach began by completing the Executive Skills Questionnaire with the student, explaining any words the student didn't understand and helping the student apply the items to themselves (by offering examples or situations that the student was familiar with). Together they identified response inhibition as one of this student's weaker executive skills. The coach asked the student how this skill showed itself in the classroom, and the student stated that they frequently got in trouble for calling out without raising their hand. The student agreed that this was a problem that they wanted to work on, and the coach asked the student what might help them remember to raise their hand. The student suggested that the coach remind the student at the beginning of class that their goal was raising their hand to speak. They followed the plan, with the student keeping track of callouts during the class. In a very short time, the student had achieved their goal of remembering to raise their hand before speaking.

FINAL COMMENTS

Students with other disabilities (e.g., specific learning disability, emotional or behavioral disorders) may also benefit from coaching, but the issues associated with their disabilities tend to be more disparate and thus do not lend themselves to the kind of guidelines we have provided here. For these students, the coaching model as outlined in this book may require adaptation to meet their unique needs.

CHAPTER 14

Other Forms of Coaching

The most effective coaching we have seen takes place in the school with an adult the student knows well and is comfortable with acting as the student's coach. We have known students who have selected other students to act as their coaches, but when this is done, we recommend that an adult serve as "backup coach" to monitor the process and step in when problems arise.

There are other forms that coaching can take, with a number of options described below.

GROUP COACHING

Many middle schools and high schools assign students to "advisor groups" that meet daily or frequently (e.g., during homeroom period). With some modifications, including group instruction in how the coaching process works and a training period to get the process up and running, group coaching can be successful, either by pairing students in a peer coaching model (see below) or by having the teacher lead the group in setting individual goals and reporting back to the group students' success in meeting those goals. Group applications have the added advantage of enabling the classroom teacher to address the needs of many students without having to allot individual time to each one.

Merriman (2010) compared a group coaching model to an after-school homework club for students with executive skills challenges. This study is described in some detail because it provides a blueprint for what a group coaching model might look like.

Participants in the study were selected because they had significant problems with homework completion. The group coaching model followed the format described in the first edition of this book, with students setting both long-term and short-term goals or action plans. Students were also asked to consider what obstacles might prevent them from carrying out their plans and to identify strategies to overcome those obstacles. Three groups with 9–10 participants each met 4 days a week for 42 minutes after school for 10 weeks. At each coaching session, students completed a version of the Daily Coaching Form (Appendix 10; pp. 171–172) in which they identified the work they needed to do and made plans for what they expected to accomplish before the next coaching session. After the first session, where students were shown how to complete this form, the coaching session began with having students review their previous plans, indicate which tasks they'd completed, and rate how well they did the work using a 1–5 scale. They then went on to make plans for that day.

The coaches' role in these daily coaching sessions was to ensure that students filled out the forms, to call on volunteers to share with the group how their plans had gone, and to provide encouragement and answer questions. With the time remaining when students had completed their planning, the group started on their homework while the coaches met individually with students to discuss their progress and, if necessary, help them refine their goals.

In the first coaching session each week, the coach shared homework completion data provided by teachers, and students were asked to input the data into preformatted graphs. The study also incorporated the use of a reinforcer: Students were given a raffle ticket for each day they attended the coaching session and once a week a drawing was held for a $15 gift card.

Outcome measures included GPA, homework completion rates, and scores on two rating scales, one measuring general academic performance and the second measuring homework problems, that were completed by students before and after the 10-week study. Although GPA did not change significantly, rating scales showed improvement and, most importantly, students showed significant gains in homework completion rates. Prior to the study, students in the group coaching condition completed, on average, 41 percent of their homework. During the study, homework completion rates rose to 89 percent.

PEER COACHING

Peer coaching has a number of advantages. Peers are available to act as models for each other throughout the day since they are part of the natural school environment. With peers as coaches, large numbers of children can be served while the labor intensity of the model is significantly reduced. Peer coaching is potentially a very effective model for learning executive skills, particularly with reciprocal coaching, since each child is both coach and "player" or teacher and student. Moreover, as a classwide intervention, peer coaching means that an awareness of executive skills pervades the environment.

Peer coaching can take two forms. One of these is at a classwide level, involving all students acting as reciprocal coaches for each other. The second involves a more targeted intervention, using selected students as coaches to work with other students who evidence more significant executive skills weaknesses. A study by Plumer and Stoner (2005) provided an excellent example for both applications. The objective of their study was to assess the impact of two different types of peer coaching on the social behavior of targeted students with ADHD who showed social skills deficits. At the classwide level, they used the classwide peer tutoring model (CWPT), which involves what we have called reciprocal peer coaching. Significant positive effects on the behavior and academic performance of elementary school students with ADHD using CWPT have been documented (DuPaul, Ervin, Hook, & McGoey, 1998).

Plumer and Stoner used the CWPT component with an academic task (spelling) but were interested in the impact that this intervention would have on the social behavior of the children diagnosed with ADHD. In the treatment phase of this study, the authors adapted our coaching model for use by selected peer coaches. Peer coaches were chosen by teacher nomination based on their high frequency of appropriate classroom behavior. Peer coaches received specific training for their coaching role with the students who were to be coached.

In this study, Plumer and Stoner found that the CWPT had positive effects on children's academic and social behaviors in the academic setting, but improvements in social interactions did not generalize to recess and lunch. However, with the addition of the peer coaching component, the ADHD students did show significant improvements in social interactions in school social settings. The authors concluded that our coaching model can effectively be extended to young children using elementary-age peers who were provided with coach training and adult supervision.

In terms of classwide reciprocal peer coaching, two models are relevant. As noted above, CWPT has been extensively evaluated and proven to be an effective model for academic improvement across elementary and middle school environments. CWPT has a number of demonstrated advantages, including the following:

- The model can be implemented in any school district or classroom.
- It can be implemented at little or no cost using existing materials.
- Although it has been used for academics, success of the model has suggested it could be used with almost any subject matter, particularly behaviorally defined executive skills.
- The model has been effectively used with students as young as first grade and the effects were shown to last at least 3 years after students received the training.

For executive skills training, a second and perhaps even more relevant model has been described in the literature as classwide peer-assisted self-management (CWPASM) training (Mitchem, Young, West, & Benyo, 2001). This model has particular appeal in the executive skills realm since it focuses on self-management of behavior, and the heart of executive skills processes involves self-regulation. CWPASM teaches self-management strategies to students and uses peers as coaches to help one another work on specific behaviors and to oversee the accuracy of self-monitoring measures, which are a key to the success of this process. A study by Mitchem and colleagues (2001) with middle school students showed significant improvements in on-task behavior, appropriate attention-getting strategies, and acceptable social interactions between peers for a classroom as a whole and for targeted students who had particular difficulties in these areas. The authors cited additional research demonstrating the efficacy of this model for younger students.

An approach similar to the one used by Plumer and Stoner in their study is well suited to the more intensive Tier 2 interventions in a multitiered system of supports (MTSS) model. In this model, students with strengths in those particular executive skills that the to-be-coached students are weak in would be nominated by teachers. In this case, the peer coach's role would have some similarities to the adult coach in our model. The steps involved in setting up a peer coaching program are listed in Table 14.1.

In sum, based on our own clinical experience and on the research and clinical experience of others working in the field, we understand peer coaching to be a viable, effective intervention for children with executive skills weaknesses. In fact, by virtue of the advantages it offers for modeling, transfer, and generalization of skills, along with decreased labor intensity for adult staff, peer coaching may in some cases be the intervention of choice.

TABLE 14.1. Overview of the Peer Coaching Program

Step	Task
Step 1:	Design coaching process: • Define role and specific functions of peer coach. • Outline coaching process, including meeting times and steps to be followed in the coaching interaction. • Design forms to document coaching as well as record-keeping forms to track outcomes. • Specify how, when, and by whom coaches will be supervised.
Step 2:	Select peer coaches on basis of executive skills strengths and solicit willingness to participate.
Step 3:	Identify students and determine which executive skills and which daily activities will be addressed through coaching (e.g., target skill: working memory; daily activity: remembering to hand in homework).
Step 4:	Meet with students to explain coaching; invite them to participate and to identify specific goals and objectives. Include a discussion of possible incentives to be earned if this is judged necessary (for many students, coaching by itself is a successful intervention while others require rewards on top of the coaching).
Step 5:	Contact parents of both students to explain the process and obtain permission to participate.
Step 6:	Conduct training sessions with peer coaches. Adult plays role of coached student to assess peer coach's understanding of the process and their ability to follow the template.
Step 7:	Meet with both students to discuss how the process will work. Adult models the coached student's role with the coached student observing while the peer coach undertakes the coaching role. Answer questions and clear up any confusion. Coached student and adult exchange roles, with adult observing while peer coach and coached student go through a practice run of the coaching process. Explain use of forms and record keeping.
Step 8:	When adult is satisfied that both students understand their role and has reinforced them for their effectiveness, coaching begins, with the teacher monitoring the first few sessions.
Step 9:	Evaluate the process and make any necessary adjustments.
Step 10:	Peer coach and coached student follow the coaching schedule set up, with the adult checking in one to two times per week with both students to ensure that the process is on track and being correctly followed. Arrange for regular communication with parents regarding efficacy of intervention.

Note. From Dawson and Guare (2018). Copyright © 2018 The Guilford Press. Reprinted with permission.

CHAPTER 15

Parting Thoughts

Let's step back and take a longer view of the coaching process. We have used a variety of terms to describe what coaching helps young people develop. We've talked about coaching as a strategy for helping students learn *self-management* and *self-regulation*, as well as a strategy for empowering them to become *self-regulated learners*. The tools we work with them to use include *self-monitoring, self-instruction, self-talk,* and *self-evaluation*.

But the culmination of coaching coincides with the end goal of effective education in general, and that is to enable students to achieve the broader independence or autonomy that they will need to function successfully in their world beyond high school. The term that describes this ability to function autonomously is *self-determination*.

Self-determination theory, originally developed by Deci and Ryan (Deci & Ryan, 1985; Ryan & Deci, 2017), is a widely accepted theory that explains human motivation. Ryan and Deci propose that there are three core needs that facilitate human growth: *autonomy, competence,* and *relatedness*.

Coaching supports all three of these components. *Relatedness* (the need to interact and be connected to others) is built into the relationship between the coach and the student. In fact, that relationship is so important that when the coach and the student don't feel a personal connection, coaching is unlikely to be successful. Through the coaching process, the coach helps the student build skills and as those skills develop, the sense of personal *competence* is strengthened. And finally, *autonomy* is the driver of the coaching process as well as the end result. Right from the start of coaching, coaches communicate that the student is in control of key aspects of the process. Coaching is a voluntary process, and coaches make clear that students can choose to participate at the outset and throughout the duration of coaching. When a student elects to participate, the coach invites the student both to set goals and to select plans and strategies to meet those goals. By the time coaching ends, when the process is successful, the student has not only set and achieved personal goals, they've also learned how to engage in this process autonomously.

Coaching, like any educational or therapeutic intervention, doesn't always work as well as we would like it to. Sometimes the student and the coach never quite "connect," and that lack of personal connection diminishes the student's motivation to meet with their coach and to work on goals and plans. Sometimes students feel pressured by someone else (e.g., a parent) to work with a coach. In these cases, they are acting on someone else's motivation and not their own, and this undermines their commitment to the process. Sometimes students come to view coaching as just one more obligation in a life that already feels overscheduled. Sometimes student expectations are not met quickly enough, or they see the process as more effortful than they had expected it to be. And sometimes the student realizes, after a brief introduction to the process, that they actually have the skills and drive to be successful on their own without the support of a coach.

When students choose not to continue working with a coach before they've achieved their identified goals, we recommend, whenever possible, that coaches conduct an exit interview with the student. Using MI techniques can be particularly useful, both to help the coach understand where the student is coming from and to help the student reflect on the process. One of the coaches we've worked with used MI techniques in a conversation with a student she was coaching. The student began by stating that she thought she'd gotten everything she needed from coaching and was ready to stop meeting with the coach. By using reflections (and a judicious use of silence to give the student time to answer more deeply), the student identified what she found helpful in the coaching relationship and made the decision to continue seeing the coach after all. Not all exit interviews end this way, but the self-reflection that is built into these interviews can be immensely valuable for both the coach and the student they are coaching.

Ultimately, coaching is respectful of students as agents of their own self-determination. Coaching is not alone in emphasizing the power of self-determination. We would like to close with a quote from a leader in the field of restorative practices/restorative justice, a methodology that has shown great promise in addressing problems with school discipline and conflict mediation. Ted Wachtel, the founder of the International Institute for Restorative Practices, said in a speech that is widely quoted: "Human beings are happier, more cooperative and productive, and more likely to make positive changes in their behavior when those in positions of authority do things *with* them rather than *to* them or *for* them" (Wachtel, 2005).

Coaching, in our model, strives to achieve these outcomes.

Forms and Assessment Tools

Getting to Know You Survey

Name: _____

1. How do you spend your spare time? Check (✓) all that apply and draw a circle around your favorite three activities.

☐ with family ☐ TV/videos ☐ reading ☐ theater/dance ☐ part-time job

☐ with friends ☐ alone ☐ sports ☐ social media ☐ video/computer games

☐ outdoors ☐ sleeping ☐ writing ☐ listening to music ☐ volunteering

☐ arts, crafts, building things ☐ playing an instrument

☐ extracurricular activities at school ☐ dirt biking/4-wheeling

☐ OTHER: _____

2. What talents do you have? Check all that apply and provide an example if you can.

☐ Athletic: _____ ☐ Artistic: _____

☐ Musical: _____ ☐ Writing: _____

☐ Communication: _____ ☐ Leadership: _____

☐ Performing arts: _____ ☐ Technology: _____

☐ Mechanical skills: _____ ☐ Math/sciences: _____

☐ Cooking, sewing: _____ ☐ Interpersonal skills: _____

☐ OTHER: _____

3. What personal qualities do you have that you consider to be strengths? Check up to five.

☐ leadership ☐ patience ☐ creativity ☐ sense of humor ☐ independence

☐ caring, empathy ☐ hard-working ☐ loyalty ☐ imagination ☐ dependability

☐ determination ☐ optimism ☐ self-control ☐ coping skills ☐ problem solving

☐ persistence ☐ ambition ☐ honesty ☐ organization ☐ courage

☐ competitiveness ☐ extraversion (outgoing) ☐ works well with others

☐ OTHER: _____

4. What areas of skill or knowledge would you like to become an expert in? List *any* topic that interests you, even if it is something you don't usually learn about in school (e.g., skateboarding, video games, sports statistics, cheerleading, horseback riding).

(continued)

_____

5. How do you learn best? Check all that apply.

   a. Group size:

   ☐ alone   ☐ small group (2–3 people)

   ☐ medium group (4–7)   ☐ whole class

   b. Learning style:

   ☐ visual   ☐ hands-on

   ☐ listening   ☐ memorizing

   ☐ discussion   ☐ activity/experiential learning

   ☐ apprenticeship   ☐ taking notes

   ☐ reading   ☐ thinking about what I've read or heard

   ☐ OTHER: _____

   c. What is your preferred study environment?

   ☐ library   ☐ study hall at school

   ☐ bedroom   ☐ other room in my house

   ☐ with friends   ☐ public place (e.g., coffee shop)

   ☐ resource room   ☐ OTHER: _____

6. What are your preferred classroom activities? Check all that apply.

☐ lecture	☐ discussions	☐ projects
☐ debates	☐ group games	☐ presentations
☐ reading	☐ creative writing	☐ worksheets
☐ labs/experiments	☐ cooperative learning	☐ brainstorming
☐ outdoor activities	☐ field trips	☐ learn, then teach others
☐ role playing	☐ simulations	☐ taking tests
☐ self-directed learning	☐ individual research	☐ doing homework
☐ movies/videos	☐ working on the computer	☐ teacher-led instruction
☐ doodling	☐ daydreaming	☐ talking with friends

☐ OTHER: _____

Executive Skills Questionnaire

Directions: Read each item and decide how often it's a problem for you. Then add up the three scores in each set and write that number on the **Total score** line. Use the **Key** on page 4 of this questionnaire to determine your executive skills strengths (two to three highest scores) and weaknesses (two to three lowest scores).

1. I act on impulse.

Most of the time 1	Frequently 2	Sometimes 3	Very rarely 4	Never 5

2. I get in trouble for talking too much in class.

Most of the time 1	Frequently 2	Sometimes 3	Very rarely 4	Never 5

3. I say things without thinking.

Most of the time 1	Frequently 2	Sometimes 3	Very rarely 4	Never 5

Total score, items 1–3: _____

4. I say "I'll do it later" and then forget about it.

Most of the time 1	Frequently 2	Sometimes 3	Very rarely 4	Never 5

5. I forget homework assignments or forget to bring home needed materials.

Most of the time 1	Frequently 2	Sometimes 3	Very rarely 4	Never 5

6. I lose or misplace belongings such as coats, notebooks, sports equipment, etc.

Most of the time 1	Frequently 2	Sometimes 3	Very rarely 4	Never 5

Total score, items 4–6: _____

7. I get annoyed when homework is too hard or confusing or takes too long to finish.

Most of the time 1	Frequently 2	Sometimes 3	Very rarely 4	Never 5

8. I have a short fuse, am easily frustrated.

Most of the time 1	Frequently 2	Sometimes 3	Very rarely 4	Never 5

(continued)

9. I get upset easily when things don't go as planned.

Most of the time 1	Frequently 2	Sometimes 3	Very rarely 4	Never 5

Total score, items 7–9: _____

10. I have difficulty paying attention, am easily distracted.

Most of the time 1	Frequently 2	Sometimes 3	Very rarely 4	Never 5

11. I run out of steam before finishing my homework.

Most of the time 1	Frequently 2	Sometimes 3	Very rarely 4	Never 5

12. I have problems sticking with chores until they are done.

Most of the time 1	Frequently 2	Sometimes 3	Very rarely 4	Never 5

Total score, items 10–12: _____

13. I put off homework or chores until the last minute.

Most of the time 1	Frequently 2	Sometimes 3	Very rarely 4	Never 5

14. It's hard for me to put aside fun activities to start homework.

Most of the time 1	Frequently 2	Sometimes 3	Very rarely 4	Never 5

15. I need many reminders to start chores.

Most of the time 1	Frequently 2	Sometimes 3	Very rarely 4	Never 5

Total score, items 13–15: _____

16. I have trouble planning for big assignments (knowing what to do first, second, etc.).

Most of the time 1	Frequently 2	Sometimes 3	Very rarely 4	Never 5

17. It's hard for me to set priorities when I have a lot of things to do.

Most of the time 1	Frequently 2	Sometimes 3	Very rarely 4	Never 5

18. I become overwhelmed by long-term projects or big assignments.

Most of the time 1	Frequently 2	Sometimes 3	Very rarely 4	Never 5

Total score, items 16–18: _____

(continued)

19. My backpack and notebooks are disorganized.

Most of the time 1	Frequently 2	Sometimes 3	Very rarely 4	Never 5

20. My desk or workspace at home is a mess.

Most of the time 1	Frequently 2	Sometimes 3	Very rarely 4	Never 5

21. I have trouble keeping my room tidy.

Most of the time 1	Frequently 2	Sometimes 3	Very rarely 4	Never 5

Total score, items 19–21: _____

22. I have a hard time estimating how long it takes to do something (such as homework).

Most of the time 1	Frequently 2	Sometimes 3	Very rarely 4	Never 5

23. I often don't finish homework at night and rush to get it done in school before class.

Most of the time 1	Frequently 2	Sometimes 3	Very rarely 4	Never 5

24. I'm slow getting ready for things (for example, school or appointments).

Most of the time 1	Frequently 2	Sometimes 3	Very rarely 4	Never 5

Total score, items 22–24: _____

25. If the first solution to a problem doesn't work, I have trouble thinking of a different one.

Most of the time 1	Frequently 2	Sometimes 3	Very rarely 4	Never 5

26. It's hard for me to deal with changes in plans or routines.

Most of the time 1	Frequently 2	Sometimes 3	Very rarely 4	Never 5

27. I have problems with open-ended homework assignments (for example, knowing what to write about for a creative writing assignment or coming up with topics for a long-term project).

Most of the time 1	Frequently 2	Sometimes 3	Very rarely 4	Never 5

Total score, items 25–27: _____

28. I don't have effective study strategies.

Most of the time 1	Frequently 2	Sometimes 3	Very rarely 4	Never 5

(continued)

29. I don't check my work for mistakes even when the stakes are high.

Most of the time 1	Frequently 2	Sometimes 3	Very rarely 4	Never 5

30. I don't evaluate my performance and change tactics to increase my success.

Most of the time 1	Frequently 2	Sometimes 3	Very rarely 4	Never 5

Total score, items 28–30: _____

31. I can't seem to save up money for something I want.

Most of the time 1	Frequently 2	Sometimes 3	Very rarely 4	Never 5

32. I don't see the value in earning good grades to achieve a long-term goal.

Most of the time 1	Frequently 2	Sometimes 3	Very rarely 4	Never 5

33. If something fun comes up when I should be studying, it's hard for me to make myself study.

Most of the time 1	Frequently 2	Sometimes 3	Very rarely 4	Never 5

Total score, items 31–33: _____

Key			
Items	**Executive Skill**	**Items**	**Executive Skill**
1–3	Response inhibition	4–6	Working memory
7–9	Emotional control	10–12	Sustained attention
13–15	Task initiation	16–18	Planning/prioritization
19–21	Organization	22–24	Time management
25–27	Flexibility	28–30	Metacognition
31–33	Goal-directed persistence		

Your Executive Skills Strengths	Your Executive Skills Weaknesses

Executive Skills Questionnaire—Adult Version

Name: _____   Date: _____

Read each item below and then rate that item based on the extent to which you agree or disagree with how well it describes you. Use the rating scale below to choose the appropriate score. Then add the three scores in each section. Use the key on the last page to determine your executive skills strengths (2–3 highest scores) and weaknesses (2–3 lowest scores).

Strongly disagree	1	Tend to agree	5
Disagree	2	Agree	6
Tend to disagree	3	Strongly agree	7
Neutral	4		

Item   Score

1. I don't jump to conclusions.   _____
2. I think before I speak.   _____
3. I don't take action without having all the facts.   _____

TOTAL SCORE: _____

4. I have a good memory for facts, dates, and details.   _____
5. I am very good at remembering the things I have committed to do.   _____
6. I seldom need reminders to complete tasks.   _____

TOTAL SCORE: _____

7. My emotions seldom get in the way when performing on the job.   _____
8. Little things do not affect me emotionally or distract me from the task at hand.   _____
9. I can defer my personal feelings until after a task has been completed.   _____

TOTAL SCORE: _____

10. No matter what the task, I believe in getting started as soon as possible.   _____
11. Procrastination is usually not a problem for me.   _____
12. I seldom leave tasks to the last minute.   _____

TOTAL SCORE: _____

13. I find it easy to stay focused on my work.   _____
14. Once I start an assignment, I work diligently until it's completed.   _____
15. Even when interrupted, I find it easy to get back and complete the job at hand.   _____

TOTAL SCORE:

(continued)

Item	Score
16. When I plan out my day, I identify priorities and stick to them.	_____
17. When I have a lot to do, I can easily focus on the most important things.	_____
18. I typically break big tasks down into subtasks and timelines.	_____
TOTAL SCORE:	_____

19. I am an organized person.	_____
20. It is natural for me to keep my work area neat and organized.	_____
21. I am good at maintaining systems for organizing my work.	_____
TOTAL SCORE:	_____

22. At the end of the day, I've usually finished what I set out to do.	_____
23. I am good at estimating how long it takes to do something.	_____
24. I am usually on time for appointments and activities.	_____
TOTAL SCORE:	_____

25. I take unexpected events in stride.	_____
26. I easily adjust to changes in plans and priorities.	_____
27. I consider myself to be flexible and adaptive to change.	_____
TOTAL SCORE:	_____

28. I routinely evaluate my performance and devise methods for personal improvement.	_____
29. I am able to step back from a situation in order to make objective decisions.	_____
30. I "read" situations well and can adjust my behavior based on the reactions of others.	_____
TOTAL SCORE:	_____

31. I think of myself as being driven to meet my goals.	_____
32. I easily give up immediate pleasures to work on long-term goals.	_____
33. I believe in setting and achieving high levels of performance.	_____
TOTAL SCORE:	_____

34. I enjoy working in a highly demanding, fast-paced environment.	_____
35. A certain amount of pressure helps me to perform at my best.	_____
36. Jobs that include a fair degree of unpredictability appeal to me.	_____
TOTAL SCORE:	_____

(continued)

Executive Skills Questionnaire—Adult Version *(page 3 of 3)*

KEY			
Items	Executive Skill	Items	Executive Skill
1–3	Response inhibition	4–6	Working memory
7–9	Emotional control	10–12	Task initiation
13–15	Sustained attention	16–18	Planning/prioritization
19–21	Organization	22–24	Time management
25–27	Flexibility	28–30	Metacognition
31–33	Goal-directed persistence	34–36	Stress tolerance

Strongest Skills

_____

_____

_____

_____

Weakest Skills

_____

_____

_____

_____

Executive Skills Problem Checklist

Directions:

1. Check (✓) problem areas that significantly interfere with effective studying.
2. Look over all the items you checked and choose THREE that you think cause the greatest problems. Place a star (★) next to those.

Response Inhibition

_____ Rushing through work just to get it done

_____ Not having the patience to produce quality work

_____ Giving up on a homework assignment when I encounter an obstacle

_____ Having trouble doing homework when there are more fun things to do

Working Memory

_____ Writing assignment instructions without enough detail to understand later

_____ Forgetting to take home necessary materials or take materials to class

_____ Forgetting to hand in homework

_____ Forgetting long-term projects or upcoming tests

_____ Not paying attention to classroom instructions/task directions

_____ Trouble remembering multiple directions or multiple problem steps

_____ Losing materials

_____ Forgetting to complete assignments

_____ Forgetting to check agenda/assignment book

_____ Not recording when an assignment is due

Emotional Control

_____ Getting really irritated when a homework assignment is hard or confusing

_____ Finding it hard to get started on assignments because of perfectionism or fear of failure

_____ Freezing when taking tests and doing poorly despite studying long and hard

_____ Not seeing the point of an assignment and finding it hard to motivate myself to do it

(continued)

Task Initiation

Procrastinating/avoiding tasks due to:

_____ not knowing how to get started

_____ believing the task will "take forever"

_____ believing my performance won't meet expectations

_____ seeing the task as tedious, boring, or irrelevant

_____ Finding other things to do rather than starting homework

_____ Having difficulty getting back to work after breaks

Sustained Attention

_____ Taking frequent breaks when working

_____ Taking breaks that are too long

_____ Internally distracted—thoughts, states, moods, daydreams (please specify): _____

_____

_____ Externally distracted—sights, sounds, technology such as phone, computer, TV, video games (please specify): _____

_____ Rushing through work—sloppy/mistakes

_____ Not knowing limits (e.g., how long I can sustain attention) or when the best study time is

_____ Not recognizing when I'm off task

Planning/Prioritization

_____ Not making a study plan (may not know how)

_____ Can't break down long-term projects into smaller tasks and timelines

_____ Having difficulty taking notes or studying for test because I can't distinguish important from nonimportant

_____ Not using or not knowing how to use agenda/assignment book

_____ Spending too much time on less important elements—can't put the most important parts or most important assignments first

_____ Planning unrealistically (e.g., fail to take into account obstacles to the plan)

Flexibility

_____ Struggling with assignments that require creativity or are open-ended

_____ Getting stuck on one solution or one way of looking at a problem

_____ Having trouble coming up with topics or ideas of things to write about

_____ Having difficulty coming up with "Plan B" if the first attempt didn't work

(continued)

Organization

_____ Not using or knowing how to design an organizational system

_____ Not being able to find things in notebooks or backpacks

_____ Losing assignments or important papers

_____ Not having neat study area

_____ Losing electronic data—forget where work is stored or what name it's filed under

Time Management

Can't estimate how long a task will take—due to:

_____ overestimating how long it will take to do a task (therefore never getting started)

_____ underestimating how long it will take to do a task (therefore running out of time)

_____ Chronically late (for school, tutoring, other appointments and obligations)

_____ Having difficulty juggling multiple assignments and responsibilities because I can't judge time involved

_____ Overcommitted—juggling too many obligations (and I think I can pull it off!)

_____ Lacking a sense of time urgency (I don't appreciate that deadlines are important)

_____ Relying on deadline as activator or motivator

Goal-Directed Persistence

_____ Not having a long-term goal

_____ Having a long-term goal but lacking a realistic plan to achieve the goal

_____ Not seeing how daily actions impact goal attainment

_____ Not seeing studying as important and making minimal effort as a result

_____ Giving up in the face of an obstacle

_____ Having a "good-enough" mentality that gets in the way of producing quality work

_____ "Not on the radar"—seeing work as not relevant or not important enough to do

Metacognition

_____ Can't accurately evaluate skills (e.g., expect to do well on tests in spite of poor past performance, expect to go to a college or get a job without requisite skills or academic record)

_____ Can't identify appropriate study strategies

_____ Can't plan or organize a writing assignment

_____ Can memorize facts but missing the larger context (I do better on multiple-choice tests than essay questions)

_____ Having a hard time understanding more abstract concepts (math as well as content-area subjects)

(continued)

_____ Having difficulty making inferences, drawing conclusions, grasping the main idea, and reading between the lines

_____ Failing to check work/proofread

Other

_____

_____

WHAT ARE MY TARGETS?

Executive Skill	Specific Problem

What are some ways that I could use my executive skills strengths to help me be successful?

_____

_____

_____

_____

Executive Skills Semistructured Interview—Student Version

Name: _____ Date: _____

I'm going to ask you some questions about situations related to your success as a student. All of these are situations in which you have to use planning and organizational skills in order to be successful. Some will be directly related to school, whereas other questions will touch on extracurricular activities, any job situations you've been in, and how you spend your leisure time.

HOMEWORK. I'm going to ask you some questions about homework and the kinds of problems kids sometimes have with homework. Please tell me if you think these are problems for you. I may ask you to give me examples of how you see it as a problem.

Item	Not a Problem	Notes
Getting started on homework. (TI) *Related questions:* What makes it hard? When is the best time to do homework? Are some subjects harder to start than others?		
Sticking with it long enough to get it done. (SA) *Related questions:* Is this worse with some subjects than others? What do you say to yourself that leads you to either give up or stick with it? Does the length of the assignment make a difference in your ability to complete it?		
Remembering assignments. (WM) *Related questions:* Do you have trouble remembering to write down assignments, bring home necessary materials, or hand in assignments? Do you lose things necessary to complete the task?		
Becoming distracted while doing homework. (SA) *Related questions:* What kinds of things distract you? Have you found places to study that minimize distractions? How do you handle the distractions when they come up?		
Having other things you'd rather do. (P, GDP) *Related questions:* Are there things you have trouble tearing yourself away from to do homework? Do you resent having homework or too much homework? Do you think there are other things in your life that are more important than homework?		

(continued)

LONG-TERM PROJECTS. Now let's talk about long-term assignments. Which of the following, if any, are hard for you?

Item	Not a Problem	Notes
Choosing a topic (M)		
Breaking the assignment into smaller parts (P)		
Developing a timeline (P)		
Sticking with a timeline (TM)		
Estimating how long it will take to finish (TM)		
Following directions (e.g., Do you forget to do part of the assignment and lose points as a result?) (WM, M)		
Proofreading or checking your work to make sure you followed the rules and haven't made careless mistakes (M)		
Finishing the project by the deadline (GDP)		

STUDYING FOR TESTS. Here are some problems students sometimes have when studying for tests. Which ones, if any, are a problem for you?

Item	Not a Problem	Notes
Making yourself sit down and study (TI)		
Knowing what to study (M)		
Knowing how to study (M)		
Putting off studying/not studying at all (TM)		

(continued)

STUDYING FOR TESTS. *(continued)*

Item	Not a Problem	Notes
Taking breaks that are either too frequent or too long (SA)		
Giving up before you've studied enough (GDP)		
Memorizing the material (WM)		
Understanding the material (M)		

HOME CHORES/RESPONSIBILITIES. What kinds of chores, if any, do you have to do on a regular or irregular basis?

Chore	Regular (When do you do it?)	Occasional
1.		
2.		
3.		
4.		
5.		

What aspects of completing chores, if any, do you have trouble with?

Item	Not a Problem	Notes
Remembering to do them (WM)		
Doing them when you're supposed to (TI)		
Running out of steam before you're done (SA)		
Doing a sloppy job and getting in trouble for it (M)		

(continued)

ORGANIZATIONAL SKILLS. Now I'm going to ask some questions about how organized you are. Tell me if you have problems with any of the following.

Item	Not a Problem	Notes
Keeping your bedroom neat (O)		
Keeping your notebooks organized (O)		
Keeping your backpack organized (O)		
Keeping your desk clean (O)		
Keeping your locker clean (O)		
Leaving your belongings all over the house (O)		
Leaving belongings other places (e.g., school, friend's houses, at work) (O)		
Losing or misplacing things (O)		

MANAGING EMOTIONS. Sometimes emotions can get in the way of doing well in school or getting along with others. Tell me if you have problems with any of the following.

Item	Not a Problem	Notes
Losing your temper (EC)		
Getting nervous in some situations (e.g., when taking tests, speaking up in class, with peers or adults you don't know well) (EC)		
Getting easily frustrated (e.g., when you don't understand homework or when parents get on your nerves) (EC)		
Saying or doing something without thinking that you later regret (RI)		
Giving up quickly when a task is hard or boring (RI)		
Difficulty adjusting to changes in plans or disruptions to routines (F)		
Having trouble with open-ended assignments (such as writing assignments where there's no one right answer) (F)		

(continued)

WORK/LEISURE TIME. Let's talk about how you spend your time when you're not in school. What kinds of extracurricular activities, if any, are you involved in? Do you have a job? How do you spend your leisure time?

Activity	Amount of time (approximate per day or week)
1.	
2.	
3.	
4.	
5.	
6.	
7.	

Here are some problems that students sometimes have with how they spend their spare time. Which ones, if any, are problems for you?

Item	Not a Problem	Notes
Spending too many hours at a job (TM)		
"Wasting" time (e.g., hanging out, playing computer/video games, talking on the phone, time on Facebook, watching too much TV) (TM)		
Hanging out with kids who get in trouble (RI)		
Not getting enough sleep (RI)		
Spending money as soon as you get it (RI)		

(continued)

LONG-TERM GOALS. Do you know what you want to do after high school?

Possible goals
1.
2.
3.
4.

Have you formulated a plan for reaching your goal(s)? If so, what is it?

What are some of the potential obstacles that might prevent you from reaching your goal(s)?

Potential obstacle	Ways to overcome the obstacle
1.	
2.	
3.	
4.	
5.	

If you have not yet identified a goal or developed a plan for reaching the goal, when do you think you will you do this?

Note. TI, Task initiation; WM, Working memory; O, Organization; GDP, Goal-directed persistence; RI, Response inhibition; SA, Sustained attention; P, Planning; F, Flexibility; EC, Emotional control.

Executive Skills Coaching
What Parents Should Know (Parent Handout)

WHAT EXECUTIVE SKILLS ARE

Executive skills refer to the cognitive processes required to plan and organize activities, including task initiation and follow-through, working memory, sustained attention, performance monitoring, impulse inhibition, and goal-directed persistence. Located primarily in the prefrontal cortex (the part of the brain just behind the forehead), these are skills that begin to develop in some form soon after birth, but neuroscientists are now realizing that it takes about 25 years for these skills to fully mature. And for kids with attention disorders, these skills tend to develop even more slowly.

WHAT COACHING IS

One of the responsibilities of parenting is to teach children the skills they need to become effective, independent, and self-regulated adults. And for the first decade or so, most children are receptive to their parents teaching them. As they come up on adolescence, however, they begin to resist their instruction. This is because a primary developmental task of adolescents is to establish their own identity. The reason this is such a strong drive in so many teenagers may be baked into our DNA—scientists have speculated that this was the drive that propelled our ancestors to move from our origins in Africa to explore and settle in new lands and habitats.

When children begin to push back at their parents' effort to teach them new skills, coaching is an option many parents turn to. Coaching serves as a way station between kids relying on parents to manage (or micromanage) them and them being able to function independently. It's an approach ideally suited to helping teens grow the executive skills they need to become the independent, self-sufficient individuals both they and their parents want them to become.

Coaching is a process whereby adults work with students to help them identify goals that are important to them and to make daily plans to help them achieve their long-term goals. With younger teenagers, long-term goals may be those the student hopes to accomplish by the end of the marking period. With older teenagers, coaches may continue to work on marking period goals, but they may also work with students to identify the goals they want to accomplish by the time they complete high school. Examples of marking period goals might be *make the honor roll*, *earn no grades less than a C*, or *pass math*. An example of a long-term goal for an older adolescent might be *get accepted by the state university*, *get a job as an auto mechanic*, or *get into hairdressing school*.

(continued)

KEY FEATURES OF COACHING

Coaching approaches vary. Through years of working with and refining our coaching process, we have identified some key elements that contribute to its success. Some of these features are:

- Coaching has to be voluntary. Students who feel pushed into coaching tend to sabotage the process, so we find it helpful to establish up front that the student is a willing participant.
- It is the student who sets coaching goals and not parents. A primary goal of coaching is to help students become autonomous. The only way this can happen is for students to make key decisions, particularly around the goals they want to work toward.
- Students help identify the strategies that work for them as they pursue their goals. In this way, the coach acts as a consultant—offering advice and suggesting strategies, but always leaving the final decision in the hands of the student.
- Coaches provide ways to track progress so that the students they're working with have clear evidence that they're being successful. Coaches have an array of measurement techniques they can draw on, selecting the appropriate technique based on the specific goals the student is working on. Giving students clear feedback about their progress is one of the most powerful components of our coaching model.
- Success with achieving small goals builds a foundation for solid skill development, making it easier for the student to achieve larger goals, but *this takes time.*

WHAT IS THE PARENT ROLE IN COACHING?

- Be willing and able to step back. You own the car, but you have to allow your child to drive it— and let the coach rather than you sit in the passenger seat to guide and instruct as your child learns to drive.
- Take cues from the coach. There may still be a role for you to play, but this should be the result of a negotiation between you, the coach, and your child to ensure that everyone agrees that this is the right course of action.
- Be patient. New habits are not acquired overnight. We often say with respect to executive skills development, *progress is measured in years instead of months.* While it is likely that with coaching that time frame can be shortened a bit, at a minimum it will take a marking period or two to see growth—and longer for that growth to solidify.

(continued)

WHAT PARENTS CAN DO
TO SUPPORT EXECUTIVE SKILLS DEVELOPMENT

Just because a coach has taken over part of the role you used to play with your child doesn't mean there aren't things you can do to support executive skills development. Here are some of the tips we often share with parents:

- Pick your battles. While health and safety concerns rightly impact parents' decisions about when to impose their will, kids mature by making decisions and experiencing the consequences of those decisions.
- Be willing to negotiate, keeping in mind the things that motivate teens. These include having the chance to do what adults do, making their own choices and decisions, having their opinions valued, and having some say in what rules will apply and how.
- Work on positive communication skills. These include being available to talk when the teen is ready (or offering a specific time to talk), using active listening that focuses on reflecting the teen's feelings without judging them or offering a solution ("It sounds like that made you really angry"), negotiating when possible, and avoiding the "knee-jerk no."
- Keep your eye on the biggest prize—building goal-directed persistence. The best way to do this is to model this yourself. If your child sees that you work hard to achieve the goals that matter to you, that's a lesson that will bear fruit in years to come. What's important to a teenager may be very different than what's important to their parents, but as those frontal lobes mature, kids will draw on past experience and begin to apply what they picked up from all that observational learning that was going on throughout childhood and adolescence.

Our approach to coaching is nicely captured by the following quote:

> Human beings are happier, more cooperative and productive, and more likely to make positive changes in their behavior when those in positions of authority do things with them rather than to them or for them.
>
> —TED WACHTEL, International Institute for Restorative Practices

Consent for Services: Executive Functioning Coaching

1. What is executive functioning coaching?

Executive functioning coaching supports students in developing executive functioning skills such as organization, time management, and goal setting. This coaching program is provided by a district school psychologist who is participating in an executive functioning skills coaching program under the direction of Dr. Peg Dawson and Dr. Richard Gaure.

2. What can I expect will happen?

After you sign this consent form, the coach will contact you and your child to arrange a meeting to confirm your consent and to identify priorities for the coaching sessions. The first session may last 1 to 2 hours to facilitate collection of information about your child and their goals. Subsequent coaching appointments will be arranged at mutually agreed-upon times with an approximate frequency of one to two meetings per week. Meetings may be online or in-person as mutually agreed.

Coaching is most effective when the student is engaged and motivated. Thus, the focus of coaching will involve goals that are determined and agreed to by the student. While the coach is committed to helping students to develop executive functioning skills, particular improvements or results cannot be guaranteed.

While the coaching session may include completion of questionnaires to obtain information about your child, *coaching does not involve assessment of academic or cognitive abilities* (i.e., a psychoeducational assessment). If you are seeking information about your child's current academic skills, you should discuss this with your child's teacher.

3. What should I know about the use of technology during the assessment?

As part of the coaching program, your child and the coach will track progress toward goals using web-based software on servers in Canada and/or the United States of America. Information stored in Canada is subject to Canadian laws (i.e., Freedom of Information and Protection of Privacy Act [FOIPPA] and Personal Information Protection Act [PIPA]). Information stored in the United States is subject to US Freedom of Information laws (i.e., USA Freedom of Information Act [FOIA] and the Children's Online Privacy Protection Act [COPPA]). Please note: *Procedures to protect the confidentiality of this information are followed to the level possible, such as providing identification numbers or initials for your child's name and using passwords to protect the information.*

4. How is information communicated, and what are the implications of using electronic communication?

Communication may be in person, by telephone, email, or using online video conferencing software. Similarly, communication regarding your child may also occur with other school district staff, in person, or through electronic methods. Any information shared will be done so in accordance with school district guidelines for protection of personal information (e.g., using equipment and applications that are deemed by the school district to be compliant with federal and provincial privacy regulations). While every effort is made to protect personal privacy, when personal information is shared via electronic communication there are risks to personal privacy during transmission and storage.

(continued)

If you choose to use technology for meetings or to download or store information, you are responsible for the security of your own equipment, email service, internet server, and cellular phone. If documents or personal information are shared electronically via email they should be in a password-protected attachment. Similarly, if you wish to email confidential information to the school psychologist, a password-protected process may be arranged. *Video or audio conversations shall not be recorded unless agreed by all involved.* All email documents that you send to the school psychologist will be maintained in your child's coaching file.

5. What will happen to the information from the coaching sessions?

Every effort will be made to respect the privacy of the information that is shared by the family and student during the coaching process. Student records and documentation of the coaching sessions will be maintained by the coach in accordance with district policy, the School Act, the Freedom of Information and Protection of Privacy Act, and other applicable legislation. All information is confidential and is only available to school district personnel unless required by law (see section 6 below). With your signed consent, or at your written request, the school psychologist may assist in sharing your child's report with other professionals (e.g., pediatrician, behavior consultant) outside the school district.

6. What are the legal reasons for disclosing confidential information?

There are cases when the law requires that information be disclosed.

a) In the interest of safety, the school psychologist has a duty to report suspicion that a child may harm themselves or other(s) or if a child has been or is likely to be abused or neglected and the parent is unwilling or unable to protect the child.

b) Legal obligations may include responding to a valid subpoena or court order.

c) Public health authorities may require information in relation to tracing or managing illness outbreaks.

d) In accordance with school district regulations and procedures, a student's record may be disclosed to a government representative (e.g., Ministry of Children and Family Development, Health or the Attorney General) that is planning the delivery of, or providing, health services, social services, or other support services to the student.

e) The Motor-Vehicle Act requires a registered psychologist to report if a client (student) has a medical condition that endangers oneself or the public and continues to drive after being warned of the danger.

7. What if I have questions or concerns about the coaching, or I change my mind?

If you have any questions or concerns about this process, please contact the coach directly. Coaching is voluntary and you have the right to withdraw consent for any reason.

8. What if I have concerns regarding behavior of the coach?

The school psychologist is required to abide by a code of ethical conduct. If you feel that a school psychologist has acted unethically or unprofessionally, you may try to resolve the problem with (a) the school psychologist, (b) the director of instruction or designate, (c) the district superintendent's office, or (d) by filing a formal complaint with a regulatory/certifying body. You may learn more about the ethical codes of conduct at the following websites: *www.collegeofpsychologists.bc.ca* or *www.bcasp.ca/standards*.

(continued)

Consent for Services: Executive Functioning Coaching *(page 3 of 3)*

Statement of Consent:

_____   _____
Student Name (Print)   Date of Birth

☐ I am the parent/legal guardian of this child and I have the responsibility of making educational decisions for this child. All authorized parents/legal guardians have reviewed and understand the information contained in this document and have signed below.

☐ I am aware of the nature and purpose of the coaching program, the risks and benefits as well as how information is communicated and stored. I feel that the explanation has been relayed in a language that is understandable to me, and that I have had the opportunity to ask questions or raise any concerns regarding this assessment.

I, therefore, voluntarily give consent for my child to participate in the coaching program at this time. This consent is valid for one year from the date it is signed.

1. _____   _____   _____
   Parent/Legal Guardian Name (Print)   Signature   Date

2. _____   _____   _____
   Parent/Legal Guardian Name (Print)   Signature   Date

_____
Signature of Student

OFFICE USE ONLY
Date of meeting with school psychologist:
School psychologist's signature:
Password for email communication (optional):
Person providing language interpretation if required:

Model of an Independent Coaching Contract

EXECUTIVE FUNCTION COACHING
POLICIES AND PROCEDURES AGREEMENT
Lisa Kennedy, MA, LMFT
Executive Function Coach

I am delighted to be working with your student and family. This Coaching Policies and Procedures Agreement will offer some further information on how the flow of coaching works. Please don't hesitate to ask as many questions as you need to ensure clarification.

The Initial Consultation

Our first consultation will be a complimentary 20-minute phone consultation and will include information gathering, paperwork, and assessments.

The Kickoff Meeting

Following the initial consultation, I will schedule our kickoff meeting, which will be a 60-minute Zoom session in which we will discuss Executive Function Strengths and Weaknesses, review how the flow of coaching works, and begin establishing rapport with the student. I recommend that the parents are present at this first meeting, if possible. Prior to the kickoff meeting, I will review any testing and reports as well as the paperwork that you fill out and send back to me. *Please note that I do not make a formal DSM diagnosis and will be happy to recommend a more thorough assessment via an educational psychologist or a local college/university.*

Weekly Ongoing Sessions

Following the kickoff meeting, we will begin meeting weekly. My standard practice is to offer one, 40-minute Zoom session per week and a 20-minute Zoom check-in between our 40-minute sessions. *This can be altered and we can work together on what works best for you.* In general, the more frequently we can have check-ins, the more growth that is possible in the students/adults. Check-ins create continuity between sessions. We can even change check-ins to texting updates as needed to fit the schedule of the student/family.

Canceled/Missed Appointments

24-hour notice is required if an appointment is going to be canceled or missed. Appointments canceled outside of the 24-hour notice period or missed appointments will be charged at the full session fee. I may offer *occasional complimentary* telephone calls lasting 10 minutes or less at my discretion. Frequent phone calls or calls that last longer than 10 minutes will be billed at a prorated amount based on the regular weekly fee.

(continued)

Model of an Independent Coaching Contract *(page 2 of 2)*

Confidentiality

Any information, written or verbal, shared by you during the course of your coaching will constitute confidential information (the "Confidential Information"). I will use Confidential Information solely for coaching purposes and for no other purpose. I will not disclose, use, or publish any Confidential Information, except as required to provide the services in accordance with this Agreement, by operation of law, if I believe that disclosure is necessary to protect me, you, or any other individual from harm, or as otherwise authorized by you in writing.

I am a mandated reporter and must notify the appropriate authorities in any of the following situations:

- If you threaten to harm an identifiable person, that information has to be revealed to the police and to the person or persons against whom the threat has been made.
- If you threaten to hurt yourself and I believe that you have the means to carry out this threat, that information has to be revealed to the local mental health authority.
- If abuse of a child is revealed in session, that information has to be revealed to child protective services.
- If abuse of an elder (age 65 and up) or dependent adult is revealed in session, that information has to be revealed to elder/dependent adult protective services.

I look forward to working with you. If you understand and agree to these policies and procedures, please sign below.

By signing below, you represent and warrant that you are the authorized legal guardian of the student named below.

Signature _____

Print Name: _____

Authorized Legal Guardian of: _____

Date _____

Goal-Planning Template

What do you want to work on through this coaching process?

Possible goals
1.
2.
3.
4.

Select one of the goals listed above and put an asterisk next to it.

If the goal you've selected is ambitious or vague, what is a reasonable place to start? For example, if you've decided you want to bring up all your grades, you might choose one or two classes to focus on first. If you're behind in all your subjects and want to hand in all your missing assignments, where might you start? If you want to start handing in all your homework on time, but at present you only hand in 1–2 assignments per week, could you choose one subject to start with?

This is where I want to start:

If you're going to do this successfully, what will you need to do? It may help you to think about what you need to do differently than you've done in the past. This might include things like doing homework more consistently, handing homework in on time, bringing test grades up (e.g., by changing how or how much you study), starting assignments early enough so that you'll have time to proofread or revise them, keeping track of assignments better, taking notes in class, keeping notebooks better organized, making and following a plan for long-term assignments, getting more help with difficult subjects, figuring out how to avoid temptations that get in the way of you reaching your goal.

I am likely to meet my goal if I:

(continued)

What are some of the potential obstacles that might prevent you from reaching your goal? How can those obstacles be overcome or avoided?

Potential obstacle	Ways to overcome the obstacle
1.	
2.	
3.	
4.	

What help do you need to achieve your goal? This might include classroom modifications, assistance from teachers, parents, or a "coach," or additional help in the resource room or from a tutor.

Creating a SMART Goal

SMART Goal Planner		
Specific	What EXACTLY do you want to happen?	
Measurable	I will know I have reached my goal when . . .	
Attainable	Can I reach my goal by the deadline?	How confident am I that I can reach my goal? 1　　2　　3　　4　　5 Not very　　So-so　　Very!
Relevant	Is this goal important to me?	How important is it to me to reach my goal? 1　　2　　3　　4　　5 Not very　　So-so　　Very!
Time-bound	I will reach my goal by:	

(continued)

Goal-Planning Template *(page 3 of 3)*

Action Plan for Achieving SMART Goal

Steps to follow to complete goal	Target completion date	Done!
1.		
2.		
3.		
4.		
5.		

Action Plan Follow-Up

Did you follow the plan?	☐ Yes	☐ Partially	☐ No
What worked well?			
What didn't work so well?			
What's the next step?	☐ Continue plan	☐ Revise plan	☐ Make new SMART goal

Daily Coaching Form

DATE: _____

GOAL I'M WORKING ON NOW:

SNAPSHOT:

1. **How are things going?**

1	2	3	4	5	6	7

Things are really difficult   Things are going really well

2. **Is there anything you'd like to talk with your coach about?**

ACTION PLANNING

THE BIG PICTURE:

Upcoming tests/quizzes:		Long-term assignments:		Other responsibilities:	
Subject:	Date:	Assignment:	Date:	Task	Date/Time:
_____	_____	_____	_____	_____	_____
_____	_____	_____	_____	_____	_____
_____	_____	_____	_____	_____	_____
_____	_____	_____	_____	_____	_____
_____	_____	_____	_____	_____	_____

TODAY'S PLANS: (include homework assignments as well as any work to be done on long-term projects or studying for tests)

LOOKING BACK:

What are you going to do?	When will you do it?	Did you do it?	How did it go?*
1. _____	1. _____	Yes No	1 2 3 4 5
2. _____	2. _____	Yes No	1 2 3 4 5
3. _____	3. _____	Yes No	1 2 3 4 5

(continued)

4. _____ 4. _____ Yes No   1 2 3 4 5

5. _____ 5. _____ Yes No   1 2 3 4 5

*Use this scale to evaluate: 1—Not well at all; 2—So-so; 3—Average; 4—Very well; 5—Excellent

THINGS I NEED TO REMEMBER (check off when taken care of)   **OTHER NOTES:**

1. _____ _____

2. _____ _____

3. _____ _____

4. _____ _____

5. _____ _____

Coach Feedback Form—Student Version

Tell us how much you agree or disagree with the following statements, using the following scale:

5—Strongly agree

4—Somewhat agree

3—Not sure

2—Somewhat disagree

1—Strongly disagree

Compared with before I started coaching, I . . .

1. Completed more of my homework assignments.	5	4	3	2	1
2. Handed in more of my homework assignments on time.	5	4	3	2	1
3. Spent more time studying for tests.	5	4	3	2	1
4. Got better grades on tests/quizzes.	5	4	3	2	1
5. Got better grades on homework assignments.	5	4	3	2	1
6. Managed long-term assignments better (e.g., not leaving them until last minute).	5	4	3	2	1
7. Got fewer detentions or other discipline referrals.	5	4	3	2	1
8. Was less likely to get in trouble in class or other school settings.	5	4	3	2	1

Tell us how helpful the different coaching components were, using the following scale:

4—Very helpful

3—Somewhat helpful

2—Not sure

1—Not helpful

1. Daily (or regular) contact with my coach.	4	3	2	1
2. Setting daily goals.	4	3	2	1
3. Talking about whether I met my goals (reviewing the daily plans).	4	3	2	1
4. Making daily work plans.	4	3	2	1
5. Having my coach remind me of things I might have forgotten.	4	3	2	1
6. Getting help from my coach to solve academic or social problems.	4	3	2	1
7. Getting tips from coach on specific strategies (e.g., how to study for tests, write papers, manage time).	4	3	2	1
8. Having my coach check with my teachers to make sure I was on track.	4	3	2	1
9. Having my coach listen to me vent about school problems.	4	3	2	1

(continued)

What worked best about coaching?

How could coaching be improved?

Other comments:

Coach Feedback Form—Coach Version

Tell us how much you agree or disagree with the following statements, using the following scale:

5—Strongly agree

4—Somewhat agree

3—Not sure

2—Somewhat disagree

1—Strongly disagree

Coaching helped this student . . .

1. Complete homework assignments.	5 4 3 2 1
2. Hand in homework assignments on time.	5 4 3 2 1
3. Spend time studying for tests.	5 4 3 2 1
4. Get better grades on tests/quizzes.	5 4 3 2 1
5. Get better grades on homework assignments.	5 4 3 2 1
6. Manage long-term assignments (e.g., not leaving them until last minute).	5 4 3 2 1
7. Avoid detentions or other discipline referrals.	5 4 3 2 1
8. Avoid getting in trouble in class or other school settings.	5 4 3 2 1

Tell us how helpful you feel the different coaching components were for this student, using the following scale:

4—Very helpful

3—Somewhat helpful

2—Not sure

1—Not helpful

1. Daily (or regular) contact with the coach.	4 3 2 1
2. Setting daily goals.	4 3 2 1
3. Talking about whether the student met goals (review the daily plans).	4 3 2 1
4. Making daily work plans.	4 3 2 1
5. Having the coach remind the student of things that might have been forgotten.	4 3 2 1
6. Helping the student solve academic or social problems.	4 3 2 1
7. Providing tips on specific strategies (e.g., how to study for tests, write papers, manage time).	4 3 2 1
8. Checking with teachers to make sure the student was on track.	4 3 2 1
9. Listening to the student vent about school problems.	4 3 2 1

(continued)

What worked best about coaching?

How could coaching be improved?

Other comments:

Executive Skills Questionnaire for Children—
Preschool/Kindergarten Version

Read each item below and then rate that item based on how well it describes your child. Then add the three scores in each section. Find the three highest and three lowest scores.

Strongly agree	5
Agree	4
Neutral	3
Disagree	2
Strongly disagree	1

Score

1. Acts appropriately in some situations where danger is obvious (e.g., avoiding hot stove). _____
2. Can share toys without grabbing. _____
3. Can wait for a short period of time when instructed by an adult. _____

TOTAL SCORE: _____

4. Runs simple errands (e.g., gets shoes from bedroom when asked). _____
5. Remembers instructions just given. _____
6. Follows two steps of a routine with only one prompt per step. _____

TOTAL SCORE: _____

7. Can recover fairly quickly from a disappointment or change in plans. _____
8. Is able to use nonphysical solutions when another child takes toy away. _____
9. Can play in a group without becoming overly excited. _____

TOTAL SCORE: _____

10. Can complete a 5-minute chore (may need supervision). _____
11. Can sit through preschool "circle time" (15–20 minutes). _____
12. Can listen to one to two stories at a sitting. _____

TOTAL SCORE: _____

13. Will follow an adult directive right after it is given. _____
14. Will stop playing to follow an adult instruction when directed. _____
15. Is able to start getting ready for bed at set time with one reminder. _____

TOTAL SCORE: _____

16. Can finish one task or activity before beginning another. _____
17. Is able to follow a brief routine or plan developed by someone else (with model or demo). _____
18. Can complete a simple art project with more than one step. _____

TOTAL SCORE: _____

(continued)

Score

19. Hangs up coat in appropriate place (may need one reminder). _____

20. Puts toys in proper locations (with reminders). _____

21. Clears off place setting after eating (may need one reminder). _____

TOTAL SCORE: _____

22. Can complete daily routines without dawdling (with some cues/reminders). _____

23. Can speed up and finish something more quickly when given a reason to do so. _____

24. Can finish a small chore within time limits (e.g., make bed before turning on TV). _____

TOTAL SCORE: _____

25. Will direct other children in play or pretend play activities. _____

26. Will seek assistance in conflict resolution for a desired item. _____

27. Will try more than one solution to get to a simple goal. _____

TOTAL SCORE: _____

28. Is able to adjust to change in plans or routines (may need warning). _____

29. Recovers quickly from minor disappointments. _____

30. Is willing to share toys with others. _____

TOTAL SCORE: _____

31. Can make minor adjustment in construction project or puzzle when first attempt fails. _____

32. Can find novel (but simple) use of a tool to solve a problem. _____

33. Makes suggestions to another child for how to fix something. _____

TOTAL SCORE: _____

KEY			
Items	Executive Skill	Items	Executive Skill
1–3	Response inhibition	4–6	Working memory
7–9	Emotional control	10–12	Sustained attention
13–15	Task initiation	16–18	Planning/prioritization
19–21	Organization	22–24	Time management
25–27	Goal-directed persistence	28–30	Flexibility
31–33	Metacognition		

Your child's executive skills strengths
(highest scores)

_____

_____

_____

Your child's executive skills weaknesses
(lowest scores)

_____

_____

_____

Executive Skills Questionnaire for Children—
Lower Elementary Version

Read each item below and then rate that item based on how well it describes the child. Then add the three scores in each section. Find the three highest and three lowest scores

Strongly agree	5
Agree	4
Neutral	3
Disagree	2
Strongly disagree	1

Item   Score

1. Can follow simple classroom rules. _____

2. Can be in close proximity to another child without need for physical contact. _____

3. Can wait until teacher finishes with another student before asking/telling them something (may need one reminder). _____

Total Score: _____

4. Is able to run a school errand with 2–3 steps. _____

5. Remembers instructions given a couple of minutes earlier. _____

6. Follows two steps of a routine with one prompt. _____

Total Score: _____

7. Can tolerate criticism from an adult. _____

8. Can deal with perceived "unfairness" without undue upset. _____

9. Is able to adjust behavior quickly in new situation (e.g., calming down after recess). _____

_____

10. Can spend 10–15 minutes on independent classwork. _____

11. Can complete a school chore that takes 10–15 minutes. _____

12. Can sit through lunch at school. _____

Total Score: _____

13. Can remember and follow simple 1- and 2-step routines (e.g., hang up your coat and sit at circle). _____

14. Can get right to work on classroom assignment following teacher instruction to begin. _____

15. Almost always hands in homework on time. _____

Total Score: _____

16. Can carry out a 2- to 3-step project of own design (e.g., arts and crafts, construction). _____

17. Can figure out how to use free time. _____

18. Can carry out 2- to 3-step in-class assignment with support. _____

Total Score: _____

(continued)

Item

19. Puts coat, backpack, work materials in proper location (may need reminders). _____

20. Puts personal belongings in designated location (e.g., cubby, locker). _____

21. Doesn't lose permission slips, notices from school. _____

Total Score: _____

22. Can complete a short task within time limits set by an adult. _____

23. Can build in appropriate amount of time to complete a classroom chore before deadline. _____

24. Can complete a morning routine within time limits (may need practice). _____

Total Score: _____

25. Will stick with challenging task to achieve desired goal (e.g., building difficult LEGO construct. _____

26. Will come back to a task later if interrupted. _____

27. Will work on a desired project for several hours or over several days. _____

Total Score: _____

28. Plays well with others (doesn't need to be in charge, can share, etc.). _____

29. Tolerates redirection by teacher when not following instructions. _____

30. Adjusts easily to unplanned-for situations (e.g., substitute teacher). _____

Total Score: _____

31. Can adjust behavior in response to feedback from parent or teacher. _____

32. Can watch what happens to others and change behavior accordingly. _____

33. Can verbalize more than one solution to a problem and make the best choice. _____

Total Score: _____

KEY			
Items	Executive Skill	Items	Executive Skill
1–3	Response inhibition	4–6	Working memory
7–9	Emotional control	10–12	Sustained attention
13–15	Task initiation	16–18	Planning/prioritization
19–21	Organization	22–24	Time management
25–27	Goal-directed persistence	28–30	Flexibility
31–33	Metacognition		

Child's executive skill strengths

_____
_____
_____

Child's executive skills challenges

_____
_____
_____

Executive Skills Questionnaire for Children— Upper Elementary Version

Read each item below and then rate that item based on how well it describes your child. Then add the three scores in each section. Find the three highest and three lowest scores.

Strongly agree	5
Agree	4
Neutral	3
Disagree	2
Strongly disagree	1

Item   Score

1. Handles conflict with peer without getting into physical fight (may lose temper).   _____

2. Follows home or school rules in the absence of an adult's immediate presence.   _____

3. Can calm down or de-escalate quickly from an emotionally charged situation when prompted by an adult.   _____

Total Score: _____

4. Remembers to follow a routine chore after school without reminders.   _____

5. Brings books, papers, assignments to and from school.   _____

6. Keeps track of changing daily schedule (e.g., different activities after school).   _____

Total Score: _____

7. Doesn't overreact to losing a game or not being selected for an award.   _____

8. Can accept not getting what they want when working/playing in a group.   _____

9. Acts with restraint in response to teasing.   _____

Total Score: _____

10. Can spend 30–60 minutes on homework assignments.   _____

11. Can complete a chore that takes 30–60 minutes (may need a break).   _____

12. Is able to attend sports practice, church service, etc., for 60–90 minutes.   _____

Total Score: _____

13. Is able to follow a 3- to 4-step routine that has been practiced.   _____

14. Can complete 3 to 4 classroom assignments in a row.   _____

15. Can follow established homework schedule (may need reminder to get started).   _____

Total Score: _____

16. Can make plans to do something special with a friend (e.g., go to movies).   _____

17. Can figure out how to earn/save money for a more expensive purchase.   _____

18. Can carry out long-term project for school, with most steps broken down by someone else.   _____

Total Score: _____

(continued)

Item   Score

19. Can put belongings in appropriate places in bedroom or other locations in house.   _____

20. Brings in toys from outdoors after use or at end of day (may need reminder).   _____

21. Keeps track of homework materials and assignments.   _____

                                                                         Total Score: _____

22. Can complete daily routines within reasonable time limits without assistance.   _____

23. Can adjust homework schedule to allow for other activities (e.g., starting early if there's an evening Scout meeting).   _____

24. Is able to start long-term projects enough in advance to reduce time crunch (may need help with this).   _____

                                                                         Total Score: _____

25. Can save allowance for 3–4 weeks to make a desired purchase.   _____

26. Is able to follow a practice schedule to get better at a desired skill (sport, instrument)—may need reminders.   _____

27. Can maintain a hobby over several months.   _____

                                                                         Total Score: _____

28. Doesn't "get stuck" on things (e.g., disappointments, slights).   _____

29. Can "shift gears" when plans have to change due to unforeseen circumstances.   _____

30. Can do "open-ended" homework assignments (may need assistance).   _____

                                                                         Total Score: _____

31. Is able to anticipate in advance the result of a course of action and make adjustments accordingly (e.g., to avoid getting in trouble).   _____

32. Can articulate several solutions to problems and explain the best one.   _____

33. Enjoys the problem-solving component of school assignment or video games.   _____

                                                                         Total Score: _____

KEY			
Items	Executive Skill	Items	Executive Skill
1–3	Response inhibition	4–6	Working memory
7–9	Emotional control	10–12	Sustained attention
13–15	Task initiation	16–18	Planning/prioritization
19–21	Organization	22–24	Time management
25–27	Goal-directed persistence	28–30	Flexibility
31–33	Metacognition		

Your child's executive skills strengths
(highest scores)

_____

_____

_____

Your child's executive skills weaknesses
(lowest scores)

_____

_____

_____

Executive Skills Problem Checklist—Elementary Version for Teachers

Directions:

1. Read each item and decide whether the student in question exhibits this problem *to a significantly greater degree* than other children in the same grade level.
2. Look over all the items you checked and choose THREE that you think cause the greatest problems. Place a star (★) next to those.

Response Inhibition

_____ Blurts out inappropriate comments

_____ In a teacher-directed activity, does not wait until the person talking finishes and is acknowledged by the teacher before offering a response

_____ Can't wait turn in games

_____ Does not use acceptable language to handle conflict situations

_____ Does not remain at their seat or assigned area during seatwork time and classroom lessons

_____ Does not complete seatwork or assignments accurately

Working Memory

_____ Doesn't write down all homework in assignment books or other designated location

_____ Doesn't bring all necessary materials to and from school every day (e.g., homework, notebooks/binders, permission slips, gym clothes, lunch money, coats/hats/mittens)

_____ Doesn't hand in assignments on the dates they are due

_____ Doesn't remember where to find all necessary materials to get through the school day and to complete homework

_____ Doesn't follow all instructions accurately for multistep tasks by using checklists or rubrics, if necessary

Emotional Control

_____ Leaves class or becomes visibly upset rather than asking for help when they don't understand an assignment

_____ Engages in verbal or physical aggression or unsafe behavior when playing with other students at recess

_____ Doesn't use coping strategies to recover when they begin to get upset (or angry, frustrated, anxious)

(continued)

_____ Anxiety interferes with test performance

_____ Anxiety interferes with classroom presentations

_____ Becomes very upset or responds with verbal or physical aggression when teased or taunted by other students

Flexibility

_____ Becomes very upset when confronted with the unexpected (e.g., changes in plans or routines, disappointment, being told "no")

_____ Has difficulty managing transitions between activities or settings

_____ Is unable to come up with one or more alternative plans or solutions when the first strategy doesn't work (no Plan B)

_____ Is unable to complete open-ended tasks successfully according to the rubric assigned

Sustained Attention

_____ Doesn't complete classwork and homework within the time allotted or within suggested time frames

_____ Loses focus on class lessons (as demonstrated by not being able to answer questions related to the content of the lesson or by not understanding assignments associated with the lesson)

Task Initiation

_____ Has difficulty starting class assignments within 3 minutes of the prompt to begin working

_____ Stretches out breaks and fails to return to work promptly with longer or less preferred work tasks

Planning/Prioritization

_____ Has difficulty setting priorities (in what order to do tasks, how much time to spend on any given task)

_____ Doesn't know what to focus on when studying for tests

_____ Writing does not follow a logical sequence; paragraphs don't contain main ideas and supporting details

Organization

_____ Does not place materials in a specified place in notebooks, backpack, desk, and study area

_____ Does not follow an organizational system with consistency (e.g., throwing out unnecessary papers, placing homework assignments in assigned spot, organizing papers for each subject separately)

_____ Does not have a tidy study area

(continued)

184

Time Management

_____ Does not complete assignments within the time allotted or by the due date

_____ Can't adjust work speed to fit the time available

Goal-Directed Persistence

_____ Does not persist with effortful tasks

_____ Gives up in the face of an obstacle

_____ Has a "good-enough" mentality that gets in the way of producing quality work

Metacognition

_____ Cannot judge the quality of their own work

_____ Does not know how to improve work

_____ Has difficulty making inferences, drawing conclusions, grasping the main idea, reading between the lines

_____ Fails to check work/proofread/use spell-check

APPENDIX 17

Executive Skills Problem Checklist—Elementary Version for Parents

Directions:

1. Read each item and decide whether your child exhibits this problem *to a significant degree* such that it interferes with daily life at home. Keep in mind that some of the items may not be age appropriate for your child.

2. Look over all the items you checked and choose THREE that you think cause the greatest problems. Place a star (★) next to those.

Response Inhibition

_____ Interrupts when others are talking

_____ Blurts out inappropriate comments

_____ Can't wait turn in games or conversations

_____ Doesn't use acceptable language to handle conflict situations

_____ Doesn't consider consequences before acting

_____ Rushes through homework or chores without regard to quality of work

Working Memory

_____ Can't remember short instructions even right after they're given

_____ Does not bring all necessary materials to and from school every day (e.g., homework, notebooks/binders, permission slips, gym clothes, lunch money, coats/hats/mittens)

_____ Has trouble keeping track of schedule when it changes from day to day

_____ Doesn't remember things necessary for activities outside the home (e.g., sports equipment)

_____ Doesn't remember to do chores, even when they follow a consistent schedule

Emotional Control

_____ Becomes easily upset over small things that would not bother others

_____ Engages in verbal or physical aggression when angry

_____ Fails to use coping strategies to recover when they begin to get upset (or angry, frustrated, anxious)

_____ Overreacts when provoked by things people say or do to them

_____ Gets "revved up" in some situations (e.g., social gatherings) and has trouble calming down

_____ Has trouble dealing with disappointment, such as losing at a game or not getting what they want

(continued)

Flexibility

_____ Doesn't use coping strategies to recover when they begin to get upset (or angry, frustrated, anxious)

_____ Has difficulty managing transitions between activities or settings

_____ Can't do open-ended homework assignments (e.g., using each spelling word in a sentence or doing a creative writing assignment)

_____ Is unable to come up with one or more alternative plans or solutions when the first strategy doesn't work (no Plan B)

_____ Gets stuck or fixated on certain thoughts or ideas

Sustained Attention

_____ Doesn't complete homework or chores within the time allotted or within suggested time frames

_____ Gets up and down during homework—difficulty sticking with it long enough to get it done

_____ Doesn't listen when parents or other adults are talking to them

_____ Shifts quickly from one play activity to another

_____ Doesn't stay focused when engaged in organized activities (e.g., sports)

Task Initiation

_____ Doesn't perform daily routines at scheduled times unless prompted

_____ Leaves homework or chores until the last minute unless prompted by an adult

_____ Finds other things to do rather than chores, homework, and daily routines

_____ Stretches out breaks and fails to return to work promptly with longer work tasks

_____ Dawdles when asked to do a chore, perform a boring daily routine, or switch from a preferred to a nonpreferred activity

Planning/Prioritization

_____ Has difficulty setting priorities (in what order to do tasks, how much time to spend on any given task)

_____ Can't make a plan to accomplish a task (even when it's something they want to do)

_____ Gets sidetracked when following a plan and doesn't get back to it

_____ Doesn't know what to focus on when studying for tests

_____ Can't break down a task into individual steps (what to do first, second, etc.)

(continued)

Organization

_____ Doesn't hang up coat/put belongings away in designated place

_____ Doesn't place materials in a specified place in notebooks, backpack, desk, and study area

_____ Doesn't follow an organizational system with consistency (e.g., throwing out unnecessary papers, placing homework assignments in assigned spot, organizing school papers)

_____ Doesn't have a tidy study area to work at

_____ Bedroom and play spaces are a mess and this doesn't bother them

Time Management

_____ Does not arrive places on time (e.g., coming home from friend's house at agreed-upon time)

_____ Can't complete daily routines within time limits

_____ Does not complete assignments by the due date

_____ Can't adjust work speed to fit the time available

_____ Can't juggle multiple time demands (e.g., starting homework early on days when child has evening Scout meetings)

Goal-Directed Persistence

_____ Does not persist with effortful tasks

_____ Gives up in the face of an obstacle

_____ Starts projects but doesn't finish them (including preferred activities)

_____ Wants to quit rather than do the work to get better at something

_____ Has a "good-enough" mentality that gets in the way of producing quality work

_____ Can't save up money to make a desired purchase

Metacognition

_____ Can't judge the quality of their own work

_____ Does not know how to improve work

_____ Can't solve everyday problems

_____ Has difficulty making inferences, drawing conclusions, grasping the main idea, reading between the lines

_____ Can't read or misinterprets the emotions or reactions of others

_____ Fails to check work/proofread

Basic Self-Assessment

Techniques	Check off if used (✓)	Examples
Open-ended questions/statements		
Affirmations		
Reflections		
Summaries		
Asking permission		
Cognitive rehearsal methods		
Closed-ended/ directive statements*		
What was my best moment during the session?		
Next session I would like to:		

*For this question, consider these questions: Could I have rephrased this? Could I have asked permission? or Did I really need to make this point at all?

Advanced Self-Assessment Score Sheet

1	2	3	4	5	6	7	8	9	10	11	12	13	14	15
16	17	18	19	20	21	22	23	24	25	26	27	28	29	30
31	32	33	34	35	36	37	38	39	40	41	42	43	44	45
46	47	48	49	50	51	52	53	54	55	56	57	58	59	60

O = Open-Ended Question	C = Closed-Ended Question	A = Affirmation	S = Summary
CR = Cognitive Rehearsal	R = Reflection	P = Permission	DSI = Directive Statement

Motivational Interviewing Resources

Motivational Interviewing Network of Trainers (MINT): *https://motivationalinterviewing.org*

Health Education and Training Institute (HETI): *www.hetimaine.org*

Brier, N. M. (2015). *Enhancing self-control in adolescents: Treatment strategies derived from psychological science.* Routledge/Taylor & Francis Group.

Herman, K. C., Reinke, W. M., Frey, A. J., & Shepard, S. A. (2014). *Motivational interviewing in schools.* Springer.

Miller, W. R., & Rollnick, S. (2012). *Motivational interviewing: Helping people change* (3rd edition). Guilford Press.

Naar, S., & Suarez, M. (2021). *Motivational interviewing with adolescents and young adults* (2nd ed.). Guilford Press.

North, R. A. (2017). *Motivational interviewing for school counselors.* Self-published.

Rollnick, S., Kaplan, S. G., & Rutschman, R. (2016). *Motivational interviewing in schools: Conversations to improve behavior and learning.* Guilford Press.

Terry, J., Smith, B., Strait, G., & McQuillin, S. (2013). Motivational Interviewing to improve middle school students' academic performance: A replication study. *Journal of Community Psychology, 41*(7), 902–909.

YouTube: Search for "Motivational Interviewing."

Environmental Modifications Menu

Strategy	Examples (check off ✓ choices)
Change the physical or social environment	☐ Remove distractions (e.g., turn off social media) ☐ Create visual reminders ☐ Avoid settings with temptations ☐ Seek out people who support your goal; avoid people who don't ☐ Other: _____
Modify the task	☐ Make task shorter/build in breaks ☐ Use 1–10 scale to adjust effort ☐ Pair unpleasant task with something pleasant ☐ Kill two birds with one stone (pair unpleasant task with another obligation) ☐ Break task into very small pieces and turn into a to-do checklist ☐ Use technology ☐ Turn open-ended tasks into closed-ended tasks ☐ Build in variety or choice (or turn into a game) ☐ Other: _____
Enlist the help of others	☐ Someone to cue you: _____ ☐ Someone to report to: _____ ☐ Someone who will be a cheerleader: _____ ☐ Post goal/progress on social media ☐ Other: _____

Example of Elaborate Incentive System

John was an eighth grader whose goal was to improve his report card grades. The coach and the student identified a number of behaviors that were affecting his ability to earn the grades he wanted, including not writing down homework assignments, failing to turn in homework on time, producing poor-quality work, and not studying for tests. The reward John wanted to work for was a new smartphone, which his parents were willing to give him if he improved his academic performance. Specific behaviors were identified, with point values assigned to each one (based on effort and frequency). A chart was created and every Saturday, John and his mother filled in the chart. The chart allowed John to see weekly as well as cumulative point totals so that he had a clear picture of how close he was to earning the smartphone. Since a smartphone is expensive, points were allotted to make it likely that John would have to work for a full marking period in order to earn the reward. Figure 1 outlines the point system developed with John, and Figure 2 (on p. 194) depicts the chart created to help him track his progress.

Point category	Points earned
All homework handed in for the week	15
Homework done well (at least 80% accuracy)	3 per assignment
All homework recorded in assignment book	1 for each day (max. 5)
Grades on tests/quizzes/projects/long-term assignments B– (80–82) B (83–85) B+ (86–89) A– (90–92) A (93–95) A+ (96–100)	5 10 15 20 25 30
Number of points needed to earn smartphone: 500	

FIGURE 1

POINT CHART

Goal: 500

Week	Dates	HW handed in	HW quality	Agenda book completed	Grades on Tests/Quizzes/Papers/Projects (use / marks to tally assignment grades for the week)							Weekly point total	Cumulative total
					B− (80–82)	B (83–86)	B+ (87–89)	A− (90–92)	A (93–96)	A+ (94–99)			
1													
2													
3													
4													
5													
6													
7													
8													
9													
10													

FIGURE 2

Strategies for Specific Executive Skills

Executive skill	Possible strategies
Response inhibition	• Post home or classroom rules and review regularly • Arrange for *in vivo* practice or behavioral rehearsal • Wristband reminder (e.g., to raise hand to talk) • Talking stick (cue to talk) • Sticky notes to write something down rather than interrupting • Sit near teacher • Prompts in advance about expected behavior • Visual cue on desk to remind student to work quietly • Help student build in technology breaks rather than combining homework with technology use
Working memory	• To-do lists (paper, whiteboard to post prominently) • Colored wristbands to remind student of homework assignments • Sticky note reminders • Laminated lists (e.g., by door at home or on inside of locker door) to remind kids what they need to take with them • Songs and rhymes as memory aids • Ask student what cues work for them (e.g., how they might use smartphone to provide cues) • Teach principle of "off-loading" **Off-loading:** This refers to the idea that the brain doesn't have to work as hard when you can find a way to "off-load" some of the tasks we're asking it to do. Examples: The brain doesn't have to allot space to remembering homework assignments when we write them down. It doesn't have to work at remembering something we have to do after school if we build an alarm into our smartphone to remind us.
Emotional control	• Help student write a script to follow • Have a "cooling-off" space • Prepare student by asking them to predict what will happen/ how they will handle it • Review expectations in advance • Teach students to label emotions • Teach kids: "respond don't react" • Teach kids to recognize situations or early signs • Teach coping strategy • Rehearse the strategy repeatedly until it is internalized • Teach mindfulness meditation • Self-talk to plan in advance (*if–then: "If* this happens, *then* I will . . .")
Flexibility	• "Normalize" errors • Preview changes in schedule • Praise kids for being flexible • Role-play handling situations that require flexibility • Use language to showcase flexibility (stuck/unstuck; big deal/ little deal; Plan B) • Create a "Do It Later" folder (for kids who have trouble leaving a task undone)

(continued)

Strategies for Specific Executive Skills *(page 2 of 3)*

Executive skill	Possible strategies
Sustained attention	• Reduce distractions (seating arrangements, white noise) • Modify/limit task length or demand (end in sight) • Build in variety/choice • Help student choose best time of day to work on effortful tasks • Use fidget toys such as stress balls • Movement breaks • Wiggle cushions/study carrels; dead headphones; listen to iPod; quiet desk/noisy desk/standing desk; "theraband" on front two legs of chair to allow movement • Time timer (make time visible) • Sand timer (real or app) • Identify distractors and figure out how to remove or work around them • Have student identify something to look forward to doing after work is done • Teach to track time on task using index card or sticky note • Have students set goals (how long can you go before you need a break?)
Task initiation	• Establish set time to do nonpreferred tasks • Teach 1-2-3-Start strategy (student lists the first three things they need to do in a work session and then they do them in order) • Make a list and break into bite-sized chunks • Use alarm on smartphone to remind student to start (If they're not ready to start, have them hit "Snooze" rather than turning the alarm off) • Help student make a plan for doing the task and include the start time • Practice getting started in isolation—start with a short, easy task and just practice starting it at the planned start time • Help student figure out what's preventing them from getting started and design an appropriate strategy.
Planning	• Teach to use a planning template • Help student design a plan/template • Start with big picture; plan backward • Help student find planning tools that work for them (calendar, agenda book, apps) • Break task down with a visual (e.g., dividing reading assignment into pages per day) • Put each step of a project on a separate index card or sticky note and rearrange to create the right sequence • Make a road map • Help student select a graphic organizer that meets the need • Walk through the planning process (use a template) • Have them plan a simple task and gradually prompt to do more of the planning themselves • Ask questions to get student to prioritize (What do you need? What should you do first?)

(continued)

196

Strategies for Specific Executive Skills *(page 3 of 3)*

Executive skill	Possible strategies
Time management	• Create a color-coded chart showing student their weekly schedule and where the discretionary time is (school; sports or extracurricular activities; travel to and from school; chores or family obligations; study time) • Practice estimating how long it takes to do something • Write each task on a sticky note and place it on a large dry-erase calendar so that it can be moved as needed • Use a dry-erase board for planning with columns for Task, This Month, This Week, Today, Done; have student move sticky notes from left to right
Goal-directed persistence	• Make sure the goal or benchmark is in sight—post it visually (e.g., a picture of the reward they're working for) • Help them set "personal best" goals (i.e., incremental improvement) and teach them about outcome goals ("Last week I got a 75 on my math quiz; this week I'll shoot for a 78") and process goals ("Last week I studied 20 minutes for my math quiz; this week I'll study for 30 minutes"); talk about the advantage of focusing on process goals	For students who are resistant to goal setting: • Define a goal as something that people want to get better at or to change • Start with helping them set a goal for something they want to do outside of school • Skip the word *goal* and talk with them about making a plan (starting with one thing they want to do before the next coaching session)

Metacognition	• Help student create sample to match or an error monitoring checklist
	• Embed metacognitive questions into instruction/conversations
	• Help student decide on how performance will be evaluated
	• Have student evaluate their own performance
	• Model thinking aloud to solve problems
		• Use different strategies—ask student to evaluate which worked best
		• Use Problem-Solving Worksheet (Appendix 29, p. 215)
		• Teach students to ask questions
		  ○ What's my problem?
		  ○ What's my plan?
		  ○ Am I following I my plan?
		  ○ How did I do?

How to Write an Essay

Executive skills addressed: task initiation, sustained attention, planning, organization, time management, metacognition

Students with a variety of executive skills weaknesses struggle with writing papers because this is one of the most complicated tasks we expect students to do. Use the following steps to help them through the process.

1. **Brainstorm topics.** If the student has to come up with a topic to write about, the process should begin with brainstorming. The rules of brainstorming are that any idea is accepted and written down in the first stage—the wilder and crazier the better because wild and crazy ideas often lead to good, usable ideas. No criticism is allowed at this point. If the student has trouble thinking of ideas on their own, the teacher or aide can throw out some ideas to "grease the wheels." We recommend that the adult working with the student write down the ideas rather than expecting the student to because youngsters with weak writing skills often struggle with the act of writing itself. When a reasonable number of ideas have been generated, have the student read the list and circle the most promising ones. The student may know right away what they want to write about. If not, talk about what they like and dislike about each idea to make it easier to zero in on a good choice.

2. **Brainstorm content.** Once a topic has been selected, the brainstorming process begins again. Ask the student, "Tell me everything you know or would like to know about this topic." Again, write down any idea or question: the crazier the better at this point.

3. **Organize the content.** Now look at all the ideas or questions that have been written down. With the student, decide whether the material can be grouped together in any way. If the assignment is to do a report on aardvarks, for instance, the information might cluster into categories such as what they look like, where they live, what they eat, who their enemies are, and how they protect themselves. Create topic headings and then write the details under each topic heading. Sometimes it's helpful to use sticky notes for this process. During the brainstorming phase, each individual idea or question is written on a separate note. The note can then be organized on a table under topic headings to form an outline of the paper. The paper can then be written (or dictated) from this outline.

4. **Write the opening paragraph.** This is often the most difficult part of the paper to write. The opening paragraph, at its most basic level, describes very succinctly what the paper will be about. For instance, an opening paragraph on a report about aardvarks might read:

   This paper is about a strange animal called an aardvark. By the time you finish reading it, you will know what they look like, where they live, what they eat, who their enemies are, and how they protect themselves.

   The one other thing that the opening paragraph should try to do is "grab the reader"—give the reader an interesting piece of information to tease their curiosity. At the end of the prior opening paragraph, for instance, two more sentences might be added:

   The reader will also learn the meaning of the word "aardvark" and what language it comes from. And if that hasn't grabbed your interest, I will also tell you why the aardvark has a sticky tongue—although you may not want to know this!

(continued)

Children with writing problems will have trouble writing the opening paragraph by themselves and may need help. Help can be provided by asking general questions, such as "What do you want people to know after they read your paper?" or "Why do you think people might be interested in reading this?" If they need more help than that, they may need a model to work from—for example, an opening paragraph on a topic similar to the one the student is working on or the paragraph on aardvarks provided here. If the student needs more guided help writing this paragraph, provide it. Then see if they can continue without the need for as much support.

5. **Write the rest of the paper.** To give the student a little more guidance, suggest that the rest of the paper be divided into sections with a heading for each section. Help the student make a list of the headings and then see if they can continue with the writing task alone. If not, continue to provide support until the paper is written. Each paragraph should begin with a main or topic sentence that makes one main point. Following the topic sentence should be three to five sentences that expand or explain the main point. It's helpful to use connecting words to link sentences or paragraphs. Examples of simple linking words are *and, because, also, instead, but, so.* Examples of more complex linking words are *although, moreover, on the other hand, therefore, as a result, finally, in conclusion.*

In the early stages of learning to write, children with writing problems need a great deal of help. This skill should get better with time, especially if each writing session concludes by giving the student some positive feedback about something done well. Note in particular any improvement since the last writing assignment (e.g., "I really like the way you were able to come up with the headings on your own this time, with no help from me").

For students with more significant writing impairments: More modeling, guidance, and support will need to be provided for students with writing disabilities. Furthermore, the process may need to be broken down a good deal more. For those with significant impairments or those who are highly resistant to the writing process, we recommend the following sequence:

- **Step 1:** Spend a few minutes (e.g., 5 minutes) each day practicing any kind of writing. Here, the goal is to get words down on paper. For many students, just having them write any words they can think of is the place to start. If children have difficulty generating words on their own, give them organizing or retrieval strategies, such as looking around the room and writing down the name of anything you see or having them write rhyming words by giving them the first word (e.g., *cat, man*). Count the number of words written and keep a graph, challenging them to write a few more words each day.

- **Step 2:** Give them a picture and have them write down words to describe the picture or have them describe the picture and you write down the words. Use pictures that reflect their interests.

- **Step 3:** Give them a picture and have them write a sentence or two describing the picture.

- **Step 4:** Have them draw a picture and write sentences describing the picture or telling a story to go along with the picture.

- **Step 5:** Finally, give them a story starter and have them write for 5 minutes based on it. They may want to choose a story starter or to think up one on their own.

This approach can be very effective when combined with curriculum-based measurement—that is, keeping the time frame constant, counting the number of words written, and graphing the results. The graph should be constructed with the child and might incorporate small stickers (obtainable at office supply stores like Staples) to construct the graph. Watching the graph progress indicator go up can be very motivating for young children, in particular those with writing production problems.

(continued)

Additional Resources

- Harvey, V. S., & Chickie-Wolfe, L. A. (2007). *Fostering independent learning: Practical strategies to promote student success*. Guilford Press.—This book has a chapter devoted to writing that includes a number of useful checklists and handouts. One of these lists presents a wide variety of "genre ideas" to remind teachers that there are myriad forms of writing and that going beyond the traditional essay may help stimulate writing in reluctant writers.

- Harris, K. R., Graham, S., Mason, L. H., & Friedlander, B. (2008). *Powerful writing strategies for all students*. Brookes.—This book describes the process of self-regulated strategy development and applies it to the writing process. Packed with helpful lesson plans and handouts, it details explicit strategies for specific writing genres as well as general writing strategies with an overarching goal of developing self-regulated learners. Thus, not only does the book teach writing, but it also helps students learn self-regulation strategies (i.e., executive skills!) such as goal setting, self-monitoring, self-reinforcement, and self-instruction.

(continued)

WRITING TEMPLATE FOR A FIVE-PARAGRAPH ESSAY

Introductory Paragraph

Sentence 1 summarizes what your essay is about:

Sentence 2 focuses on the main point you want to make:

Sentence 3 adds more detail or explains why the topic is important:

Body Paragraphs

Paragraph 1, topic sentence:

Supporting detail 1:

Supporting detail 2:

Supporting detail 3:

(continued)

Paragraph 2, topic sentence:

Supporting detail 1:

Supporting detail 2:

Supporting detail 3:

Paragraph 3, topic sentence:

Supporting detail 1:

Supporting detail 2:

Supporting detail 3:

(continued)

Concluding Paragraph

Restate the most important point from the paper you want to make (what the reader should go away understanding).

How to Plan and Complete Long-Term Projects

Executive skills addressed: task initiation, sustained attention, planning, time management, metacognition

Even more than writing assignments, long-term projects involve many of the more advanced executive skills. For this reason, students in general benefit from teacher support, not only when this kind of assignment is first introduced but to some degree or other throughout their schooling (at least until well into high school).

The steps involved in teaching students to complete long-term projects are as follows:

1. With the student, look at the description of the assignment to make sure the student understands what is expected. If the student is allowed a choice of topic, topic selection is the first task. Many children have trouble thinking up topics, and you may need to brainstorm ideas—and include a variety of suggestions—starting with topics that are related to the student's areas of interests.

2. Using the Long-Term Project Planning Sheet, write down the possible topics. Once three to five topics have been generated, ask the student what they do or do not like about each choice.

3. Help the student make a final selection, taking into consideration not only the topic of greatest interest but also (a) a topic that is neither too broad nor too narrow, (b) the level of difficulty involved in tracking down references and resources for the topic, and (c) whether there is an interesting "twist" to the topic that will make it either fun to work on or appealing for the teacher.

4. Using the Long-Term Project Planning Sheet, decide what materials or resources will be needed, where the student will get them, and when (this last variable may be determined after completing Step 5). Possible resources include Internet websites, library books, travel brochures, and similar items that may need to be ordered, people who might be interviewed, and relevant places to visit (e.g., museums, historical sites). You may need to "walk" the student through the process of tracking down sources (e.g., going to the library or accessing the Internet to show how to conduct a search). Also consider any construction or art materials needed if the student's plan includes a visual presentation.

5. Using the Long-Term Project Planning Sheet, list all the steps required to carry out the project and then develop a timeline so the student knows when each step will be done. It may be helpful at this point to transfer this information onto a monthly calendar that can be placed in the student's binder to make it easier to keep track of what needs to be done when.

6. Assist the student in following the timeline. Before they begin each step, you may want to discuss what exactly is involved in completing the step—this may mean making a list of things to be done for each step. Planning for the next step could be done as each step is completed, so that the student has some idea what's coming next and to make it easier to get the next step started.

(continued)

LONG-TERM PROJECT PLANNING SHEET

Step 1: Select Topic

What are possible topics?	What I like about this choice:	What I don't like:
1.		
2.		
3.		
4.		
5.		

Final Topic Choice:

Step 2: Identify Necessary Materials

What materials or resources do you need?	Where will you get them?	When will you get them?
1.		
2.		
3.		
4.		
5.		

(continued)

Step 3: Identify Project Tasks and Due Dates

What do you need to do? (List each step in order.)	When will you do it?	Check off when done
Step 1:		
Step 2:		
Step 3:		
Step 4:		
Step 5:		
Step 6:		
Step 7:		
Step 8:		
Step 9:		
Step 10:		

Reminder List. Include here any additional tasks or details you need to keep in mind as you work on the project. Cross out or check each one off as it is taken care of.

1. _____
2. _____
3. _____
4. _____
5. _____
6. _____
7. _____
8. _____
9. _____
10. _____

Studying for Tests

Test date: _____   Subject: _____

Check off the strategies you will use.		
Passive strategies (use sparingly)	**Active strategies (better)**	**Active strategies with feedback (best)**
☐ 1. Reread text ☐ 2. Reread notes ☐ 3. Highlight notes/text ☐ 4. Read study guide ☐ 5. Rewrite notes ☐ 6. Read/watch Spark Notes, Kahn Academy, etc.	☐ 7. Make study guide ☐ 8. Make flashcards/Quizlet ☐ 9. Make concept maps ☐ 10. Organize notes ☐ 11. Complete review packet (no answers) ☐ 12. Attend review session or study group	☐ 13. Quiz myself with Quizlet/study guide/flash cards ☐ 14. Take practice test (check answers) ☐ 15. Redo old tests or homework (check answers) ☐ 16. Have someone else quiz me ☐ 17. Complete review packet (check answers) ☐ 18. Meet 1:1 with teacher
☐ 19. Other: _____		

STUDY PLAN

Date	Day	Which strategies will I use? (Write number)	How much time for each strategy?
	4 days before test	1. 2. 3.	1. 2. 3.
	3 days before test	1. 2. 3.	1. 2. 3.

(continued)

Studying for Tests

Date	Day	Which strategies will I use? (Write number)	How much time for each strategy?
	2 days before test	1. 2. 3.	1. 2. 3.
	1 day before test	1. 2. 3.	1. 2. 3.

POSTTEST EVALUATION

How did your studying work out? Answer the following questions:

1. What strategies worked best?

2. What strategies were not so helpful?

3. Did you spend enough time studying? Yes No

4. If no, what more should you have done?

5. What will you do differently the next time?

How to Organize Notebooks/Homework

1. With input from the student, decide on what needs to be included in the organizational system: A place to keep unfinished homework? A separate place to keep completed homework? A place to keep papers that need to be filed? Notebooks or binders to keep notes, completed assignments, handouts, and worksheets? A sample list is included in the checklist that follows.

2. Once you've listed all these elements, decide how best to handle them, one at a time. For example, you and the student might decide on a colored folder system, with a different color for completed assignments, unfinished work, and other papers. Or you might decide to have a separate small three-ring binder for each subject or one large binder to handle all subjects.

3. Make a list of the materials the student needs—these might include a three-hole punch, lined and unlined paper, subject dividers, and small sticky notes the student can use to flag important papers.

4. Ask the student to procure the necessary materials if they are not available at school. It may be necessary to email the student's parents to ensure that the materials are obtained.

5. Set up the notebooks and folders, labeling everything clearly.

6. Help the student maintain the system over time. This generally means a daily check-in, which might include having the student take out the folders for completed assignments, unfinished work, and material to be filed. Have the student make a decision about each piece of material and where it should go.

(continued)

SETTING UP A NOTEBOOK/HOMEWORK MANAGEMENT SYSTEM

System element	What will you use?	Got it (✓)
Place for unfinished homework		
Place for completed assignments		
Place to keep materials for later filing		
Notebooks or binder(s) for each subject		
Other things you might need: 1. 2. 3. 4.		

MAINTAINING A NOTEBOOK/HOMEWORK MANAGEMENT SYSTEM

Task	Monday	Tuesday	Wednesday	Thursday	Weekend
Clean out "to be filed" folder.					
Go through notebooks and books for other loose papers and file them.					
Place all assignments (both finished and unfinished) in appropriate places.					

How to Take Notes

- Solicit from student the reasons why note taking is important. If the student has difficulty answering the question, point out that note taking not only enables students to record important information needed to understand the lecture topic and provides material to use when studying for tests, but it also is a way to help them pay attention and focus on the class.
- Ask the student how they takes notes now and assess the usefulness of the method. Explain that learning is most likely to occur when three things happen: (1) The student is able to absorb the relevant information in a way that is organized appropriately for the material being presented; (2) the student is able to extract the key concepts or main ideas as a way to help them understand and retain the factual information presented in lecture; and (3) the student is able to apply what they are learning to prior learning or relate it to personal experiences in order to have a meaningful context within which the new material can be placed. The more a student can make the information *emotionally* relevant, the more they will likely understand and remember.
- If the student's current note-taking style does not incorporate these three elements, explain that you will be teaching a couple of different note-taking strategies for the student to try and then to decide which one works best.

NOTE-TAKING STRATEGY 1: CORNELL METHOD

This strategy uses a three-column system and begins with sequential note taking (writing down what the teacher is saying in the sequence provided) in the center column (see the following sample). As the lecture progresses, the student writes down key concepts and "big ideas" in the left-hand column. Sometimes a teacher is direct in identifying those key concepts; other times students have to listen carefully and draw conclusions on their own. In the right-hand column, the student is instructed to jot down personal reflections—a word or two that relates the material to a personal experience, an emotional reaction to what is being said, or a question that the material brings to mind. The first and third columns can be filled in during the lecture as well as later, when the student reviews the notes from the day's class.

The strategy should be modeled using relevant material from the class in which the note taking will be used. The student may need particular help identifying key concepts or relating the material to personal experiences and can be guided through this process by asking probing questions (e.g., "Can you think of anything in your life that you could relate this to?" "What's your opinion about this—do you agree or disagree?").

If teachers provide PowerPoint notes, the student can use a highlighter to emphasize key concepts and write down personal reactions/questions in the margins. This, too, may need to be modeled.

NOTE-TAKING STRATEGY 2: CONCEPT MAPPING

This visual strategy uses graphic organizers to link key concepts to details. Concept maps begin with a central topic (e.g., the title of the day's lecture), to which main branches are added to represent the main subdivisions of the lecture. Each branch can be extended with details illustrating or clarifying the subdivision. (See the following example, based on the theme of Chapter 12 of this book.)

The concept map is a more difficult approach to note taking for students to learn, but the graphic display makes it easier for them to learn the content to study for tests. The best way to teach this skill is to model it. When working with individual students, it may be easier to teach concept mapping using a chapter from the student's text (e.g., social studies or science) before applying the method to lectures. Giving students partially completed concept maps and having them fill in the missing pieces is a way to shape the skill (or fade the support).

(continued)

SAMPLE CORNELL METHOD FORM

Name: _____   Date: _____   Class: _____

Lecture topic: _____

Key terms and concepts	Running notes	Reflections, questions, links to personal experience

(continued)

EXAMPLE OF CONCEPT MAP

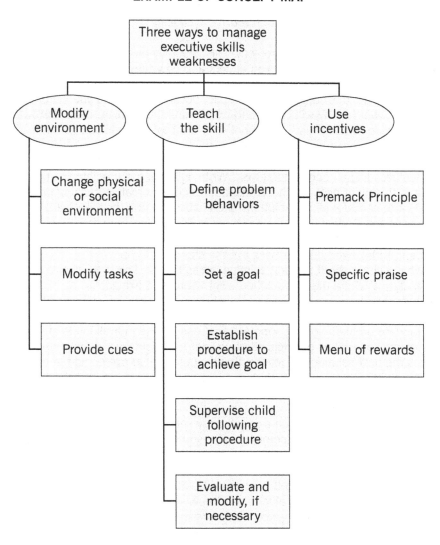

Learning to Solve Problems

Executive skills addressed: metacognition, flexibility, planning

1. Talk with the student to identify the problem. This generally involves three steps: (a) empathizing with the student or letting them know you understand how they feel ("I can see that makes you really mad" or "That must be really upsetting for you"); (b) getting a *general* sense of what the problem is ("Let me get this straight—you're upset because the friend you were hoping to play with at recess doesn't want to play with you); and (c) defining the problem more narrowly so that you can begin to brainstorm solutions ("You're not sure what to do when you go out to recess").
2. Brainstorm solutions. Together with the student, think of as many possible solutions as you can. You may want to set a time limit (e.g., 2 minutes) because this sometimes speeds up the process or makes it feel less like an open-ended task. Write down all the possible solutions. Do not criticize the solutions at this point because this tends to squelch the creative thinking process.
3. Ask the student to consider all the solutions and choose the one they like best. You may want to start by having the student circle the top three to five choices and then narrow them down by talking about the pluses and minuses associated with each.
4. Ask the student if they need help carrying out the choice.
5. Talk about what will happen if the first solution doesn't work. This may involve choosing a different solution or analyzing where the first solution went wrong and fixing it.
6. Praise the student for coming up with a good solution (and again after the solution is implemented.

    This is a standard problem-solving approach that can be used for all kinds of problems, including interpersonal problems as well as obstacles that prevent a student from getting what they want or need. Sometimes the best solution will involve figuring out ways to overcome the obstacles, while at other times it may involve helping the student come to terms with the fact that what they want is unobtainable.

    Sometimes the problem-solving process may lead to a "negotiation," where you and the student both agree on what will be done to reach a satisfactory solution. In this case, you should explain to the student that whatever solution you come up with, you both have to be able to live with it. You may want to talk about how labor contracts are negotiated so that both workers and bosses get something they want out of the bargain.

    After you've used the process (and the worksheet) with the student for a number of different kinds of problems, the student may be able to use the worksheet independently. Because your goal is to foster independent problem solving, you may want to ask the student to fill out the following Problem-Solving Worksheet alone before coming to you for help (if needed). Eventually, the student will internalize the whole process and be able to solve problems "on the fly."

(continued)

PROBLEM-SOLVING WORKSHEET

What is the problem?
What are some possible things I could do to solve the problem?
What will I try first?
If this doesn't work, what can I do?
How did it go? Did my solution work?
What might I do differently the next time?

References

Abela, A. R., Duan, Y., & Chudasama, Y. (2015). Hippocampal interplay with the nucleus accumbens is critical for decisions about time. *European Journal of Neuroscience, 42*(5), 2224–2233.

American Psychiatric Association. (2022). *Diagnostic and statistical manual of mental disorders* (5th ed., text rev.). Author.

Anderson, D. H., Munk, J. H., Young, K. R., Conley, L., & Caldarella, P. (2008). Teaching organizational skills to promote academic achievement in behaviorally challenged students. *Teaching Exceptional Children, 40*, 6–13.

Andrew, S. A. (2015). *Motivational interviewing: A basic synopsis*. Health Education and Training Institute.

Barkley, R. A. (1997). *ADHD and the nature of self-control*. Guilford Press.

Barkley, R. A. (Ed.). (2014). *Attention-deficit hyperactivity disorder: A handbook for diagnosis and treatment* (4th ed.). Guilford Press.

Bevill-Davis, A., Clees, T. J., & Gast, D. L. (2004). Correspondence training: A review of the literature. *Journal of Early and Intensive Behavioral Intervention, 1*, 17–26.

Blair, C., & Raver, C. C. (2016). Poverty, stress, and brain development: New directions for prevention and intervention. *Academic Pediatrics, 16*(3), S30–S36.

Brier, N. M. (2015). *Enhancing self-control in adolescents: Treatment strategies derived from psychological science*. Routledge/Taylor & Francis Group.

Briesch, A. M., & Chafouleas, S. M. (2009). Review and analysis of literature on self-management interventions to promote appropriate classroom behaviors (1988–2008). *School Psychology Quarterly, 24*(2), 106–118.

Bruhn, A. L., McDaniel, S. C., Fernando, J., & Troughton, L. (2016). Goal-setting interventions for students with behavior problems: A systematic review. *Behavioral Disorders, 41*(2), 107–121.

Capstick, M. K., Harrell-Williams, L. M., Cockrum, C. D., & West, S. L. (2019). Exploring the effectiveness of academic coaching for academically at-risk college students. *Innovative Higher Education, 44*(3), 219–231.

Crisci, G., Cardillo, R., & Mammarella, I. C. (2022). The processes underlying positive illusory bias in ADHD: The role of executive functions and pragmatic language skills. *Journal of Attention Disorders, 26*(9), 1245–1256

Dawson, P., & Guare, R. (2009). *Smart but scattered: The revolutionary "executive skills" approach to helping kids reach their potential.* Guilford Press.

Dawson, P., & Guare, R. (2017). *The work-smart academic planner: Write it down, get it done* (rev. ed.). Guilford Press.

Dawson, P., & Guare, R. (2018). *Executive skills in children and adolescents: A practical guide to assessment and intervention* (3rd ed.). Guilford Press.

Deci, E. L., & Ryan, R. M. (1985). *Intrinsic motivation and self-determination in human behavior.* Plenum Press.

Devine, M., Meyers, R., & Houssemand, C. (2013). How can coaching make a positive impact within educational settings? *Procedia-Social and Behavioral Sciences, 93*, 1382–1389.

Dike, D. E. (2012). *A descriptive study of intrinsic motivation in three California accredited model continuation high schools.* Unpublished doctoral dissertation, University of La Verne, La Verne, CA.

Dotson, R. (2016). Goal setting to increase student academic performance. *Journal of School Administration Research and Development, 1*(1), 45–46.

Duckworth, A. L., Kirby, T. A., Gollwitzer, A., & Oettingen, G. (2013). From fantasy to action: Mental contrasting with implementation intentions (MCII) improves academic performance in children. *Social Psychological and Personality Science, 4*(6), 745–753.

DuPaul, G. J., Ervin, R. A., Hook, C. L., & McGoey, K E. (1998). Peer tutoring effects on the classroom performance of children with attention deficit hyperactivity disorder. *Journal of Applied Behavior Analysis, 31*, 579–592.

Emeh, C. C., Mikami, A. Y., & Teachman, B. A. (2018). Eplicit and implicit positive illusory bias in children with ADHD. *Journal of Attention Disorder, 22*(10), 994–1001.

Fantuzzo, J. W., & Polite, K. (1990). School-based behavioral self-management: A review and analysis. *School Psychology Quarterly, 5*, 180–198.

Fantuzzo, J. W., Rohrbeck, C. A., & Azar, S. T. (1987). A component analysis of behavioral self-management interventions with elementary school students. *Child & Family Behavior Therapy, 9*, 33–43.

Gawande, A. (2011, October 3). Personal best: Top athletes and singers have coaches. Should you? *The New Yorker*, pp. 44–53.

Giedd, J. N. (2004). Structural magnetic resonance imaging of the adolescent brain. In R. E. Dahl & L. P. Spear (Eds.), *Adolescent brain development: Vulnerabilities and opportunities* (pp. 77–85). New York Academy of Sciences.

Gollwitzer, P. M., & Oettingen, G. (2012). Goal pursuit. In R. Ryan (Ed.), *The Oxford handbook of human motivation* (pp. 208–231). Oxford University Press.

Grassley, T. (2019, July 26). *Academic coaches help students raise grades, stay in school, study finds.* www.colorado.edu/asmagazine/2019/07/26/academic-coaches-help-students-raise-grades-stay-school-study-finds

Gutierrez, D., Foxx, S. P., & Kondili, E. (2018). Investigating the effectiveness of a motivational interviewing group on academic motivation. *Journal of School Counseling, 16*(14). http://www.jsc.montana.edu/articles/v16n14.pdf

Hallowell, E. M., & Ratey, J. J. (1994). *Driven to distraction.* Pantheon.

Hume, K., Loftin, R., & Lantz, J. (2009). Increasing independence in autism spectrum disorders: A review of three focused interventions. *Journal of Autism and Developmental Disorders, 39*(9), 1329–1338.

Icenogle, G., Steinberg, L., Duell, N., Chein, J., Chang, L., Chaudhary, N., . . . Bacchini, D. (2019). Adolescents' cognitive capacity reaches adult levels prior to their psychosocial maturity: Evidence for a "maturity gap" in a multinational, cross-sectional sample. *Law and Human Behavior, 43*(1), 69–85.

Kennedy, M. R. T. (2017). *Coaching college students with executive function problems*. Guilford Press.

Kenworthy, L., Anthony, L. G., Alexander, K. C., Werner, M. A., Cannon, L., & Greenman, L. (2014). *Solving executive function challenges*. Brookes.

Kercood, S., Grskovic, J. A., Banda, D., & Begeske, J. (2014). Working memory and autism: A review of literature. *Research in Autism Spectrum Disorders, 8*(10), 1316–1332.

Klein, S. B., Robertson, T. E., & Delton, A. W. (2010). Facing the future: Memory as an evolved system for planning future acts. *Memory & Cognition, 38*(1), 13–22.

Knäuper, B., Roseman, M., Johnson, P. J., & Krantz, L. H. (2009). Using mental imagery to enhance the effectiveness of implementation intentions. *Current Psychology, 28*(3), 181–186.

Kumm, S., & Maggin, D. M. (2021). Intensifying goal-setting interventions for students with emotional and behavioral disorders. *Beyond Behavior, 30*(1), 14–23.

Locke, E. A., & Latham, G. P. (2002). Building a practically useful theory of goal setting and task modification. *American Psychologist, 57*, 705–717.

Lower, A., Young, K. R., Christensen, L., Caldarella, P., Williams, L., & Wills, H. (2016). Effects of a tier 3 self-management intervention implemented with and without treatment integrity. *Education and Treatment of Children, 39*(4), 493–520.

Luerssen, A., Gyurak, A., Ayduk, O., Wendelken, C., & Bunge, S. A. (2015). Delay of gratification in childhood linked to cortical interactions with the nucleus accumbens. *Social Cognitive and Affective Neuroscience, 10*(12), 1769–1776.

Mazefsky, C. A., Herrington, J., Siegel, M., Scarpa, A., Maddox, B. B., Scahill, L., & White, S. W. (2013). The role of emotion regulation in autism spectrum disorder. *Journal of the American Academy of Child and Adolescent Psychiatry, 52*(7), 679–688.

Merriman, D. E., & Codding, R. S. (2008). The effects of coaching on mathematics homework completion and accuracy of high school students with attention deficit/hyperactivity disorder. *Journal of Behavioral Education, 17*, 339–355.

Merriman, D., Codding, R. S., Tryon, G. S., & Minami, T. (2016). The effects of group coaching on the homework problems experienced by secondary students with and without disabilities. *Psychology in the Schools, 53*(5), 457–470.

Miller, W. R., & Rollnick, S. (2002). *Motivational interviewing: Preparing people for change*. Guilford Press.

Miller, W. R., & Rollnick, S. (2012). *Motivational interviewing: Helping people change* (3rd ed.). Guilford Press.

Mitchem, K. J., Young, K. R., West, R. P., & Benyo, J. (2001). CWPASM: A classwide peer-assisted self-management program for general education classrooms. *Education and Treatment of Children, 24*(2), 111–140.

Murty, V. P., Calabro, F., & Luna, B. (2016). The role of experience in adolescent cognitive development: Integration of executive, memory, and mesolimbic systems. *Neuroscience & Biobehavioral Reviews, 70*, 46–58.

Naar-King, S., & Suarez, M. (2011). *Motivational interviewing with adolescents and young adults*. Guilford Press.

North, R. A. (2017). *Motivational interviewing for school counselors*. Self-published.

Oettingen, G., & Gollwitzer, P. M. (2010). Strategies of setting and implementing goals: Mental contrasting and implementation intentions. In J. E. Maddux & J. P. Tangney (Eds.), *Social psychological foundations of clinical psychology* (pp. 114–135). Guilford Press.

Oettingen, G., Kappes, H. B., Guttenberg, K. B., & Gollwitzer, P. M. (2015). Self-regulation of time management: Mental contrasting with implementation intentions. *European Journal of Social Psychology, 45*, 218–229.

Paniagua, F. A. (1992). Verbal–nonverbal correspondence training with ADHD children. *Behavior Modification, 16*, 226–252.

Palminteri, S., Kilford, E. J., Coricelli, G., & Blakemore, S. J. (2016). The computational development of reinforcement learning during adolescence. *PLoS Computational Biology, 12*(6), e1004953.

Plumer, P. J., & Stoner, G. (2005). The relative effects of classwide peer tutoring and peer coaching on the positive social behaviors of children with ADHD. *Journal of Attention Disorders, 9*, 290–300.

Prochaska, J. O., Norcross, J. C., & DiClemente, C. C. (1994). *Changing for good*. HarperCollins.

Rabiee, A., Vasaghi-Gharamaleki, B., Samadi, S. A., Amiri-Shavaki, Y., & Alaghband-Rad, J. (2020). Working memory deficits and its relationship to autism spectrum disorders. *Iranian Journal of Medical Sciences, 45*(2), 100–109.

Raffaelli, M., Crocket, L. J., & Shen, Y.-L. (2005). Developmental stability and change in self-regulation from childhood to adolescence. *Journal of Genetic Psychology, 166*, 54–75.

Reynolds, G. D., & Romano, A. C. (2016). The development of attention systems and working memory in infancy. *Frontiers in Systems Neuroscience, 10*, 15.

Riley-Tillman, T. C., Christ, T. J., Chafouleas, S. M., Boice-Mallach, C. H., & Briesch, A. (2011). The impact of observation duration on the accuracy of data obtained from direct behavior rating (DBR). *Journal of Positive Behavior Interventions, 13*(2), 119–128.

Ryan, R. M., & Deci, E. L. (2017). *Self-determination theory: Basic psychological needs in motivation, development, and wellness*. Guilford Press.

Schunk, D. H. (2003). Self-efficacy for reading and writing: Influence of modeling, goal setting, and self-evaluation. *Reading & Writing Quarterly, 19*, 159–172.

Society for Neuroscience. (2018). *Brain facts: A primer on the brain and nervous system* (8th ed.). Author.

South, M., & Rogers, J. (2017). Sensory, emotional and cognitive contributions in autism spectrum disorders. *Frontiers in Human Neuroscience, 11*, 20.

Sutherland, K. S., Conroy, M. A., McLeod, B. D., Kunemund, R., & McKnight, K. (2019). Common practice elements for improving social, emotional, and behavioral outcomes of young elementary school students. *Journal of Emotional and Behavioral Disorders, 27*(2), 76–85.

Swartz, S. L., Prevatt, F., & Proctor, B. E. (2005). A coaching intervention for college students with attention deficit/hyperactivity disorder. *Psychology in the Schools, 42*, 647–656.

Terry, J., Smith, B., Strait, G., & McQuillin, S. (2013). Motivational interviewing to improve middle school students' academic performance: A replication study. *Journal of Community Psychology, 41*(7), 902–909.

Terry, J., Strait, G., McQuillin, S., & Smith, B. H. (2014). Dosage effects of motivational interviewing on middle-school students' academic performance: Randomized evaluation of one versus two sessions. *Advances in School Mental Health Promotion, 7*(1), 62–74.

Troller-Renfree, S. V., Costanzo, M. A., Duncan, G. J., Magnuson, K., Gennetian, L. A., Yoshikawa, H., & Noble, K. G. (2022). The impact of a poverty reduction intervention on infant brain activity. *Proceedings of the National Academy of Sciences, 119*(5), e2115649119.

Underwood, A. G., Guynn, M. J., & Cohen, A. L. (2015). The future orientation of past memory: The role of BA 10 in prospective and retrospective retrieval modes. *Frontiers in Human Neuroscience, 9*, 668.

Van Den Bos, W., Rodriguez, C. A., Schweitzer, J. B., & McClure, S. M. (2015). Adolescent impatience decreases with increased frontostriatal connectivity. *Proceedings of the National Academy of Sciences, 112*(29), E3765–E3774.

Velasquez-Sheehy, S. (2015). A study of the impact of mental contrasting and implementation intentions on academic performance. *College of Education Theses and Dissertations*, 82. https://via.library.depaul.edu/soe_etd/82.

Vilardo, B. A., & DuPaul, G. J. (2010). *Cross-age peer coaching: Enhancing the peer interactions of first graders exhibiting symptoms of ADHD*. Poster session presented at the annual convention of the National Association of School Psychologists, Chicago.

Vygotsky, L. (1978). *Mind in society*. Harvard University Press.

Wachtel, T. (2005, November). *The next step: developing restorative communities*. Paper presented at the Seventh International Conference on Conferencing, Circles and other Restorative Practices, Manchester, UK.

Watkins, V. (2019). *The effects of goal setting and data tracking on student performance.* Master's thesis, Northwestern College, Orange City, IA. https://nwcommons.nwciowa.edu/cgi/viewcontent.cgi?artic le=1141&context=education_masters

Wells, J. C., Sheehey, P. H., & Sheehey, M. (2017). Using self-monitoring of performance with self-graphing to increase academic productivity in math. *Beyond Behavior, 26*(2), 57–65.

Williams, G. C. (2002). Improving patients' health through supporting the autonomy of patients and providers. In E. L. Deci & R. M. Ryan (Eds.), *Handbook of self-determination research* (p. 233–254). University of Rochester Press.

Wolters, C. A. (2003). Regulation of motivation: Evaluating an underemphasized aspect of self-regulated learning. *Educational Psychologist, 38*(4), 189–205.

Zimmerman, B. J. (1986). Becoming a self-regulated learner: Which are the key subprocesses? *Contemporary Educational Psychology, 11*(4), 307–313.

Zimmerman, B. J. (2001). Theories of self-regulated learning and academic achievement: An overview and analysis. In B. J. Zimmerman & D. H. Schunk (Eds), *Self-regulated learning and academic achievement* (2nd ed., pp. 1–37). Erlbaum.

Zinn, M. E., Huntley, E. D., & Keating, D. P. (2020). Resilience in adolescence: Prospective self moderates the association of early life adversity with externalizing problems. *Journal of Adolescence, 81,* 61–72.

Index

Note. Page numbers followed by *f* or *t* indicate a figure or a table